Maintenance Systems and Documentation

D1407225

Maintenance Systems and Documentation

Anthony Kelly

AMSTERDAM • BOSTON • HEIDELBERG • LONDON • OXFORD •
NEW YORK • PARIS • SAN DIEGO • SAN FRANCISCO • SINGAPORE •
SYDNEY • TOKYO

First Edition 2006
Copyright © 2006, Anthony Kelly.
Published by Elsevier Ltd. All rights reserved

Notice
No responsibility is assumed by the publisher for any injury and/or damage
to persons or property as a matter of products liability, negligence or otherwise,
or from any use or operation of any methods, products, instructions or ideas
contained in the material herein. Because of rapid advances in the medical
sciences, in particular, independent verification of diagnoses and drug dosages
should be made

British Library Cataloguing in Publication Data
A catalogue record for this book is available from the British Library

Library of Congress control number: 2006921208

ISBN 13: 978 0 75 066994 8
ISBN 10: 0 75 066994 2

Plant Maintenance Management (set of three volumes)
ISBN 13: 978 0 75 66995 5; ISBN 10: 0 75 066995 0

For information on all Elsevier Butterworth-Heinemann
publications visit our web site at www.books.elsevier.com

Typeset by Charon Tec Ltd, Chennai, India
www.charontec.com
Printed and bound in Great Britain

Contents

Preface

Maintenance Systems and Documentation is the third of three companion books covering material which has been developed (and updated) from my 1997 publications *Maintenance Strategy* and *Maintenance Organization and Systems*, which were subsequently expanded and converted into distance-learning units which comprised the first half of a 2-year Masters program offered by an Australia and a UK university.

The main approach adopted throughout all three books, and which determines the direction and content of all the material, is that of business-centered maintenance (BCM), the starting point of which is the identification of the business aims. These are then translated into the maintenance objectives which, in their turn, are used to underpin the formulation firstly of strategy (the subject of Book 1, *Strategic Maintenance Planning, viz.* the *planning* aspects of maintenance management), secondly of the design of the appropriate organization (the subject of Book 2, *Managing Maintenance Resources, viz.* the *doing* aspects of maintenance management), and finally the creation of the necessary systems (the subject of this book, *viz.* the *controlling* aspects).

Because the material has come from a distance-learning program all three books contain numerous review questions (with answers), exercises and case studies – these last having been selected to ensure coverage of the care of physical assets across a wide range of industries (process, mining, food, power generation and transmission, etc.). In addition, every chapter has its own clearly specified objectives and learning outcomes – as well as a route map which enables the reader to see where the chapter is in relation to the rest of the topics covered.

Although the BCM approach integrates all three books into a unified maintenance management methodology, I have tried to ensure that each one can stand alone, i.e. be studied and understood in isolation from its companion works. It is therefore inevitable that there is some overlap, *viz.*:

- To explain the principles and concepts of BCM, the same case study (of a food processing plant) is used at the beginning of each book.
- To illustrate the linkage between maintenance planning, organization and systems, a full audit of a chemical plant is presented at the end of each book.

The overall aim of each book is to provide managers of physical assets with a better understanding of the operation of the maintenance function, an understanding which will enable them to identify problems within their own organization and prescribe effective solutions. As asserted by Henry Mintzberg (Managers Not MBAs, *Financial Times*, Prentice Hall, 2004):

> *What managers really need from a course or a book is insight – theories or models that enable them to make sense of practice, learn from experience and reach better judgements.*

The provision of such insight is the over-riding purpose of these three books.

Managing Systems and Documentation, the third book of the series, addresses the main systems that are necessary for the successful operation of a maintenance organization. The book identifies the key maintenance systems (e.g. performance control, work control, documentation, etc.) and, for each one, shows:

- How it can be mapped and modeled.
- Its function and its operating principles.
- The main problems encountered in its operation.

Chapter 1 is the key section, setting the maintenance organization within the context of BCM (the principles and concepts of which are explained via a case study of a food processing plant). Chapter 2 then identifies the main systems and shows them within the context of a company organization. Chapter 3 describes maintenance budgeting and its linkages with the costing system. Chapter 4 outlines the main maintenance control systems, and deals with the use of performance indices. Chapter 5 covers the key maintenance information system, *viz.* work planning and work control, this providing much of the information for the successful operation of the other systems.

Chapters 6 and 7 describe, respectively, the theory and then the practice of the planning and control of major shutdowns. Chapter 8 provides a comprehensive and detailed coverage of the management of spare parts. Chapter 9 looks at the function, principles and concepts of maintenance documentation systems. Chapter 10 reviews the advantages and problems of using computerized maintenance documentation systems, and in Chapter 11 this book concludes with a case study showing how the maintenance systems of a company can be audited in order to identify their problems.

Anthony Kelly
a.kelly99@ntlworld.com

Acknowledgments

Firstly, I wish to acknowledge a special gratitude to John Harris who has edited the complete text, made a contribution to Chapter 8 and provided Appendix. I also thank Tom Lenehan who contributed the major part of Chapter 7.

Thanks also go to the people in industry, most recently: Bill Sugden, Ian Peterson, Gudmunder Bjornason, Leonard Bouwman, Kevin Hardman, Nigel Beard and many others who provided access to their plants and without whose help this book could not have been written.

Finally, I thank Vicky Taylor for typing the text and Denise Jackson for producing the artwork.

Author's biography

Dr. Anthony Kelly served a trade apprenticeship before obtaining a first degree in mechanical engineering from the University of Wales and a Masters Degree (in corrosion engineering) from the University of London. He then held several industrial positions, in which he was responsible for the management of maintenance resources, before joining, in 1969, the University of Manchester, UK, where he specialized in maintenance management, its teaching and research, and obtained his doctorate for a thesis on maintenance organizational design. Dr. Kelly has published numerous technical papers and seven textbooks which have been translated into several languages.

Over the last 15 years Dr. Kelly has run his own consultancy partnership, operating worldwide and carrying out more than 60 major investigations and audits of a wide variety of industrial activities: mining, power generation and distribution, chemical processing, manufacturing, building services, etc. Over the last 15 years he has also held visiting/industrial professorships at Central Queensland University (Australia), University of Stellenbosch (South Africa) and Hogskolen i Stavanger (Norway).

PART 1

Introductory chapters

1 A business-centered approach to maintenance systems

'Good plans shape good decisions. That's why good planning helps to make elusive dreams come true.'

Lester Bittel (1929)

Chapter aims and outcomes

To explain the business-centered maintenance (BCM) procedure and show how it can be used to understand, develop and modify (if necessary) the maintenance systems for a complex industrial plant.

On completion of this chapter you should be able to:

- understand the methodology of BCM and why it is called 'business-centered';
- understand that maintenance strategy is concerned with deciding how to maintain the plant, setting up an appropriate maintenance organization and developing the required systems;
- understand how the BCM methodology can be used to map and model the maintenance department of an industrial plant in order to improve the maintenance systems – the strategic thought process.

Chapter route map

Book divisions	This chapter in the division	Chapter topics
Introductory chapters	Chapter 1 A business-centered approach to maintenance systems	1.1 Introduction
Budgeting and control		1.2 Business-centered maintenance
Work planning and work control	Chapter 2 Introduction to maintenance management systems	1.3 An example of the application of BCM: background
Spare parts management		1.4 Part A: Audit of the FPP maintenance department
Documentation		1.5 Part B: An alternative maintenance strategy for continuous operation
Case study		1.6 Part C: A longer-term view of organizational change
		1.7 The strategic thought process

Key words

- Business-centered maintenance
- Maintenance systems
- Maintenance documentation
- Maintenance auditing
- Strategic thought process

1.1 Introduction

As explained in the preface, this is the third of three companion books on maintenance management. In Book 1, *Strategic Maintenance Planning*, we dealt with the identification of objectives and the formulation of the maintenance strategy. In Book 2, *Managing Maintenance Resources*, we dealt with the maintenance organization. Here, we shall examine the documentation and control systems that are needed for carrying out maintenance management. Before doing so – and for the benefit of those who may not have read Book 1 or 2, it is important to recall the overall BCM methodology, which was described as:

> . . . a framework of guidelines for deciding maintenance objectives, formulating equipment life plans and plant maintenance schedules **(Maintenance Planning)**, designing the maintenance organisation **(Maintenance Doing)** and setting up appropriate systems of documentation and control **(Maintenance Control)**.

and secondly to outline (via a case study) the concepts, procedures and models of all three of these areas of maintenance management.

1.2 Business-centered maintenance

The structure of a methodology for developing a maintenance strategy – which I call the business-centered maintenance (BCM) approach – is outlined in Figure 1.1. It is based on well-established administrative management principles (see Figure 1.2) and provides a framework for identifying, mapping and then auditing the elements of any maintenance management system.

> In order to better understand the purpose of Figure 1.1 it is useful to put yourself in the position of a maintenance manager thinking through how he is going to set up a maintenance department for a new plant. Obviously he needs to understand the way the plant operates, its relationship with its market and the function of maintenance within this context. The large circle is his strategic thought process starting with the plant maintenance objective (which is subordinate to the business objectives) and proceeding via life plans and organization through

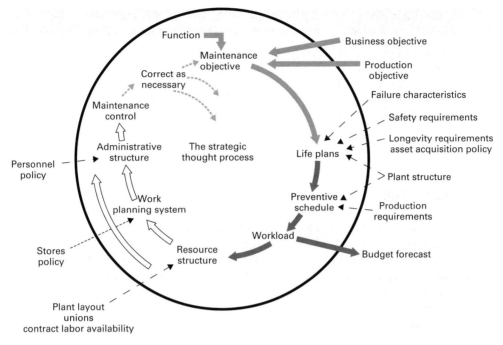

Figure 1.1 A BCM methodology

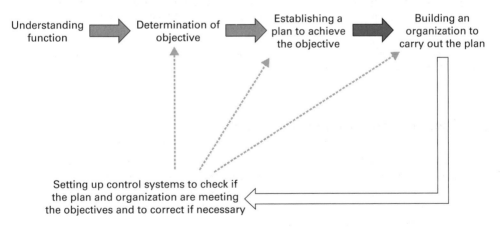

Figure 1.2 Basic steps of the management process

to control (this procedure is essentially the same as the basic management procedure of Figure 1.2). From outside of the large circle come the numerous factors (from other departments or from the environment, e.g. industrial relations) that can affect the strategic thought process.

1.3 An example of the application of BCM: background

A more detailed and comprehensive explanation of BCM may be gained by referring to an industrial application, in this case its use in auditing the maintenance department of a food processing plant (FPP).

The plant layout was shown in Figure 1.3 and an outline process flow diagram being shown in Figure 1.4. At the time of the audit the production pattern was three shifts per day, 5 days per week, 50 weeks per year. There was also considerable spare capacity.

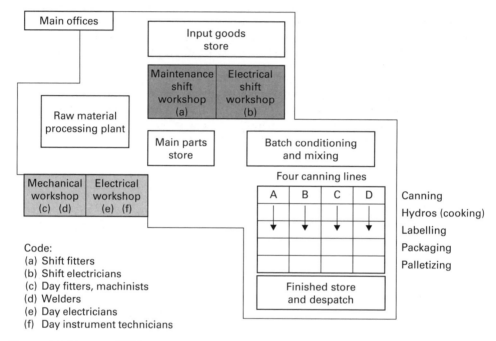

Figure 1.3 Layout of FPP

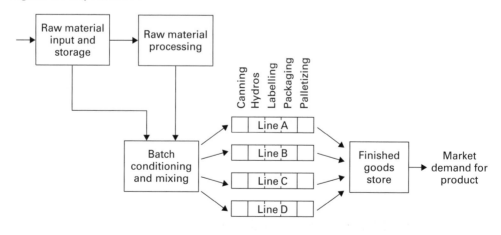

Figure 1.4 Process flow for FPP

For example, only three lines out of four (see Figure 1.4) were needed to achieve full capacity. However, each line had its own product mix to satisfy the market demand. Thus, the availability of any given line for maintenance depended on the market demand and the level of finished product stored. Offline maintenance could be carried out in the weekend windows of opportunity or, by exploring spare capacity, during the week. In general, the maintenance manager found it easier to carry out most of the offline work during the weekend.

> The relationship between the plant and the market demand for its product (and/or raw material supply) has a considerable influence on maintenance strategy. It governs the way production will use the plant, the plant operating pattern. This in turn determines the frequency, duration and cost of scheduling the plant for offline maintenance, maintenance windows.
>
> The market demand is different across different industries. For example, baseload power stations (stations that provide the cheapest electricity) are required to operate for as long as possible because of a constant and continuous demand. The FPP of this example is a multi-product company where the demand for each product may well vary with time, often seasonally.

The problem the company faced was that they wanted to increase their output by using the weekends for production and by operating each line for as long as possible. Experience had led to the feeling that each line could operate continuously for about 4 weeks before coming out, for two shifts, for maintenance. The company wanted to know how this was going to affect their maintenance strategy and the following tasks were requested:

A To audit their existing maintenance department in order to compare it to international best practice.
B To propose an alternative maintenance strategy that would facilitate the new mode of continuous operation.
C To provide an organizational vision (via models) of where the company should be heading in the next 5 years.

> The audit of the FPP (task A above) will be used to provide a detailed and comprehensive explanation of BCM. This will include descriptions of each of the main elements of BCM, e.g. objectives, and will also introduce a number of generic models that can be used to map and understand the operation of these elements. You may find it necessary during your progress through the audit to refer back to the master diagram of Figure 1.1. It is important as you progress through the audit that you consider how you would modify the organization to comply with tasks B and C above – the answer to these tasks will be incorporated into this section as exercises.

1.4 Part A: Audit of the FPP maintenance department

The audit procedure follows the main elements of the methodology model shown in Figure 1.1.

1.4.1 Maintenance objectives

At plant level this could be stated as being:

> *to achieve the 15-shift operating pattern, product mix and output (cans/week) within the accepted plant condition for longevity and safety requirements, and at minimum resource cost.*

It is the responsibility of the production, safety, and engineering departments to specify the plant requirements, and the maintenance department to develop the strategy to achieve these requirements at minimum cost.

If the maintenance department were to develop the 'best way of maintaining the plant' the maintenance objectives needed to be interpreted in a form that is meaningful at a lower level of equipment, the plant unit – a hydro, say, or the cooker (see Figure 1.5). This allowed the maintenance *life plans* for the various units of plant to be established.

> The audit established that the FPP were using a management-by-objectives (MBO) procedure. Business objectives were set, and translated into maintenance objectives by the chief engineer. These in turn were translated into key result areas (KRAs) which, rather than being objectives, were a series of future actions to achieve the maintenance objectives. The auditors considered the procedure to be excellent but the KRAs were not well enough directed toward maintenance objectives and were not sufficiently numerical.

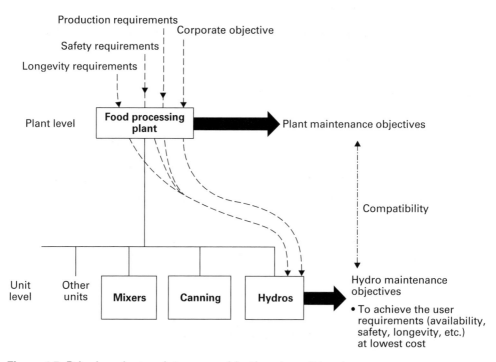

Figure 1.5 Bringing plant maintenance objectives to unit level

1.4.2 Life plans and preventive schedule

A generic model of a life plan for a unit of plant (a hydro, say) is shown in Figure 1.6. Such a plan can be considered as a program of maintenance jobs (lubrication, inspection, repair, replace and carried out at set frequencies) spanning the expected life of the unit. The main decision regarding the life plan is the determination of the preventive policy (replace or repair at fixed-time or fixed-operating periods, or via some form of inspection), which, in its turn, determines the resulting level of corrective work. The life plans should be established, using the well-documented principles of preventive maintenance and should be reviewed periodically to ensure their effectiveness.

The preventive maintenance schedule for the FPP was assembled from the preventive jobs identified in the life plans (see Figure 1.7). Such a schedule is only one part of

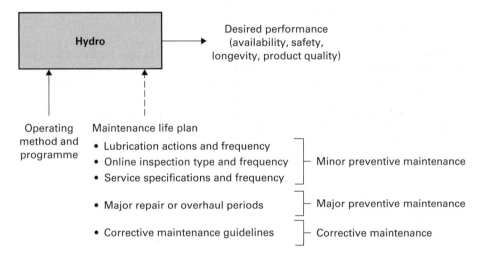

Figure 1.6 Outline of a life plan for a unit of plant

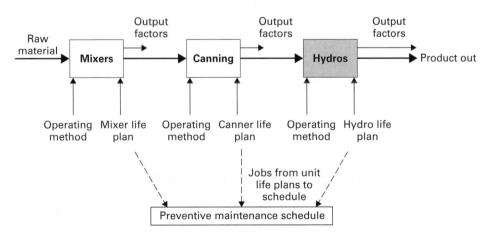

Figure 1.7 Build up of plant preventive schedule from unit life plans

the maintenance workload and has to be carried out in conjunction with the corrective work which has a shorter scheduling horizon – and often higher priority (sometimes restricting the maintenance department's ability to carryout corrective work – an aspect which will be discussed in more detail when we come to work planning).

The schedule is influenced by the production plan, which itself is a function of the market demand (multi-product fluctuating demand requiring a flexible production plan), operating pattern, plant redundancy, inter-stage and final stage storage, etc. In the FPP case the important factor was the operating pattern which gave six-shift-week-end windows and a 2-week annual window that provided enough time to carry out the necessary preventive (and corrective) work without affecting the production plan.

> In spite of the criticism of the objectives the unit life plans investigated were good, e.g. see Table 1.1 for the life plan for the hydro. The work content of the hydro overhauls (the major maintenance) was based on the monitoring and inspection of condition. The frequency of the overhauls, once every 8 years, was determined only via an experience-based, and approximate, judgment. Nevertheless, it did give an indication of the future major workload and its resource scheduling and budgeting. The preventive schedule was based on the scheduling guidelines outlined in Table 1.2. This meant that most of the second-line work was

Table 1.1 Outline the hydro life plan

Weekly	Cleaning, check operation of critical parts, lubrication.	4 hours	Minor work
2 weekly/ monthly	Lubrication routine.	4 hours	
3 monthly	Inspection of main drive to include oil analysis.	8 hours	
6 monthly	Inspection of all flights and conveyor drives. Clean hydro internally. Oil analysis of conveyor drives.	3 shifts	
12 monthly	Fixed time replacement of sprocket bearings. Overhaul drive unit and rewind motors.	1 week	
2 yearly	Replace with speed drive belts.	1 week	
8 yearly	Major rebuild. Exact frequency on condition.	3 weeks	Major work

Table 1.2 Scheduling guidelines for the FPP

	Maintenance philosophy	*Work type*
Monday to Friday	'Keep the plant going' and 'Keep an eye on its condition'	Reactive maintenance Operator monitoring routines Trade-force line-patrolling routines Condition-based routines
Weekends	'Inspect the plant carefully and repair as necessary in order to keep it going until next weekend'	Schedule corrective jobs by priority Inspect and repair schedule Fixed-time minor job schedule (services, etc.)
Summer shutdown	'Schedule out the major jobs to see us through another year'	Schedule corrective jobs Fixed-time major jobs schedule

carried out at weekends. Little attempt had been made to schedule this latter work into the weekend, by exploiting spare capacity.

(Life plans and preventive schedules are covered in depth in *Strategic Maintenance Planning*, ISBN 07506 69926.)

1.4.3 Workload

The maintenance schedule generates the maintenance workload (see Figure 1.1). The mechanical workload for the FPP is mapped in Figure 1.8 by its scheduling characteristics (the electrical workload can be mapped in the same way). *First-line work* is made up from emergency jobs (which can be defined as work needing to be carried out in the shift of its occurrence) and jobs (corrective or preventive) that are small and do not require detailed planning – they can be 'fitted in'.

It can be seen that this work is carried out during the shifts over Monday to Friday. Management had manned up the shift resource to ensure all the emergency work received attention during the shift of its occurrence.

Second-line work involves the larger preventive jobs (services, small overhauls, etc.) and corrective jobs that require planning and, via a priority system can be scheduled to be carried out at weekend (or in some other available window).

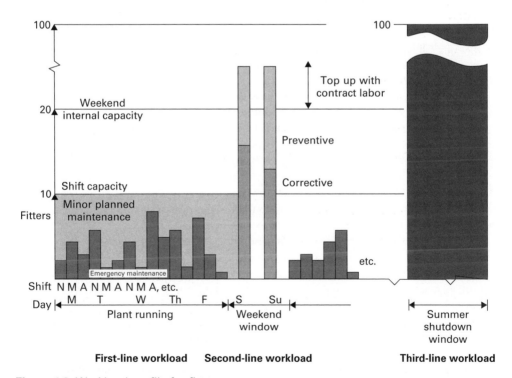

Figure 1.8 Workload profile for fitters

> When the weekend workload exceeded the internal weekend resource (two of the four shift-groups – 20 fitters) contract labor was used to cover the excess.

Third-line work involves major plant (or parts of the plant) overhauls. It requires the plant to be offline for considerable periods and is carried out at medium or long-term intervals – in the FPP case in the annual 2-week windows. The planning lead time for such work can be many months.

A more detailed categorization of a maintenance workload is shown in Table 1.3.

> The audit revealed a 50% over-manning on the mid-week shifts, caused by lack of clear definition of emergency work – much of which could have been carried out at the weekends as planned second-line work.

1.4.4 Maintenance organization

The workload is the biggest single influence in the size and shape of the maintenance organization. At the FPP the first-line emergency work required shift cover and the yearly shutdown peak required contract labor. Designing the organization requires many interrelated decisions to be made (where to locate manpower, how to extend inter-trade flexibility, who should be responsible for spare parts, how to decide the responsibilities for plant operation and maintenance), each influenced by various conflicting factors. Thinking in terms of the methodology of Figure 1.1 reduces the complexity of this problem, by categorizing the decisions according to the main elements of the organization, *viz.* its resource structure, its administrative structure, its systems and then considering each one in the order indicated – the procedure is iterative.

Resource structure

The resource structure is the geographic location of workforce, spares, tools and information, their function, composition, size and logistics. Figure 1.9, e.g. shows the Monday to Friday structure that had evolved at the FPP, to best suit the characteristics of a 24-hour first-line emergency workload. The emphasis is on rapid response, plant knowledge via specialization, shift working and team working with production. In theory, the shift-groups had been sized to match the reactive workload with the lower-priority jobs being used to smooth the workload. The weekday centralized group carried out second-line work to include weekend preparation, reconditioning and also acted as a first-line work overspill for the shift-groups.

Figure 1.10 shows the structure that matched the second-line weekend workload. The shift roster was arranged to ensure that two of the four shift-groups are available for 12 hours on Saturdays and Sundays (to include some overtime). Contract labor was used to top-up, as necessary the internal labor force. A similar approach was used for the annual shutdown, but in that case the contracted workforce exceeded the internally available labor. The spare parts store and tool store was an integral part of the resource structure and in this case both were centralized, serving the whole site.

> The resource structure, e.g. see Figure 1.9, can be regarded as a simple matrix of plant specialization against work category (first line, second line, etc.). To enable

Table 1.3 Detailed categorization of maintenance workload by organizational characteristics

Main category	Subcategory	Category number	Comments
First line	Corrective emergency	1	Occurs with random incidence and little warning and the job times also vary greatly. A typical emergency workload is shown in Figure 1.8. This is a workload generated by operating plant, the pattern following the production-operating pattern (e.g. 5 days, three shifts per day, etc.). Requires urgent attention due to economic or safety imperatives. Planning limited to resource cover and some job instructions or decision guidelines. Can be offline or online (*in-situ* corrective techniques). In some industries (e.g. power generation) failures can generate major work, these are usually infrequent but cause large work peaks.
	Corrective deferred minor	2	Occurs in the same way as emergency corrective work but does not require urgent attention; it can be deferred until time and maintenance resources are available (it can be planned and scheduled). During plant operation some small jobs can be fitted into an emergency workload such as that of Figure 1.8 (smoothing).
	Preventive routines	3	Short periodicity work, normally involving inspections and/or lubrication and/or minor replacements. Usually online and carried out by specialists or used to smooth an emergency workload such as that of Figure 1.8.
Second line	Corrective deferred major	4	Same characteristics as (2) but of longer duration and requiring major planning and scheduling.
	Preventive services	5	Involves minor offline work carried out at short- or medium-length intervals. Scheduled with time tolerances for slotting and work smoothing purposes. Some work can be carried out online although most is carried out online during weekend or other shutdown windows.
	Corrective reconditioning and fabrication	6	Similar to deferred work but is carried out away from the plant (second-line maintenance) and usually by a separate trade-force.
Third line	Preventive major work (overhauls, etc.)	7	Involves overhauls of plant, plant sections of major units. Work is offline and carried out at medium- or long-term intervals. Such a workload varies in the long term as shown in Figure 1.8. The shutdown schedule for large multi-plant companies can be designed to smooth the company shutdown workload.
	Modifications	8	Can be planned and scheduled some time ahead. The modification workload (often 'capital work') tends to rise to a peak at the end of the company financial year. This work can also be used to smooth the shutdown workload.

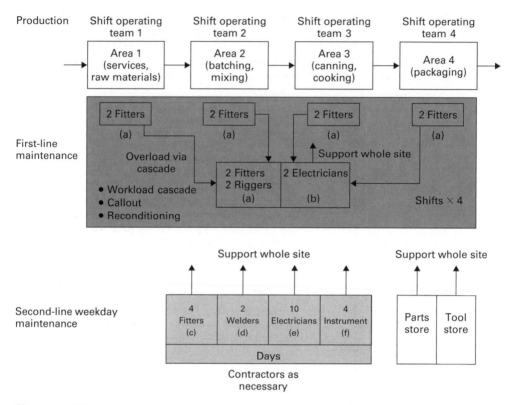

Figure 1.9 Weekday resource structure

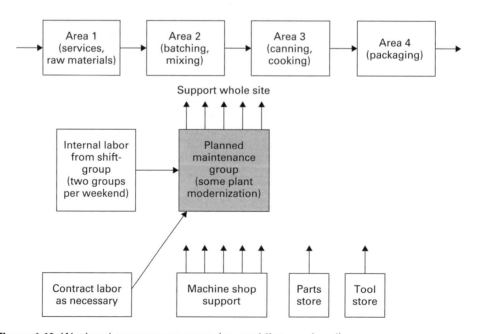

Figure 1.10 Weekend resource structure (second-line weekend)

the structure to be drawn it is necessary to construct the horizontal axis as the *plant line*, i.e. the division of the plant into its main process areas, and the vertical axis as the *work-type line*, i.e. operations above the plant line and maintenance work categories below the plant line. In this case the complete structure (weekday and weekend) could have been drawn on the same diagram. It would have then been necessary to explain on the diagram how the shift teams related into the weekend teams. Resource structures provide an outline of the way in which maintenance resources are used; they need to be supplemented by a description of trade flexibility, contract usage, shift rostering and human factors, etc.

The aim of any resource structure design (or modification) is to achieve the best resource utilization for a desired speed of response and quality of work. This, in part, involves the best match of the resources to the workload. Decisions in a number of other areas (e.g. in shift rostering, the use of contract labor, inter-plant flexibility, inter-trade flexibility and production-maintenance flexibility) can influence this matching process. Flexibility is clearly the key factor here. The structure is also influenced by the availability of trade-force skills and by various human factors.

The FPP audit revealed a number of deficiencies in the resource structure. The most important was the over-manning of the mid-week shifts (see the workload comments). The audit was carried out 13 years ago and it is not surprising that inter-trade flexibility, production-maintenance flexibility and contractor alliances were not being exploited. Human factors such as morale, motivation and a sense of equipment ownership were good.

Administrative structure

This can be considered as a hierarchy of work roles, ranked by their authority and responsibility for deciding what, when and how maintenance work should be carried out. The FPP structure is shown in Figure 1.11 (which uses the so-called organogram as the modeling vehicle). Many of the rules and guidelines of classical administrative theory can be used in the design of such structures. The model shows the maintenance administration in the context of the full administration – simplified in this case. The key decisions in the design of the maintenance administration can be divided between its upper and lower structures. Regarding the former the audit must identify how the responsibilities for plant ownership, operation, maintenance have been allocated. In the FPP case, production had responsibility for the operation of the plant, and in a sense its ownership, since they dictated how it was to be used and when it could be released for maintenance. Maintenance had responsibility for establishing and carrying out the maintenance strategy, and engineering for plant acquisition and plant condition standards. These responsibilities have to be clearly defined and overlapping areas identified.

Initially, the lower structure has to be considered separately from the upper because it is influenced – indeed, almost constrained – by the nature of the maintenance resource structure which, as explained, is in turn a function of the workload. Lower structure decisions are concerned with establishing the duties, responsibilities and work roles of the shop floor personnel and of the first level of supervision.

The FPP was using the traditional supervisor – planner – trade-force structure. This needs to be compared with the more recent structures of self-empowered

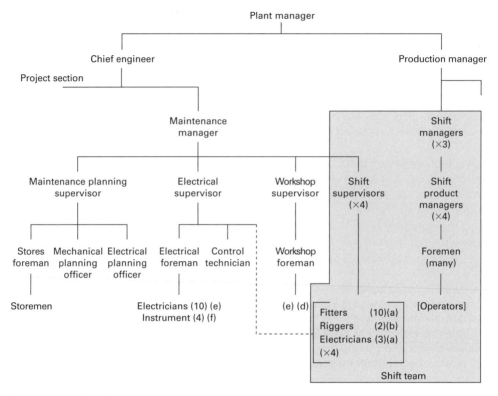

Figure 1.11 Administrative structure

operator–maintainer shift teams and self-empowered second-line maintenance teams (see Chapter 11).

(Maintenance organization is covered in depth in *Managing Maintenance Resources*, ISBN 07506 69934.)

1.4.5 Maintenance work planning

Figure 1.12 outlines a maintenance work planning system for the FPP resource and administrative structure previously shown. The design of this should aim to get the right balance between the cost of planning the resources and the savings in direct and indirect maintenance costs that result from use of such resources.

It can be seen that the planning system is designed around the resource structure it has a shift planning system (first line), a weekend planning system (second line) and an annual shutdown planning system (third line – not shown in detail). The audit must identify how well each level of planning is being carried out. At each level there are key procedures to verify, e.g. at FPP's second level:

- How good is the information base in terms of standard job procedures, spare part list, history?
- Who identifies the job method for monitoring jobs?

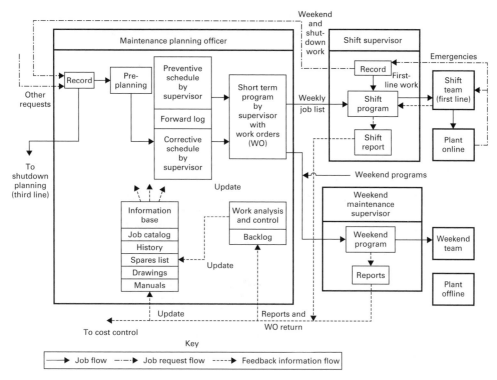

Figure 1.12 Work planning system

- Are job times estimated before they are put into the forward log?
- How are multi-trade jobs handled?
- How good is the return of information in terms of quantity and quality?

To understand operation of the 'weekday planning system' refer to Figure 1.12 and Figure 1.9. Work originates from the plant areas and goes to the maintenance shift supervisor (MSS) via the operators and production supervisors. The MSS carries out priority 1 work (emergencies, etc.) and passes back lower-priority work to the planning officer (PO) for planning and scheduling. The MSS smooths the ongoing emergency workload by feeding low-priority first-line work (from the weekly planned job list) to the trade-force (see also Figure 1.8).

To understand the operation of the weekend planning system refer to Figures 1.10 and 1.12. Corrective jobs come into this system from the MSS and from other personnel – this work is priority 2 and above (plannable and schedulable). Work that can only be carried out in a major shutdown (priority 5) is passed onto the shutdown planning system. The jobs are pre-planned (spares, method, estimated time) and slotted by priority into the corrective schedule. The planning of the jobs is aided by the 'information base'. A weekly meeting (Thursday) establishes the 'weekend program' which is passed on to the weekend supervisor (one of the four MSS on a monthly rota) for detailed planning. The PO helps in co-ordinating the multi-trade jobs. Feedback to update the information base and for cost control comes back via completed work orders. In general such systems are now carried out electronically.

Figure 1.13 shows the work control system, which is complementary to the work planning system, its main function being to control the flow of work (preventive and corrective) via a job priority procedure and via the feed-forward of information about future resource availability. At the FPP a number of performance indices were being used to assist this process, *viz*.:

- Total man-days in the forward log.
- Man-days in the forward log by priority.
- Man-days in the backlog.
- Percent planned work completed per period.
- Percent of preventive work completed per period.

The audit revealed that the FPP's work planning system was satisfactory for what was essentially a weekly planning system, the work is planned during the week for the weekend. It was my opinion that the work planning system (and the associated software) would have to be up-rated if major jobs were to be planned at short notice during the week (see Section B of this case study).

(Work planning is covered in depth in Chapters 5–7.)

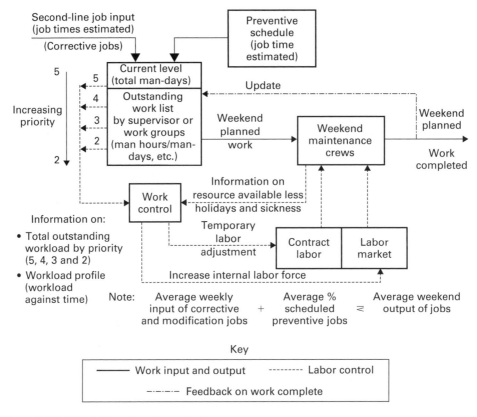

Figure 1.13 Principles of work control

1.4.6 **Maintenance control system**

This is needed to ensure that the maintenance organization is achieving its objectives (see Figure 1.1) and to initiate corrective action (e.g. change the life plan, if it is not). My own opinion is that the best practical mechanism for controlling the *overall maintenance effort* would be a properly designed maintenance costing system. This, see Figure 1.14, could be designed to provide a variety of outputs, including 'Top Tens', or Pareto plots indicating areas of low reliability, high maintenance cost, poor output performance, etc.

> The FPP audit identified that the plant had a costing system similar to that outlined in Figure 1.14 but used cost centers that were accountancy-oriented rather than equipment-oriented. In addition, the maintenance expenditure was not linked in any way to the output parameters.

Even if properly designed, a maintenance costing system has to be a high-level, longer-term system, providing a means of controlling the overall maintenance effort. This needs to be complemented by control systems operating at a lower level and on a shorter time scale.

Indeed it could be argued that a control system is needed for each sub-objective that is set, see Figure 1.15 (which has been developed from the definition of maintenance objective given in Section 1.4.1). For example, if an overtime limit is set then the actual overtime needs to be monitored and reported for corrective action. The two principal

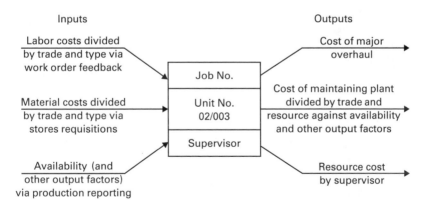

Job No.	Plant code		Trade and supervisor		Work type
	Plant	Unit	Electrician	Night shift	Preventive
521	02	003	2	NS	2

Figure 1.14 Outline of maintenance costing system

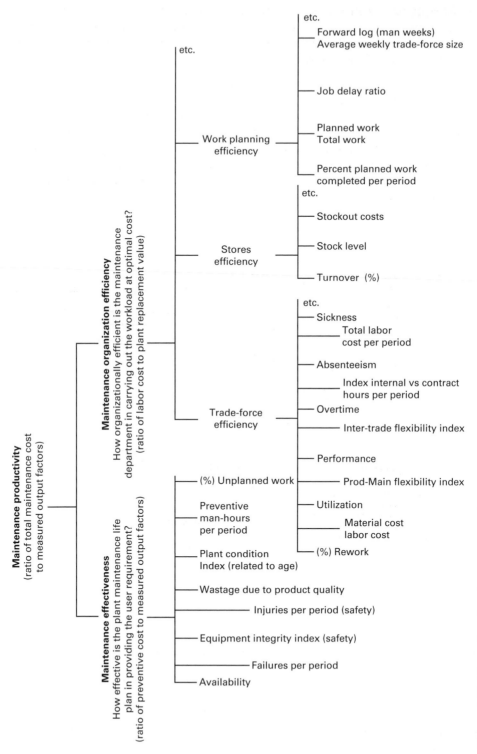

Figure 1.15 Hierarchy of maintenance performance indices

lower levels of maintenance control are best understood with reference to the objective hierarchy shown in Figure 1.15. The left-hand leg of the hierarchy is concerned with controlling *maintenance effectiveness* and the right-hand leg is concerned with controlling *organizational efficiency*.

Maintenance effectiveness

The basic model for controlling the effectiveness of maintenance is shown in Figure 1.16. It illustrates the classic ideas of reactive control – using the feedback of operational and maintenance data – and also highlights pro-active control via the feed-forward of ideas for reliability and maintenance improvement. Such mechanisms are required for each major unit of plant. Figure 1.17 shows these ideas incorporated into the FPP maintenance administration.

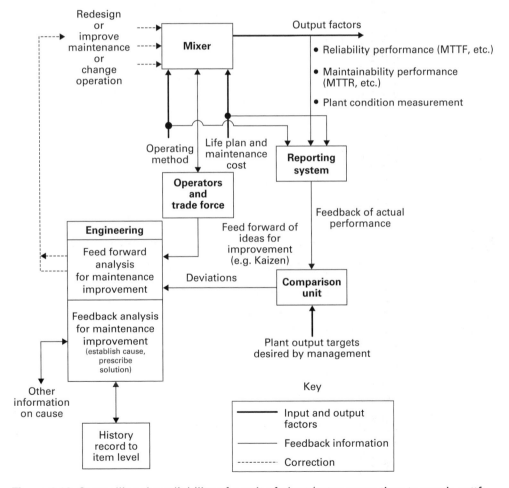

Figure 1.16 Controlling the reliability of a unit of plant (mtrr: mean time to repair, mttf: mean time to failure)

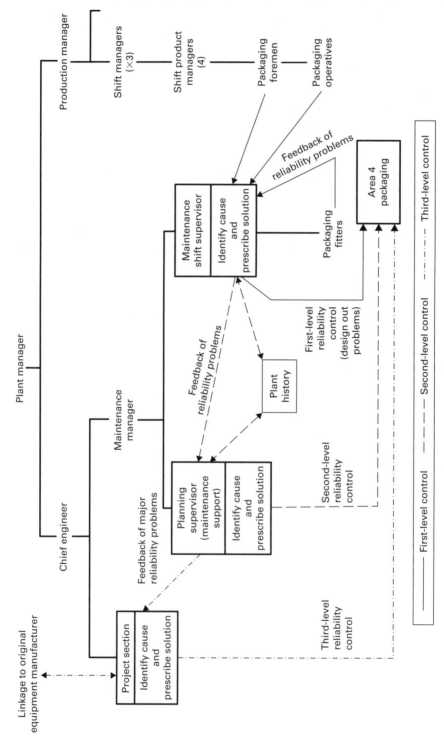

Figure 1.17 A model of plant reliability control in the FPP organization

The audit showed that the first-level system was not working well. In the 1980s few companies had incorporated the ideas of continuous improvement and equipment ownership at the trade-force/operator level of an organization. Considerable design-out maintenance effort was in evidence at the second level through the project engineers although they were not helped by the poor history/data recording.

Maintenance organizational efficiency

The prime organizational objective is outlined in Figure 1.15 and can be defined in more detail as:

> to carry out a given plant maintenance workload (governed by the life plans) at minimum cost, by using maintenance resources (man, spares, tools) in the most efficient way.

However, a single objective for organizational efficiency is somewhat fanciful. The best approach is through a series of sub-objectives (or performance indices) as shown in Figure 1.15.

> The auditors could find no such objectives/indices in use on the FPP.

(Maintenance control is discussed in depth in Chapter 4.)

1.4.7 Maintenance documentation

Figure 1.1 indicated that some forms of formal documentation system – for the collection, storage, interrogation, analysis and reporting of information (schedules, manuals, drawings or computer files) – are needed to facilitate the operation of all the elements of maintenance management. Figure 1.18, a general functional model of such a system (whether manual or computerized), indicates that it can be seen as comprising seven principal interrelated modules (performing different documentation functions). Considerable clerical and engineering effort is needed to establish and maintain certain of these functions (e.g. the plant maintenance information base). The control module, in particular, relies on an effective data collection system. Almost all of the companies that I now audit have computerized maintenance documentation systems.

> The best way of understanding the generic functional documentation model of Figure 1.18 is to start with the plant inventory (Module 1). This is a coded list of the equipment that has to be maintained, e.g. a mixer (see Figure 1.4). The essential maintenance information needed to maintain the mixer (and the other units listed in the inventory) is held in the information base (Module 2), e.g. life plans, history, spares lists, etc. The preventive work listed in the life plans of the various equipment is carried out via the preventive and inspection schedules (Modules 3 and 4). This work and the corrective and modification work are fed into the 'short-term work planning system' (Module 5) and where there are major shutdowns into the 'long-term work planning system' (Module 6). The feedback of information from the work planning system provides maintenance control (Module 7) and also updates the information base.

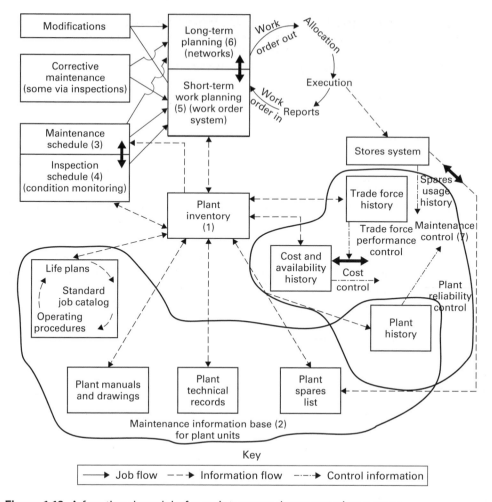

Figure 1.18 A functional model of a maintenance documentation system

The large double arrows in Figure 1.18 indicate the possible linkages between the maintenance documentation system and other company information systems *viz*.:

- Maintenance costing to financial management.
- Spare parts list to stores management.
- Work planning to shutdown scheduling (e.g. Primavera).
- Work planning to condition monitoring.

The majority of the systems I have audited have these functions connected, i.e. electronically – in fact, the most recent audit involved an integrated package – all the functions are on the same database. An audit needs to investigate each of the main modules of Figure 1.18, and also the sub-functions within each module, e.g. the spare parts list. In addition, it needs to identify the level and degree of integration with the other company functions.

The maintenance package at the FPP was a stand-alone computerized system. The audit revealed that this was satisfactory for the weekend planning system that was then being used (i.e. 13 years ago). For its time the plant information base was good and was being kept up to date (history excepted).

(The basics of maintenance documentation are covered in depth in Chapter 9 and computerized documentation in Chapter 10.)

1.4.8 Audit summary

A business-centered methodology, in conjunction with models and procedures that describes in more detail each of its elements, has been used as a framework to audit the maintenance department.

The audit revealed a number of problems, in particular, shift over-manning caused by lack of clear definition and measurement of the shift emergency maintenance work. In addition, the organization needed modification – improved inter-trade flexibility, the creation of operator–maintainer self-empowered teams, closer production-maintenance integration – to bring it up to international benchmark levels.

Review Questions

R1.1   You have been asked by your Managing Director to explain in a concise way what exactly is BCM. Write down an explanation-keep it as short as possible.

R1.2   Define maintenance strategy.

R1.3   Consider how the 'market demand for the product/service' and/or the 'supply of raw materials' can affect the maintenance strategy for the following physical asset systems:
(a) A sugar refinery.
(b) A petroleum refinery.
(c) A local passenger bus fleet.

1.5 Part B: An alternative maintenance strategy for continuous operation (see Table 1.4)

The existing maintenance strategy at the FPP was based on carrying out offline maintenance during the weekend windows of opportunity and during the once-per-year holiday window.

Little attempt had been made to exploit the excess capacity of the plant, or spare plant to schedule offline work while the plant was operating. The new, continuous, operating pattern meant that offline maintenance would have to be carried out in this way. Indeed, the life plans and schedule would have to move in the direction indicated in Table 1.4. This, in turn, would change the workload pattern as indicated in Table 1.4.

Table 1.4 Changes in maintenance strategy to accommodate continuous operation

- The first-line work would extend to 21 shifts per week. However, investigation of the mechanical emergency workload had revealed considerable over-manning.
  When the first-line work was defined as *the work that must be carried out during the shift of its occurrence* and subsequently activity sampled, it was shown that it could be carried out by five fitters.
- The second-line work (line shutdowns, unit shutdown, preparation for shutdown, services, inspection) was more difficult to forecast in terms of pattern and size. The main peaks would come during line shutdowns at a frequency of about once per week for two shifts. The size of the workload was unlikely to decrease (even with better preventive maintenance) because the plant was going to be more heavily utilized.
- The third-line major work could still be carried out during the holiday window.
- A movement toward shutdowns of complete sections of plant based on the longest running time of critical units (e.g. the hydros – about 4 weeks). The frequency of these shutdowns will, as far as possible be based on running hours or cumulative output. However, for critical items, inspection and condition monitoring routines may be used to indicate the need for shutdowns, which will provide more flexibility about shutdown dates.
- All plant designated as non-critical, e.g. as a result of spare capacity, will continue to be scheduled at unit level (e.g. the smaller mixers).
- A much greater dependence on formalized inspections and condition monitoring routines, for reasons given in (a) and also to detect faults while they are still minor and before they become critical.
- A concerted effort either to design out critical items (short life or poor reliability) or to extend their effective running time.

Exercises

E1.1   From the above comments it will be realized that immediate organizational changes are needed to match the new mode of operation (continuous operations for up to 4 weeks before a three shift shutdown of one line for essential maintenance).
    Outline a revised resource structure to match the new plant operating pattern and workload (the existing resource structure is shown in Figures 1.9 and 1.10). Modify the administrative structure to cope with any changes made to the resource structure (at this stage limit the changes to only those necessary to cope with the changed operating pattern).

E1.2   How would the new mode of operation affect the work planning system? Advise management on any changes required.

1.6 Part C: A longer-term view of organizational change

(This section uses the guideline solutions to Exercise E1.1 therefore it is advisable to answer Exercise E1.1 before reading this section.)

The organization outlined in the guideline solution to Exercise E1.1 (see Figures 1.20 and 1.21) – or in your own solutions – incorporated the immediate changes necessary for continuous operation. Their purpose was to allow the company to increase the plant availability (and output) while holding the resource costs steady. It may well be that with the experience of operation the size of the day-group of artisans will be reduced. However, in the medium and long term, when this organization is benchmarked against the best of international standards within the food processing industry, further improvements can also be identified (see Exercise E1.3).

Exercise

E1.3   Provide the management of the FPP with a model of a maintenance organization (a resource structure and administrative structure) that will bring them up to international benchmark levels.

In order to answer this question you may need to carry out a literature search of FPP maintenance organizations (or use your own experience).

1.7 The strategic thought process

The case study has shown that the maintenance department requires managerial strategic analysis in the same way as any other department. The thought process that was involved is indicated in Figure 1.19. It starts with the sales–production reaction to market demand, the resulting change in the plant operating pattern and the increased plant operation time. This, in turn, requires amended maintenance life plans and a modified maintenance schedule. Thus, the maintenance workload changes, which brings in train the need to modify the maintenance organization and systems.

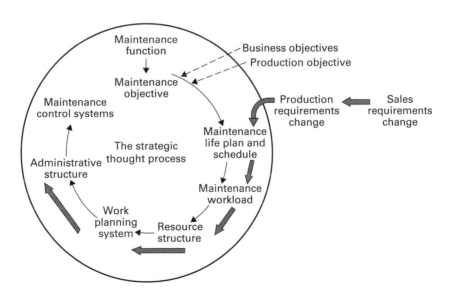

Figure 1.19   The influence of the market demand on maintenance strategy

Understanding and applying this type of strategic through process is the cornerstone of effective and fruitful maintenance management analysis [1,2].

Review Questions

R1.4   The sales department of the FPP wanted to increase output and the production department agreed to this. Can you explain the effect this had on the following:
- unit life plans;
- preventive maintenance schedule;
- maintenance workload;
- maintenance organization.

R1.5   From your answer to R1.4 and using Figure 1.19 explain the concept of the 'strategic maintenance management though process'.

References

1. Wilson, A., *Asset Maintenance Management*, Conference Communication, Farnham, 2000.
2. Mather, D., *The Maintenance Scorecard*, Industrial Press, New York, 2005.

Review Questions Guidelines

R1.1   Any decision involving the way maintenance is carried out should take into consideration its effect on the company's bottom line. For example, a reorganization might influence company profitability through changes in plant availability and maintenance resource costs.

R1.2   A maintenance strategy involves the complete maintenance management procedure which includes setting maintenance objectives, determining the preventive maintenance schedule and setting up the maintenance organization.

R1.3   (a) The supply of raw cane sugar is seasonal lasting about 6 months over the Summer/Autumn period. Sugarcane has a short storage life and has to be processed shortly after cutting. The maintenance strategy of a sugar refinery is based on maintaining the plant over the 6-month sugarcane growing season to ensure high plant availability over the 6-month plant-refining period.

(b) Petroleum refineries are mostly production limited, and involve high capital cost plant. The maintenance strategy is concerned with maintaining the plant during agreed shutdowns to achieve the longest possible production-operating period.

(c) A local passenger bus fleet provides a service rather than a product. Major maintenance is carried out using the 'spare buses in the fleet'. Minor maintenance is carried out in the low bus demand periods (the maintenance windows).

R1.4   This is explained clearly in the notes in Section 1.7.

R1.5   See Section 1.7 and Figure 1.19.

Exercise Guideline Solutions

E1.1 and E1.2   To match the new workload pattern the maintenance organization would also have to change. The most likely resource structure (see Figure 1.20) would be based on a first-line, 21 shift-group (the mechanical manning per shift being reduced to five fitters) and a second-line day-group of 15 fitters operating 5 days per week. This, in turn, would require a change the administrative structure as shown in Figure 1.21.

Because of the changes in the way the work would be scheduled (the mid-week work peaks would occur at relatively short notice via the condition monitoring of the lines) it was also necessary to advise management that their work planning system would need to be improved, in order to be far more flexible and dynamic.

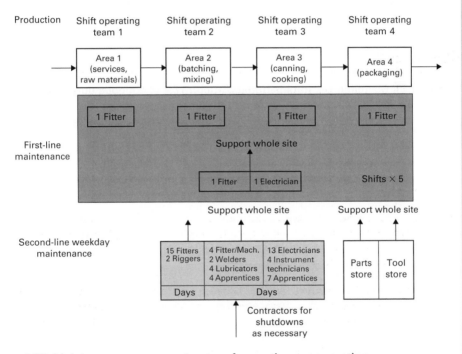

Figure 1.20 Maintenance resource structure for continuous operation

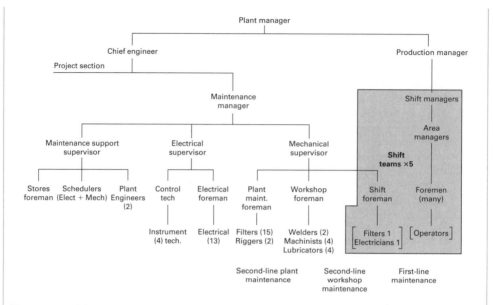

Figure 1.21 Maintenance administrative structure for continuous operation

E1.3   A proposed improved maintenance organization is shown in Figure 1.22 (resource structure) and Figure 1.23 (administrative structure). The proposals incorporate the following actions:
- The introduction of self-empowered plant-oriented operator–maintainer teams.
- The introduction of self-empowered trade teams.
- Increase in the number of engineers, plant located for maintenance support.

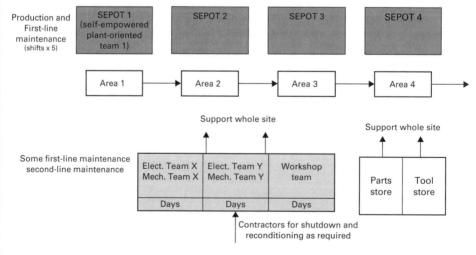

Figure 1.22   Organizational vision: resource structure

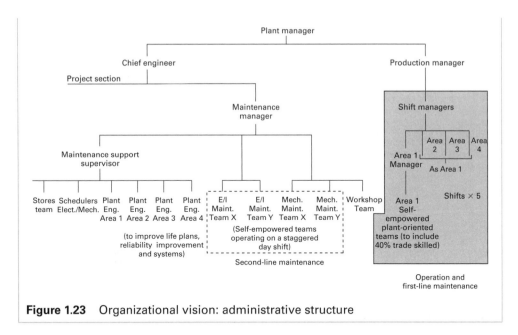

Figure 1.23   Organizational vision: administrative structure

2 Introduction to maintenance management systems

*'Always design a thing by considering it in its next larger context –
a chair in a room, a room in a house, a house in an environment,
an environment in a city.'*

Eliel Saarinin

Chapter aims and outcomes

To show how an industrial company can be modeled as an *open system* made up of numerous interacting subsystems.

On completion of this chapter you should be able to:

- understand how all management systems, and subsystems, need a control function;
- understand that the maintenance department is a subsystem of the company system;
- identify the other key company level subsystems, e.g. stores, that can have a direct affect on the performance of the maintenance subsystem;
- identify the key 'maintenance systems', e.g. work planning, that are needed to enable the maintenance department to perform its function.

Chapter route map

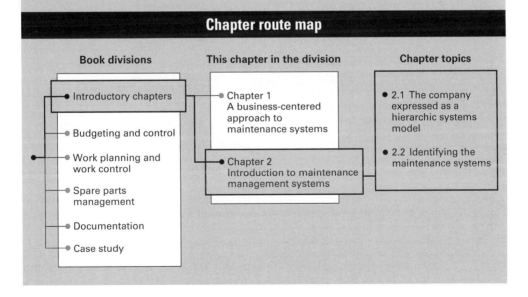

Book divisions

- Introductory chapters
- Budgeting and control
- Work planning and work control
- Spare parts management
- Documentation
- Case study

This chapter in the division

- Chapter 1
  A business-centered approach to maintenance systems
- Chapter 2
  Introduction to maintenance management systems

Chapter topics

- 2.1 The company expressed as a hierarchic systems model
- 2.2 Identifying the maintenance systems

Key words

- System control
- Hierarchic systems model
- Holism
- General systems theory

2.1 The company expressed as a hierarchic systems model

A better understanding of organizations may be obtained through the so-called *systems* approach. In this, organizations can be viewed as *open systems* taking inputs from their environments and transforming them – by a series of activities and with some objective in view – into outputs (see Figure 2.1) [1].

> *Open system*: An open system is in continual interaction with its environment and achieves a steady state whilst still retaining the capacity for work (transformation). The system is open in the sense it can react not only to the direct 'inputs and outputs' but also changes in the environment surrounding it.

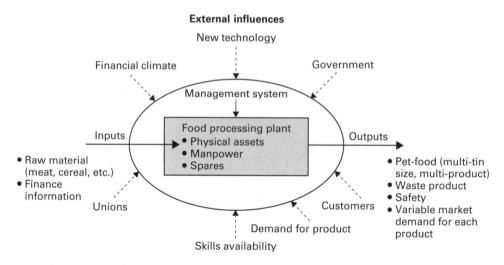

Figure 2.1 An organization producing pet-food, viewed as an open system

Figure 2.2 shows an extension of this systems model of a company to include a control element, the purpose of which is to monitor the system output, compare it to what is expected and to redirect the company's effort as necessary.

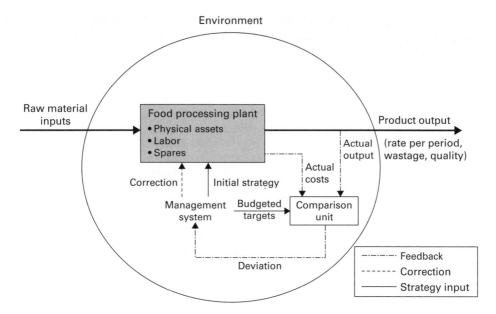

Figure 2.2 Food processing plant: management control

Several writers have shown how a systems model of a company can be considered as being made up of many interacting subsystems (e.g. maintenance, production, stores, etc.) each carrying out distinct organizational functions. Figure 2.3 shows the maintenance subsystem. This maintenance subsystem also requires a control element of the kind shown in Figure 2.2. All of these subsystems interact to carry out the overall company function.

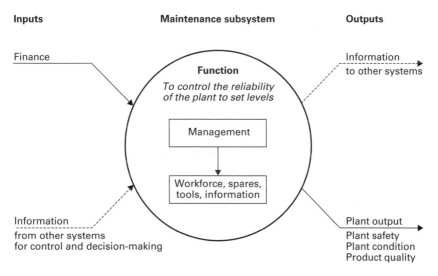

Figure 2.3 A model of the maintenance subsystem

Using the same reasoning, each of the subsystems (e.g. maintenance) can be considered as being made up of a number of sub-subsystems (e.g. short-term planning, maintenance control, etc.).

This *systems hierarchy approach* is useful for modeling a company, the environment in which it operates, and the numerous company subsystems and their interaction.

> This *hierarchy of systems* is one of the key concepts of *general systems theory* [2]. The Organization portrayed as a hierarchy of systems is shown in Figure 2.4. Another key concept is *holism – the whole is not just the sum of the parts* – i.e. the system itself is best explained as a totality. It is for this latter reason that the author uses the top-down approach of business-centered maintenance.

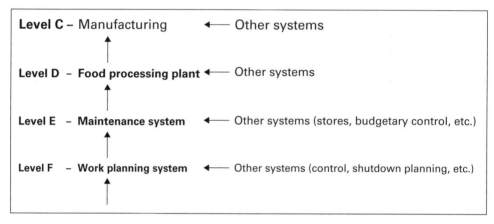

Level C – Manufacturing　　←—— Other systems

Level D – **Food processing plant** ←—— Other systems

Level E – **Maintenance system**　←—— Other systems (stores, budgetary control, etc.)

Level F – **Work planning system**　←—— Other systems (control, shutdown planning, etc.)

Figure 2.4 Hierarchy of management systems

2.2 Identifying the maintenance systems

This book is concerned with modeling, and describing the operation of the main maintenance subsystems, level F of Figure 2.4, and the other associated level E systems, e.g. spare parts management that have a major influence on the operation of the maintenance department. These systems are listed below in the order in which they will be discussed in this book:

- *Budgetary control* is a control system at company level E (see Figure 2.4). It interacts with the maintenance system with the main function of controlling maintenance expenditure. Budgetary control will be discussed in outline in Chapter 3.
- *Maintenance performance measurement and control* is an information system that sets standards of maintenance performance (via maintenance objectives, key performance indices, etc.), measures the actual performance and controls the overall maintenance management effort in the light of any deviations that may be observed. This is the system that constitutes the 'control element' of the business-centered maintenance model (see Figure 1.1) and will be covered in Chapter 4.

- *Plant reliability control* is concerned with identifying equipment 'hot spots' (areas of high maintenance cost or of low reliability), establishing root causes of problems and prescribing solutions to them. This system was outlined in Chapter 1 and will be covered in detail in Chapter 4.
- *Maintenance organizational efficiency control* is an information system that is used to measure and control the efficient use of the key maintenance resources (men, spares and tools), to be covered in Chapter 4.
- *Short-term maintenance work planning and work control* has the function of planning, scheduling, allocating and controlling the execution of the short-term maintenance workload. This topic is covered in detail in Chapter 5.
- *Long-term maintenance work planning and control (turnaround management)* has the function of planning, scheduling, allocating and controlling the execution of the major plant shutdowns (discussed in detail in Chapters 6 and 7).
- *Equipment spares management* is often managed outside the maintenance department (it can be regarded as a level E system of Figure 2.4) but is included in this book because spare parts are the key maintenance resource. This is covered as one of the main topics of this book (Chapter 8).
- *Maintenance documentation* is an information system that can be regarded as the vehicle that allows the other maintenance systems to operate and interact and as such is covered in detail in Chapters 9 and 10.

Exercise

E2.1   For your own company (or a company you can access), see how many of the systems listed in Section 2.2 you can identify?

References

1. Ackoff, R.L., Towards a system of systems concepts. *Management Science*, July 1971, pp. 661–671.
2. Kast, F.E. and Rosenzweig, J.E., *Organisations and Management* (3rd Ed), McGraw Hill, Singapore, 1974.

PART 2

Budgeting and control

3 Maintenance budgeting

'Annual income £20, annual expenditure £19.95, result happiness.
Annual income £20, annual expenditure £20.05, result misery.'

Charles Dickens

Chapter aims and outcomes

To explain the concepts and ideas of maintenance budgeting and the linkages between the maintenance budget and the company budget.

On completion of this chapter you should be able to:

- understand that the company budget is a financial statement of its long- and short-term plans and that budgetary control is an integral part of the company's management control process;
- appreciate that the maintenance budget is an essential element of the company budget and that there is a need for a long-term maintenance budget (covering major work) and a maintenance expenditure budget;
- understand an outline procedure for building the maintenance budget and how the procedure needs modification to suit different administrative structures.

Chapter route map

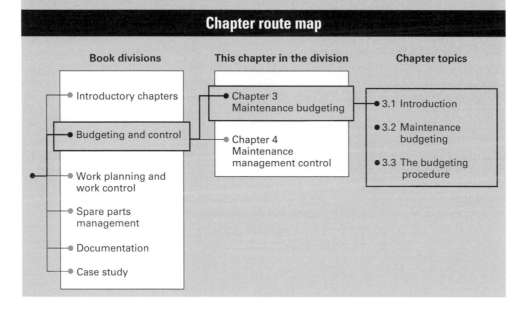

Key words
• Budgeting • Zero-based budgeting • Standard costs • Profit center • Variance • Capital budget • Company revenue budget • Cost center

3.1 Introduction

A systems model of an industrial company was shown in Figure 2.2. It incorporates the management control element, the function of which is to monitor the system outputs, compare these with what was expected, identify any deviation and then redirect the company's effort as necessary. At *company* level 'budgetary control' is one of the key management control mechanisms.

The preparation of a company budget can be regarded as an integral part of the company planning process. Management are required to plan for production volumes to meet forecasted sales demand (see Figure 2.2). This in turn requires a sales, production and maintenance budget.

The budget can be regarded as the end point of the company's planning process in as much as it is a 'statement of the company's objectives and plans in revenue and/or cost terms'. It is a baseline document against which actual financial performance is measured.

In control terms, budgets are based on *standard costs*, which provide the expected (or planned) yearly expenditure profile. This expected expenditure is compared to the actual expenditures (*cost control*) and the variances (over- or under-budget) noted. Management then have information on which to base corrective action.

Usually, the word budget is taken to refer to a particular financial year. However, the annual budget is often the first year of a rolling long-term budget. For example, if a company has a strategic 5-year plan it will normally align with a 5-year rolling financial budget.

3.2 Maintenance budgeting

The need for a maintenance budget arises from the overall budgeting need of corporate management and involves estimation of the cost of the resources (labor, spares, etc.) that will be needed in the next financial year to meet the expected maintenance workload. This is best explained via Figure 3.1 (which is extracted from the methodology diagram of Figure 1.1). The maintenance life plans and schedule have been laid down to achieve the maintenance objective (which incorporates the production needs, e.g. operating pattern and availability) and in turn generates the maintenance workload.

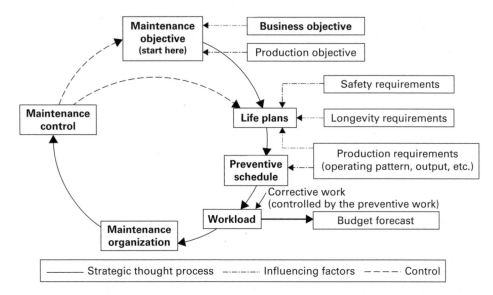

Figure 3.1 Relationship between maintenance strategy and budgeting

Typical examples of maintenance workloads are shown in Figures 3.2(a) and 3.2(b). A detailed categorization of the maintenance workload is shown in Table 3.1. Essentially, maintenance budgeting is the expression of this forecasted workload in terms of the cost of internal labor, contract labor and materials needed to deal with it.

It will be appreciated from Figure 3.2(a) that maintenance budgeting involves both the ongoing workload and also the major workload (overhauls, equipment replacement and modifications).

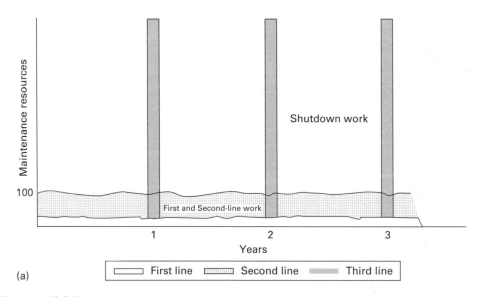

(a)

Figure 3.2(a) Power station workload

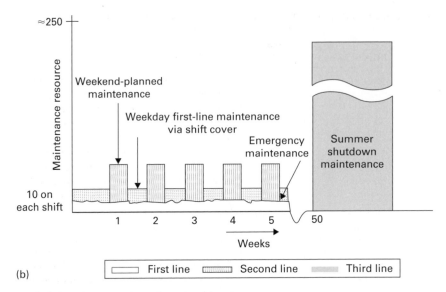

Figure 3.2(b) Food processing plant workload

It is important that the maintenance budget is set up to reflect the nature of the maintenance strategy/workload. There is a need for a *longer-term strategic maintenance budget* that covers Work Categories 7 and 8 of Table 3.1. Much of this major work involves capital expenditure that can subsequently be depreciated by corporate management in the revenue budgets. In the shorter term there is a requirement for an *annual maintenance expenditure budget* that covers Work Categories 1–6 of Table 3.1. These costs feed into the *company revenue budget* that operates over the financial year.

In plants requiring major shutdowns there is also the need for specific *turnaround budgets* which are an integral part of the turnaround planning procedure (these will be discussed in Chapter 7).

Review Question

R3.1 During his auditing experience the author has come across many companies where maintenance budgeting is based on last year's expenditure plus an allowance for inflation. What are the potential problems with this approach, and when can it be justified?

The maintenance budgeting procedure is facilitated by identifying plant cost centers and, where necessary, continuing the identification down to unit level. A cost center in an alumina refinery might be coded as follows:

Cost center	Unit	Unique unit number
Digestion area	Bauxite mills	
6	C	02

Over the designated financial period the actual maintenance cost (labor, spares, tools) are collected against these cost centers to enable cost monitoring and control *viz.* 'cost control'. Cost control is complimentary to budgeting and is discussed in Chapter 4.

Table 3.1 Categorization of maintenance workload by organizational characteristics

Main category	Subcategory	Category number	Comments
First line	Corrective emergency	1	Occurs with random incidence and little warning and the job times also vary greatly. In some industries (e.g. power generation) failures can generate major work, these are usually infrequent but cause large work peaks.
	Corrective deferred (minor)	2	Occurs in the same way as emergency corrective work but does not required urgent attention; it can be deferred until time and maintenance resources are available.
	Preventive routines	3	Work repeated at short intervals, normally involving inspections and/or lubrication and/or minor replacements.
Second line	Corrective deferred (major)	4	Same characteristics as (2) but of longer duration and requiring major planning and scheduling.
	Preventive services	5	Involves minor off-line work carried out at short- or medium-length intervals. Scheduled with time tolerances for slotting and work smoothing purposes.
	Corrective reconditioning and fabrication	6	Similar to deferred work but is carried out away from the plant (second-line maintenance) and usually by a separate trade-force.
Third line	Preventive major work (overhauls, etc.)	7	Involves overhauls of plant or plant sections or major units.
	Modifications	8	Can be planned and scheduled some time ahead. The modification workload (often 'capital work') tends to rise to a peak at the end of the company financial year.

3.3 The budgeting procedure

The budgeting procedure depends on the type of administration in use. In a functional organization of the kind used in large integrated plants, e.g. an alumina refinery (see Figure 3.3), the strategic maintenance budget is set up by the chief engineer with contributions from the maintenance manager, services manager and the refinery manager. A typical major work schedule for an alumina refinery is shown in Figure 3.4.* Such a schedule extends for at least 10 years and is used to identify the large, low-frequency, high-cost, maintenance jobs and the capital replacement work. This information is used to set up the strategic maintenance budget.

---

*An aluminum refinery never comes off line, it is designed to allow the major plant sections to be maintained while it is still operating at full or reduced load. Thus the major workload tends to be scheduled in such a way as to avoid the major work peaks.

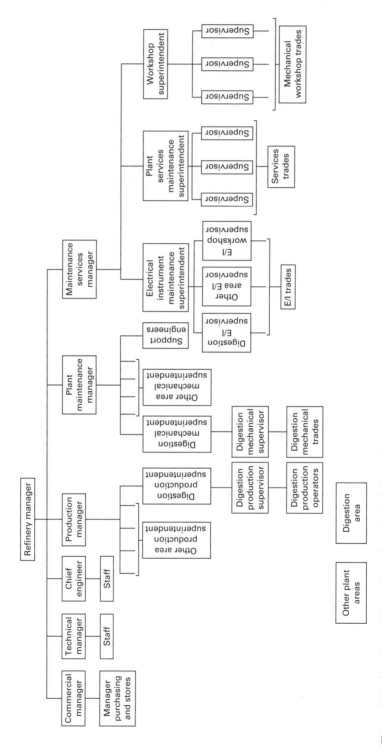

Figure 3.3 Alumina refinery: functional administration

ID	Name	Nov	Dec	Jan	Feb	Mar	Apr	May	Jun	Jul	Aug	Sep	Oct	Nov	Dec	Jan	Feb
				2000												2001	
1	BOILERHOUSE																
2																	
3	BOILERS																
4	BOILER – 4							1/5 ▬ 26/5									
5	BOILER – 7								12/7 ▬ 27/7								
6	BOILER – 2											1/9 ▬ 11/10					
7																	
8	TURBO-ALTERNATORS																
9	TURBO-ALTERNATOR – 1				5/3 ▬ 24.4												
10																	
11	DIGESTION																
12																	
13	UNIT SHUTDOWNS																
14	UNIT 1												12/10 ▬ 14/10				
15	UNIT 1 B/O TANK CONVERSION												14/11 ▬ 15/11				
16	UNIT 2								20/7 ▬ 22/7								
17	UNIT 2 B/O TANK CONVERSION									20/8 ▬ 21/8							
18	UNIT 3				23/3 ▬ 25/3												
19	UNIT 3 B/O TANK CONVERSION					23/4 ▬ 24/4											
20																	
21	DIGESTERS																
22	UNIT 1																
23	DIGESTER 1		15/1	▬ 16/3													
24	DIGESTER 1												1/10 ▬ 30/11				
25	DIGESTER 2									1/8 ▬ 30/9							
26	DIGESTER 3						1/4 ▬ 31/5										
27																	
28	UNIT 2																
29	DIGESTER 4							1/6 ▬ 31/7									
30	DIGESTER 5						1/4 ▬ 31/5										
31	DIGESTER 5													1/12 ▬ 30/1			
32	DIGESTER 6		1/1	▬ 2/3													
33	DIGESTER 6															7/2 ▬	
34																	
35	UNIT 3																
36	DIGESTER 7		15/1	▬ 16/3													

Figure 3.4 Extract from major work schedule

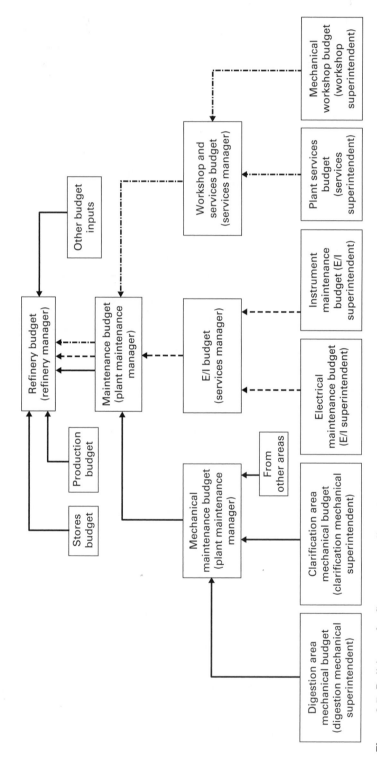

Figure 3.5 Build up of refinery expenditure budget

The author has observed that most large process plants use some form of strategic maintenance budgeting which matches their long-term preventive schedule (e.g. see the power station workload of Figure 3.2(a)). He has also noticed that some food processing plants/breweries do not use strategic maintenance budgets. This is because their maintenance strategies are based on simple routines and inspections (a 'wait and see' maintenance policy) – they do not schedule long-term major maintenance or, in some cases, the replacement of capital equipment. To say the least, the author is surprised.

The major work schedule of Figure 3.4 also includes some of the shorter frequency maintenance work which, in conjunction with the maintenance routines and services, is also covered in the annual maintenance expenditure budget. The annual budget is built up from the budget for each plant and workshop. For example, the mechanical maintenance for the digestion area can be estimated, from the expected area workload, by the digestion mechanical superintendent, translated into resources needed, and added to similar estimates from other plant areas and disciplines (see Figure 3.5).

Budgeting for the preventive work (Categories 3 and 5) is relatively straightforward. Corrective work (Categories 1, 2, 4 and 6) presents a more difficult problem. Nevertheless, if a history record is available it is often possible to estimate, with acceptable accuracy, the level of corrective work to be expected for a given level of preventive effort (see Figure 3.1). Without such experience little confidence can be placed in the estimate and this must be made clear in the budget statement.

The workshops and services areas needed to be tackled differently, in as much as their workload originates from each of the plant areas.

This approach is sometimes called zero-based budgeting (ZBB) in as much as the maintenance budget is built up from scratch each year in the light of the maintenance schedule for that year.

Exercise

E3.1   Carry out a brief Internet search for literature on ZBB.

Review Question

R3.2   Use information found in Exercise E3.1 in conjunction with Figure 3.1 to explain the concept of ZBB applied to maintenance work.

The above budgeting procedures need modification for an administrative structure based on manufacturing units (see Figure 3.6). Each manufacturing unit becomes a 'profit center', and a combined production/maintenance budget is required at operations manager level. The centralized maintenance functions become cost centers and budgets for the service they provide to the manufacturing units. These centralized maintenance functions are concerned with efficiency of resource usage rather than plant availability, they act like internal contractors and the costing system is designed to reflect this situation.

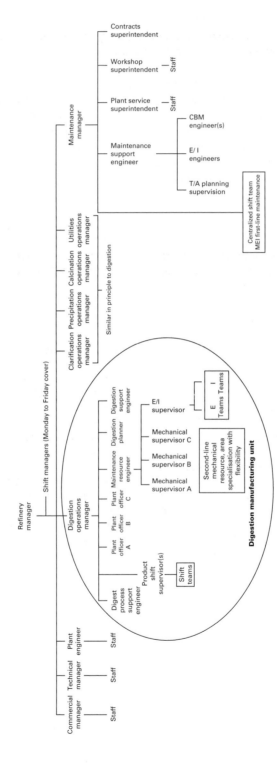

Figure 3.6 Administrative structure based on manufacturing units

Review Question

R3.3 Discuss the advantages of the 'manufacturing unit' administrative structure of Figure 2.6 in terms of maintenance budgeting.

In practice, maintenance budgeting is rarely as rational as above. Senior management see maintenance only as a cost. The linkage between maintenance expenditure and production output indicated in Figure 3.1 is often ignored. Maintenance budgeting then becomes an exercise based on last year's costs plus an allowance for inflation (at best low-frequency major work may be included). This is a poor form of budgeting, it is an attempt to forecast what is likely to be spent in the absence of any management intention to deviate from what has gone before.

Exercise

E3.2 Establish the maintenance budgeting procedure in use in your company and compare it against the key concepts and ideas presented in this section.

Review Questions Guidelines

R3.1 One of the main problems is that the budgeted expenditure may not reflect the changes in the maintenance workload.
    The approach can be justified where a company is in a stable operating situation and the maintenance workload is also relatively stable.

R3.2 Company objectives and plans change with time to suit market demand and other external factors. This affects the production requirements and objectives, which in turn affects the equipment life plans, preventive maintenance schedule and therefore the *maintenance workload*. A ZBB is built up from scratch based on this forecasted workload.

R3.3 The digestion operation manager is responsible for production and maintenance and budgets for both. He is far more likely to appreciate the relationship between maintenance expenditure and the plant output factors that affect digestion plant performance. In other words he will be concerned about maintenance organizational efficiency but he will also appreciate that more effective maintenance (and thus perhaps more maintenance expenditure) might improve availability, output and net profit.

4 Maintenance management control

'Look after the lower level performance indices and the higher indices will look after themselves.'

Anthony Kelly

Chapter aims and outcomes

To explain the principles and concepts of maintenance management control systems, and how their practical operation may be informatively modeled.

On completion of this chapter you should be able to:

- draw a conceptual model that illustrates the principles of maintenance management control;
- appreciate that a maintenance costing system that is appropriately designed may offer the best way of controlling overall maintenance performance;
- understand the need for, and operation of, a plant reliability control system and an organizational efficiency control system;
- understand how maintenance control systems may be incorporated into an organization;
- appreciate how objectives can be modified and used as performance indices (PIs) and how PIs can be used for inter-firm comparison.

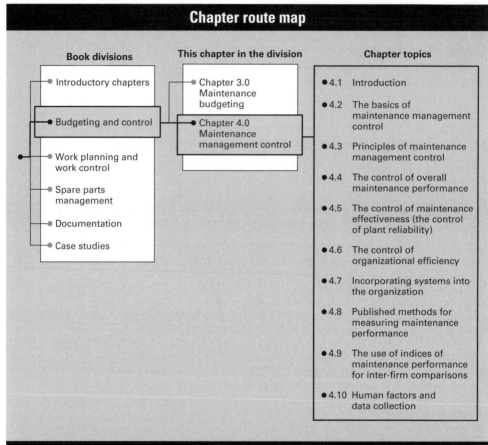

Chapter route map

Book divisions

- Introductory chapters
- Budgeting and control
- Work planning and work control
- Spare parts management
- Documentation
- Case studies

This chapter in the division

- Chapter 3.0 Maintenance budgeting
- Chapter 4.0 Maintenance management control

Chapter topics

- 4.1 Introduction
- 4.2 The basics of maintenance management control
- 4.3 Principles of maintenance management control
- 4.4 The control of overall maintenance performance
- 4.5 The control of maintenance effectiveness (the control of plant reliability)
- 4.6 The control of organizational efficiency
- 4.7 Incorporating systems into the organization
- 4.8 Published methods for measuring maintenance performance
- 4.9 The use of indices of maintenance performance for inter-firm comparisons
- 4.10 Human factors and data collection

Key words

- Paradigm
- Hierarchy of objectives
- Control principles
- Feedback and feed-forward
- Benchmarks
- Maintenance performance indices
- Maintenance effectiveness indices
- Maintenance organizational efficiency indices
- Key performance indices
- Inter-firm comparison indices

4.1 Introduction

The previous chapter showed that maintenance budgeting is an integral part of the company budgetary control procedure. Maintenance expenditure is controlled as a part of this procedure. The weakness of traditional company budgetary control procedures in controlling maintenance performance is that the linkage between maintenance expenditure and the maintenance output factors (availability, safety, longevity) is tenuous to say the least. What is required is a maintenance control system, operating under the umbrella of the company budgeting system, that can monitor maintenance costs and output factors and use this information to control the maintenance performance.

4.2 The basics of maintenance management control

The business-centered approach introduced in Chapter 1 emphasized the importance of establishing a maintenance objective – *it is the starting point of the strategic management process*. The linkage between the objective and the process of maintenance control was shown in our maintenance management paradigm – where it was shown that the control system is needed to direct the maintenance effort toward the objective.

In the case of the Alumina Refinery of Figure 4.1 the important control questions are:

- Is the maintenance effort achieving the deserved availability levels of 92%?
- Is the incurred maintenance cost within budget?
- If the answer to either or both of these questions is no, what are the reasons?

Information feedback of this kind allows the maintenance effort to be adjusted and/or redirected as necessary.

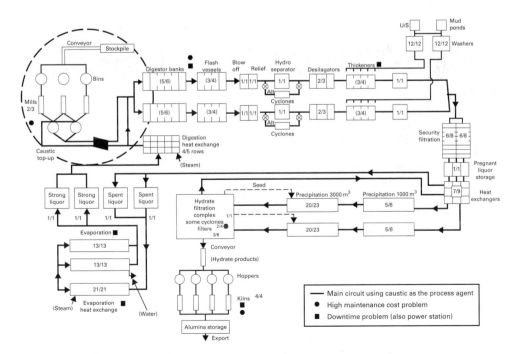

Figure 4.1 Process flow diagram of alumina refinery power station excluded

4.3 Principles of maintenance management control

The key relationships and processes of maintenance management control are delineated in Figure 4.2. The strategy (life plans, organizational policy, etc.) is established by maintenance management in order to achieve the objective (the agreed plant-user requirement at the budgeted cost). Management budgets for – and uses – resources (men, spares, tools) to implement the strategy.

The reporting system has the following principal data collection functions:

- checking whether the maintenance strategy is being carried out to specification (Point 1);
- checking whether the production operating practice is being carried out to specification (Point 2);
- measuring the parameters of maintenance output (Point 3);
- measuring the maintenance resource costs (Point 4).

The cause of any detected deviation from intent can then be determined and the necessary corrective action taken.

The above would seem to be a straightforward enough process. In practice, however, there are many complicating factors, *viz.*:

- A deterioration in some measured output (Point 3), e.g. availability, could have causes other than maintenance, e.g. maloperation. So the root-causes of the deviation must be pinpointed before any control measure is taken.

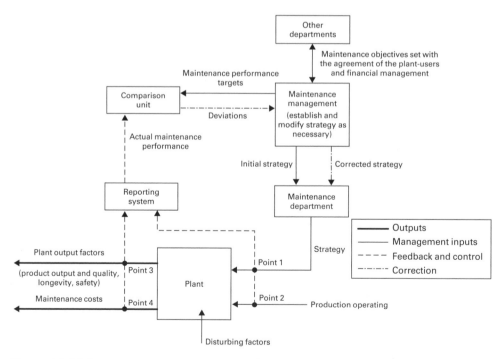

Figure 4.2 Maintenance management control: theoretical model

In some situations it may be possible to define the output factor to be specific to Maintenance, e.g. identifying downtime due to maintenance causes only, allows the definition of a maintenance availability index. Thus changes in this index is directly related to maintenance effort.

- Once set, maintenance objectives may not be unchanging; they will often have to be amended in the light of new needs of other departments, and before the overall strategy has had time to 'take effect'.
- Although the direct maintenance costs are relatively easy to measure some of the parameters of maintenance output, such as longevity or safety, are not.
- It is frequently the case that requirements relating to product output or quality will vary in the short and medium term, those relating to plant longevity and safety in the much longer term. Indeed, the maintenance strategic effort as regards plant longevity and safety is often quite divorced from that regarding product output and quality. These two aspects may well need separate objectives and control systems.
- The direct maintenance costs are a function both of maintenance policy and of organizational efficiency. These two functions may well need separate objectives and control systems (see Figure 4.3).

For these reasons, any overall maintenance control system based on the model of Figure 4.2 will have its limitations. Although it will be possible to identify deviations – from targets for output parameters and for maintenance resource costs – it will be very much more difficult to identify the causes. For this to be possible it may well be necessary to have a hierarchy of objectives and corresponding control systems.

A hierarchy of performance indices (PIs) (objectives by another name) was shown in Chapter 1 (see Figure 1.15). For convenience this is reproduced here as Figure 4.3. Each of the PIs could be monitored, compared to actual performance and used to control the maintenance effort.

The remainder of this section will discuss the practical interpretation of the maintenance management control principles outlined above.

Review Question

R4.1   Explain the limitations of the model shown in Figure 4.2 for controlling maintenance performance.

4.4 The control of overall maintenance performance

The best practical mechanism for controlling the overall maintenance performance would be a properly designed maintenance budgeting and costing system incorporating the ideas of Figure 3.1. This would mean the traditional accountancy designed costing system discussed in Chapter 3 would need some modification to move its center of gravity more toward maintenance needs.

A maintenance costing system (see Figure 4.4) could be designed which would facilitate determination – for each unit of plant (for a bauxite mill, say) of the relationships

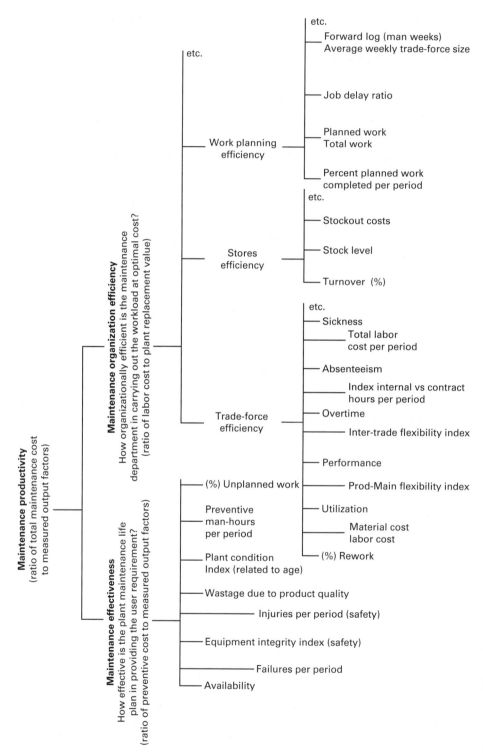

etc.
Forward log (man weeks)
Average weekly trade-force size

etc.

Job delay ratio

Planned work
Total work

Percent planned work
completed per period

etc.

Work planning
efficiency

Stockout costs

Stock level

Stores
efficiency

Turnover (%)

etc.

Sickness
Total labor
cost per period

Absenteeism

Index internal vs contract
hours per period

Overtime
Inter-trade flexibility index

Trade-force
efficiency

Performance

Prod-Main flexibility index

(%) Unplanned work

Utilization

Preventive
man-hours
per period

Material cost
labor cost

Plant condition
Index (related to age)

(%) Rework

Wastage due to product quality

Injuries per period (safety)

Equipment integrity index (safety)

Failures per period

Availability

Maintenance productivity
(ratio of total maintenance cost
to measured output factors)

Maintenance organization efficiency
How organizationally efficient is the maintenance
department in carrying out the workload at optimal cost?
(ratio of labor cost to plant replacement value)

Maintenance effectiveness
How effective is the plant maintenance life
plan in providing the user requirement?
(ratio of preventive cost to measured output factors)

Figure 4.3 Hierarchy of maintenance Performance indices

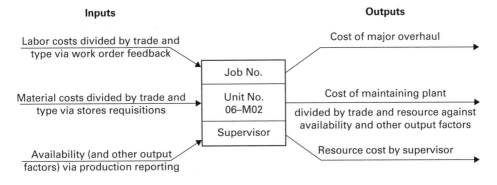

Figure 4.4 Outline of a maintenance costing system

between the rates of expenditure on maintenance and the relevant output parameters. The maintenance costs could be categorized by resource type (men, spares, etc.), maintenance type (preventive, corrective, etc.), trade (mechanical, electrical, etc.), budget type (short term for, say, availability or quality; long term for plant longevity). In addition, costs could be assigned against supervisor, trade group or major job (i.e. an overhaul). Traditionally, such a system relies on coding the plant units, work groups, work types, etc. (see Figure 4.4). All works are therefore recorded on work order (or time) cards – against unit, type and work group – and all spares usage similarly recorded on stores requisition orders, etc.

The system could be designed to provide a variety of outputs, either automatically or on demand – especially if the processing is computerized. The main outputs and their possible uses are as follows:

(i) Actual maintenance costs (separated into labor and material costs and, if required, divided according to work type and trade) and recorded levels of relevant output parameters (availability, product quality losses) – which can be compared against budgeted costs and targeted levels of performance (per period, per unit and per plant).
(ii) Identified areas (plants or units) of high maintenance cost or low availability, perhaps presented via Pareto plots or 'top ten' ranking lists).
(iii) Plots of output performance vs maintenance costs, per unit or per plant.
(iv) Actual maintenance costs per cost center per trade group or per supervisor – for comparison with budget (a part of company budgetary control).
(v) Actual cost of major overhauls – again for comparison with budget (a part of the major overhaul procedure, see Chapter 7).

The above, although not ideal, should satisfy most of the requirements of an overall maintenance performance control system, facilitating:

- the setting of objectives/PIs (or key performance indices, KPIs*)
- the monitoring of output parameters (such as availability) and of inputs (such as resource cost relative to budget) which can influence the levels achieved;
- the diagnosis of deviations from intent and the prescription of appropriate remedial action.

Most company budgeting and costing systems are designed by accountants for corporate financial control and are not sufficiently equipment-oriented to shed light on the problems of maintenance control, e.g. cost centers may not be plant-specific and, even when they are, each one may encompass too large an area of plant to be of any use in maintenance management. In addition, only rarely do such systems have the facility of comparing maintenance costs against the various parameters of output.

Even if properly designed, a maintenance costing system has to be a high level, longer-term one, providing a means of controlling the *overall* maintenance performance. It will be appreciated from Figure 4.3 that it needs to be complemented by control systems operating at a lower level (and on a shorter time scale). Indeed, it could be argued that a control system is needed for each objective that is set. For example, if an overtime limit is set then the actual overtime needs to be monitored and reported to the supervisor for necessary corrective action. In other words, control systems are integral to the operation of organizations.

The two principal maintenance control systems are those which deal with *effectiveness* and *organizational efficiency*, respectively (see Figure 4.3). The former is concerned with ensuring the effectiveness of the plant maintenance life plans and preventive schedule as regards achieving desired outputs and meeting cost targets, the latter with ensuring that maintenance work is being carried out in the most efficient way.

Review Questions

R4.2   With reference to Figure 4.3 define 'maintenance effectiveness' and 'maintenance organizational efficiency' and explain how they contribute to 'maintenance cost effectiveness'.

R4.3   Explain why conventional budgetary control and costing systems (see Chapter 3) are not effective in controlling overall maintenance performance. What are the essential differences between such traditional company costing systems and the maintenance costing system outlined in Section 4.4.

R4.4   List the ideal requirements from a system set up to control overall maintenance performance.

Exercise

E4.1   Map and compare the costing system in use in your own company against Figure 4.4 and the concepts discussed in this section.

---

*A limited or important number of higher-level indices.

4.5 The control of maintenance effectiveness (the control of plant reliability)

This is perhaps *the* most important maintenance control system. Once again, the alumina refinery of Figure 4.1 will serve as the vehicle for explaining its operation.

Figure 4.5, which outlines the mechanisms for controlling the effectiveness of one of the refinery units, illustrates the classic ideas of *reactive* control – using the feedback of operational and maintenance data – and also highlights *pro-active* control via the feed-forward of ideas for reliability and maintenance improvement.

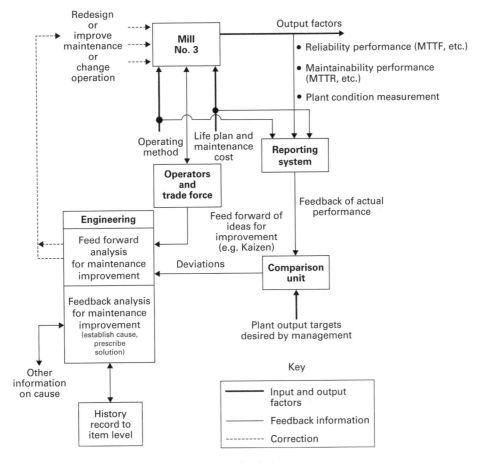

Figure 4.5 Controlling the reliability of a unit of plant

4.5.1 Reactive control of plant reliability

The requirements of the systems are to:

(a) monitor the output parameters of each unit, e.g. reliability (mean time to failure, mttf), maintainability (mean time to repair, mttr), plant condition, etc. and some of the input conditions, e.g. whether the unit life plan is being carried out to specification and at anticipated cost;

(b) determine the root cause of any failure;
(c) prescribe the necessary corrective action.

A control system for this must encompass several departments because the cause could originate in production (maloperation), in engineering (poor design) or in maintenance.

At refinery level, control can be envisaged as in Figure 4.6, i.e. each unit having its own control system. Once again, the difficulty is caused by the multiplicity of units which make up a major industrial plant, and therefore of control systems needed. The consequent data processing has been made manageable by modern computer technology which can easily handle the many independent control mechanisms. The difficulty, however, usually lies not in the processing but in the acquisition of the data. Company management may therefore need to concentrate control effort on selected units, those which they deem critical; for the rest they may use the maintenance costing system to identify the most troublesome, e.g. those of highest high maintenance cost, poorest product quality, highest downtime, and so on.

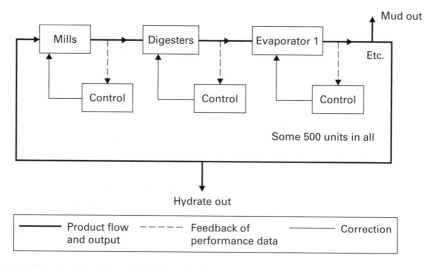

Figure 4.6 Controlling the reliability of a plant

4.5.2 Pro-active control of unit reliability

Figure 4.5 also illustrates the pro-active approach, which differs from the reactive in that it does not wait for failures or for high cost problems to occur before taking action. The basic idea is that all members of the organization – but especially the shop floor – should continuously seek ways of improving unit reliability, and hence output, safety, and so forth. The Japanese call this *kaizen*. The shop floor form small inter-disciplinary, but plant-oriented, teams to improve the reliability of selected units.

Preventive maintenance is interpreted literally – to prevent the need for any maintenance, by design-out and other actions.

4.6 The control of organizational efficiency

The concept of organizational efficiency was discussed in outline in Chapter 1 where it was stated that the prime organizational objective is:

to carry out a given plant maintenance workload at minimum cost by using maintenance resources (men, spares, tools) in the most efficient way.

It was also pointed out that a single objective for organizational efficiency is somewhat fanciful. A hierarchy of sub-objectives was therefore developed (as shown in Figure 4.3). For trade-force efficiency the objective might be stated as:

to minimize the trade-force cost per period for carrying out a given plant maintenance workload.

The extent to which this was being achieved could be measured via labor efficiency indices such as:

$$\text{Trade-force performance} = \frac{\text{Standard hours in workload}}{\text{Actual hours paid}}$$

$$\text{Trade-force utilization} = \text{Percent of time active per period}$$

For this, one or more of the techniques of maintenance *work measurement* and/or *work sampling* would have to be used. Work measurement is expensive and can bring industrial relations problems in its wake. However control that is based on standard times is superior to control based on estimated times because it can measure labor efficiency against universal standards.

Other things being equal, it is in the interest of maintenance management to pursue organizational actions – encouraging inter-trade flexibility, accelerating the introduction of self-empowered teams, making more use of contract labor, etc. – that will lead to improvements in the indices obtained from such efficiency measurements. The idea being that if the lower level indices move in the right direction so will the higher level indices, see Figure 4.3.

In other words: 'look after the lower indices and the higher indices will look after themselves'

In the case of spare parts the objective is:

to minimize the sum of stockout costs and holding costs.

An appropriate index of stores efficiency might therefore be one which involved holding costs vs number or cost of stockouts. Other sub-measures of stores efficiency could be derived via the monitoring of such parameters as percent stock turnover, average trade-force waiting time for parts, staffing costs vs stockholding costs (see Chapter 8.8).

It must be accepted that there are considerable practical difficulties in measuring and using such indices. An alternative approach, which could be applied to simple first- and second-line jobs (different information would be needed for third-line work), is illustrated in Figure 4.7. This could provide simple indices, e.g. a job-delay ratio would give a measure of organizational efficiency. In addition, profiling information on the possible causes could point to appropriate corrective action.

Exercise

E4.2   Identify the PIs used by your own company to measure organizational efficiency.

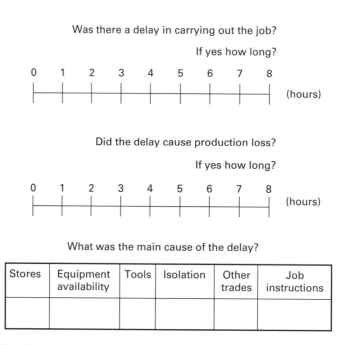

Figure 4.7 Collecting data on organizational performance

4.7 Incorporating systems into the organization

System models such as Figure 4.5 are useful for understanding the systems function and the mechanics of system operation. However it still remains to be shown how these ideas can be incorporated into a working maintenance organization.

Figure 4.8 shows the ideas of Figure 4.5 incorporated into the alumina refinery's maintenance administration. Systems for the identification and eradication of maintenance 'hot spots' is shown operating at three interlinked levels of the organization.

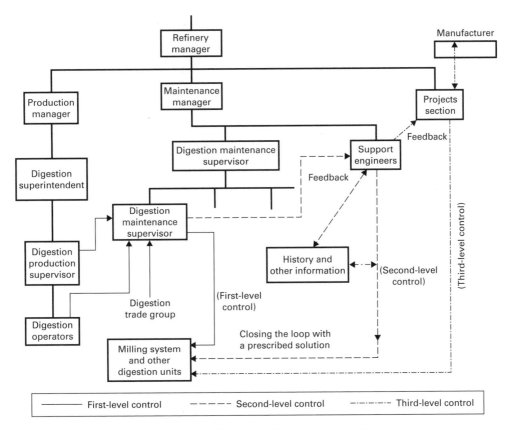

Figure 4.8 Plant reliability control within the refinery organization

A system for the *control of organizational efficiency* can be incorporated into the organization as part of traditional administrative control (see Figure 4.9). The digestion mechanical superintendent is concerned with work and decisions which involve a much longer time scale than that of the decisions of his supervisors. The former carries out his task by communicating the necessary instructions, objectives and PIs, to his supervisors (or team leaders). They, in turn, instruct their teams on what is required in terms of work performance, PIs and work programs. Information feedback to the supervisor/team leader enables them to control the completion of the work and the performance of his teams in the short term (the teams may monitor their own performance). Information feedback to the superintendent enables him to control the performance of his supervisors and teams in the long term.

For a system to operate effectively within an organization it is necessary to:

- Understand the principles of operation of the system, e.g. the principles incorporated in Figure 4.5.
- Identify the key people in the organization that have roles in operation of the system, see Figure 4.8.

- Ensure that the key people understand their roles, the way the system is expected to operate and the roles of the other key people.
- Periodically audit the system to ensure it is operating correctly.

Review Question

R4.5   Refer to Figure 4.8 and explain the importance of feed-forward control (pro-active) compared to feedback control (reactive). Explain feed-forward control in terms of total productive maintenance (TPM). Why do Japanese companies appear to have success in terms of feed-forward control of plant reliability?

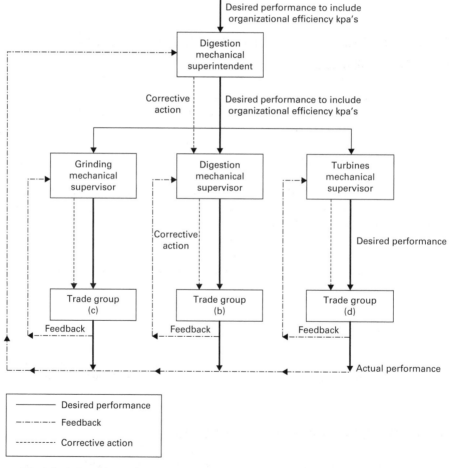

Figure 4.9 Administrative control system: digestion process

Exercise

E4.3 (a) Use Figure 4.8 as a template to draw the 'plant reliability control' system in your own organization (or an organization you can get access to). Can you identify all three levels of control? What are the main problems associated with each level? Is there a pro-active system at the first level of control?

(b) How would you improve your plant reliability control system?

4.8 Published methods for measuring maintenance performance

Various index-based methods for measuring maintenance performance [1], and hence for controlling maintenance effort, have been developed but examples of industrial organizations which have used them are hard to find. Exceptions to this are the Japanese methods [2] that have been incorporated into their concept of TPM.

4.9 The use of indices of maintenance performance for inter-firm comparisons

So far we have used objectives and PIs to help control the maintenance performance of a specific company i.e. set PIs, monitor them to see if they are getting better or worse and take corrective action as necessary [3,4].

A different use of indices is for comparing the maintenance performance across various companies. It is within such a context that the maintenance indices of Figure 4.3 could be used. They may well need extending or developing further for particular industries. The idea is that a series of indices categorized as shown (many of which may be being used for control purposes) could be profiled (perhaps into KPIs) in order to compare the maintenance performance between plants of similar technology and size – say e.g. alumina refineries. The value of doing this is not obvious, however. Even when comparing alumina refineries there are many differences – in detailed design, size, technology, manufacturer, etc. – that exercise greater influence on the indices than do such aspects as the maintenance life plan or organization.

Review Question

R4.6 Explain the limitations of using maintenance PIs (see Figure 4.3) to compare the performance of maintenance departments across different companies.

4.10 Human factors and data collection

The success of *pro-active* control, one of the cornerstones of TPM, depends on the quality, goodwill and motivation of the shop floor; that of *reactive control* on the

Table 4.1 Factors conducive to good data collection

Senior managers	Use an open approach Sell the idea Introduce the system gradually Do not use the system to assess the data inputter Show commitment to the system
Foremen	Must be committed to the system Must be convinced the system will benefit them
Artisans	Handle simple paperwork or user-friendly software Are allowed ample time for information input between jobs Have access to the system Appreciate what the data is used for
System designers	Make effective use of the data and ensure that this is seen to be the case Collect data in the easiest manner *Limit the data collected to only that which is needed*

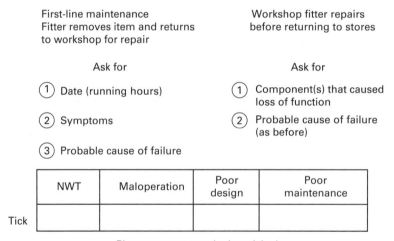

First-line maintenance
Fitter removes item and returns
to workshop for repair

Workshop fitter repairs
before returning to stores

Ask for

Ask for

1 Date (running hours)

1 Component(s) that caused
   loss of function

2 Symptoms

2 Probable cause of failure
   (as before)

3 Probable cause of failure

	NWT	Maloperation	Poor design	Poor maintenance
Tick				

Plus comment on why box ticked

Figure 4.10 Controlling the reliability of a unit of plant

quality of data returned from that level. With regard to the latter, the author's own studies have shown that data collection systems rarely operate well and that human factors problems and lack of training feature as the most important reasons for this (see Table 4.1).

Many of the companies investigated had sophisticated computer systems for control but had put little effort into defining terms such as *symptom, root cause of failure, defective part*, etc. It is not surprising, therefore, that the quality of data feedback was poor, especially concerning the cause of any problem. Perhaps the alternative means of data collection on cause, shown in Figure 4.10, would help in overcoming this problem.

References

1. Jardine, A.K.S., *Operation Research in Maintenance*, Manchester University Press, 1970, pp. 214–221.
2. Hibi, S., How to measure maintenance performance, Asian Productivity Organization, 1977.
3. Mather, M., *The Maintenance Scorecard*, Industrial Press, New York, 2004.
4. Wireman, T., *Benchmarking Maintenance Management*, Industrial Press, New York, 2005.

Review Questions Guidelines

R4.1   The deviation of some of the output parameters, e.g. availability, could have causes other than maintenance, e.g. maloperation. To overcome this problem (partly at least) it may be possible to be more specific in the definition of the output parameters, e.g. record downtime due to maintenance causes only resulting in a 'maintenance availability index'.

R4.2   Maintenance effectiveness is concerned with establishing life plans that aim to achieve the required level of plant availability/safety/longevity.
Maintenance organizational efficiency is concerned with carrying out the necessary work at least cost.
Maintenance cost effectiveness is concerned with achieving the plant output factors at least cost.

R4.3   Tradition budgetary control and costing systems regard maintenance as an expenditure. There is no clear link between maintenance expenditure and plant availability/safety/longevity. In addition accountancy 'cost centers' are not always equipment oriented. The maintenance costing system outlined in Figure 4.4 overcomes these limitations (in part).

R4.4   The ideal requirements are as follows:
  (i) The setting up of objectives as PIs.
  (ii) The monitoring of output indices (such as availability) and the input parameters (such as resource costs) which can influence the levels achieved.
  (iii) The diagnosis of deviations from intent and the prescription of appropriate remedial action.

R4.5   Feed-forward, or pro-active, control of plant reliability is concerned with identifying potential high-cost/low-reliability equipment *before* it becomes a problem. It relies on excellent human factors, e.g. a sense of equipment ownership at operator and artisans level. Feed back, or reactive, control is concerned with identifying and eradicating high-cost/low-reliability equipment *after* it becomes a problem. The advantages of pro-active control of reliability is therefore self-evident.
  A key organizational area of TPM is the idea of autonomous operator-maintenance teams. The teams are carefully selected and trained to operate, carry out essential first-line maintenance and to be involved in the 'continuous improvement' of the process and equipment, i.e. pro-active reliability control.

R3.6   Even when comparing companies within the same industrial sector, e.g. alumina refineries the plant process, equipment manufacturer, size and technology may be different. These factors often exercise a greater influence on the maintenance indices (especially cost effectiveness) than do maintenance strategy.

PART 3

Work planning and work control

5 Short-term work planning and control

'Measure twice, cut once.'

Anon

Chapter aims and outcomes

To explain the principles of operation of a short-term work planning, scheduling and work control system.

On completion of this chapter you should be able to:

- appreciate the differences between the short-term planning procedure used for first and second-line maintenance work and the turnaround planning procedure used for major overhauls (third-line work);
- understand the work planning function and objectives;
- draw a schematic work planning model based around the operation of a maintenance resource structure;
- understand the principles of work planning and work control;
- appreciate the linkage between work planning and the safety of plant and personnel.

Chapter route map

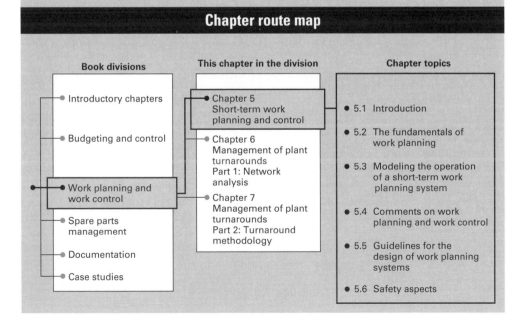

Book divisions
- Introductory chapters
- Budgeting and control
- Work planning and work control
- Spare parts management
- Documentation
- Case studies

This chapter in the division
- Chapter 5
  Short-term work planning and control
- Chapter 6
  Management of plant turnarounds
  Part 1: Network analysis
- Chapter 7
  Management of plant turnarounds
  Part 2: Turnaround methodology

Chapter topics
- 5.1 Introduction
- 5.2 The fundamentals of work planning
- 5.3 Modeling the operation of a short-term work planning system
- 5.4 Comments on work planning and work control
- 5.5 Guidelines for the design of work planning systems
- 5.6 Safety aspects

Key words
• Work planning
• Work scheduling
• Work control
• Work planning systems
• Work order
• Work request
• Job priority
• Job method
• Job list

5.1 Introduction

Perhaps the key maintenance information system is the system for *work planning* which, for the purposes of this book, we shall take also to encompass *work scheduling and controlling*. It is this that provides much of the information for the other maintenance management control systems.

Chapter 1 depicted a work planning system as an information and decision-making structure. The accompanying text stressing the need to design the system around the resource structure. The text also emphasized the need to visualize the work planning system as an integral part of the overall organization.

5.2 The fundamentals of work planning

The work planning system defines the way in which the maintenance workload – short term (first and second line) and long term (major third line) – is planned, scheduled, allocated and controlled. In companies where the third-line work involves major peaks (see Figure 3.2(a)), it is normal to have a short-term planning system for the ongoing work (first and second line) linked to a turnaround planning system (shutdown planning) for the major work. Short-term planning will be discussed in this chapter and turnaround planning in Chapters 6 and 7.

In simple terms the *function of work planning* is:

- to ensure that the right resources,
- arrive at the right place,
- at the right time,
- to do the right job,
- in the right way.

The design of the work planning system should *aim* to get maximum leverage from the cost of setting up and running the work planning system over the savings (in terms of the indirect and direct maintenance costs) that result from the use of the planning system.

The basic steps involved in the planning and execution of any job are shown in Figure 5.1. The level of administration and systems needed to aid this process will depend on the size of the job (the manpower, spares and time needed) and its characteristics (e.g. scheduling lead time, which could be zero for emergency work). In the case of a small emergency job, e.g. all of the steps indicated in Figure 5.1 may be taken by an individual artisan. The important contribution of systems in such a situation is to provide him quickly with the essential information for planning (spares requirement, drawings, instructions) and scheduling (priority, what else is on? what else can be done at the same time?). In the case of scheduled overhaul of a large unit, each step of Figure 5.1 may be taken by the appropriate specialist – planner, scheduler, artisans, clerk and so forth. A co-ordinating organization, and systems to provide it with information on jobs, planning and scheduling is then needed.

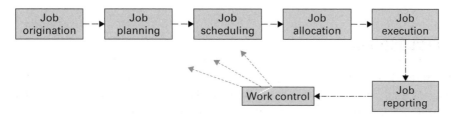

Figure 5.1 The basic steps of maintenance work planning and control

5.3 Modeling the operation of a short-term work planning system

This is best illustrated using the food processing plant (FPP) described in Chapter 1.

The plant layout, weekday and weekend resource structures, for the FPP are shown in Figures 5.2, 5.3 and 5.4, respectively. The maintenance workload is shown in Figure 5.5 and the administrative structure in Figure 5.6. The weekday shift-group carries out the first-line work (mainly high-priority corrective jobs) and the weekend group carries out the scheduled second-line work. The weekend administration is headed by one of the shift supervisors (on a one-in-four rota) and aided by an electrical supervisor.

Figure 5.6 also shows, superimposed on the administrative structure, an outline of the work planning system. This once again serves to emphasize the need to visualize work planning as an information and decision-making system operating within the organization (mainly at supervisor level). Figure 5.6 identifies the key people involved in the work planning system.

This information can be used to draw a schematic model of the work planning system (see Figure 5.7). This shows the flow of work and information between the trade groups, their supervisors and the planning office and indicates that there are three distinct levels of planning, *viz*.:

- first line (shift);
- second line (weekend);
- third line (major shutdown – not modeled).

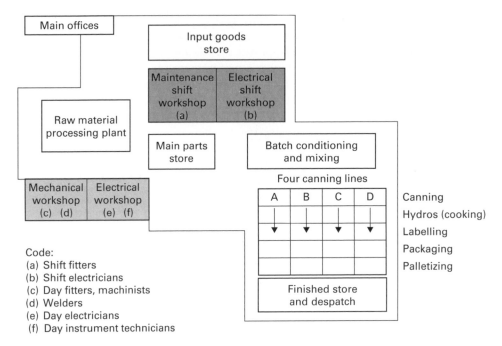

Code:
(a) Shift fitters
(b) Shift electricians
(c) Day fitters, machinists
(d) Welders
(e) Day electricians
(f) Day instrument technicians

Figure 5.2 Layout of FPP (reproduced from Chapter 1)

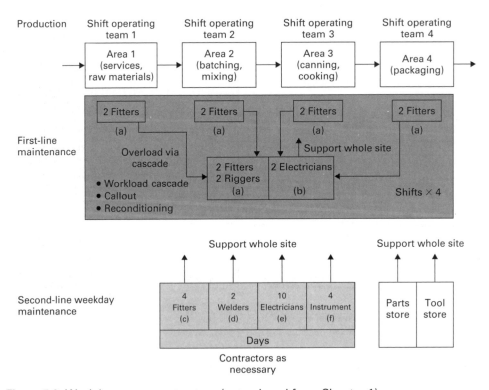

Figure 5.3 Weekday resource structure (reproduced from Chapter 1)

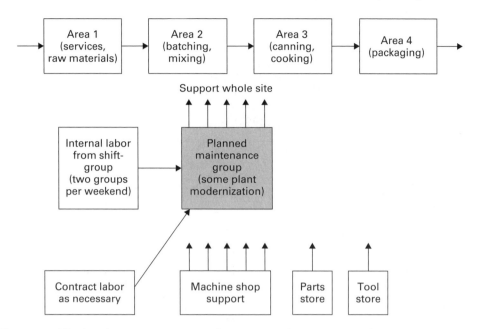

Figure 5.4 Weekend resource structure (reproduced from Chapter 1)

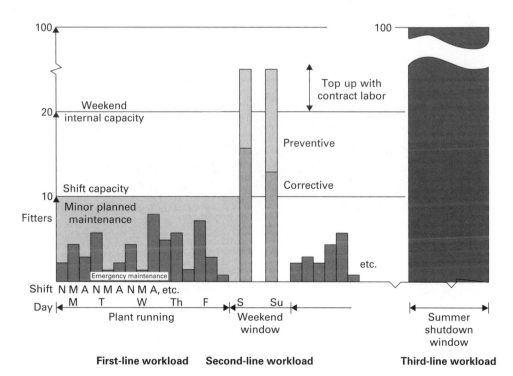

Figure 5.5 Workload profile for filters (reproduced from Chapter 1)

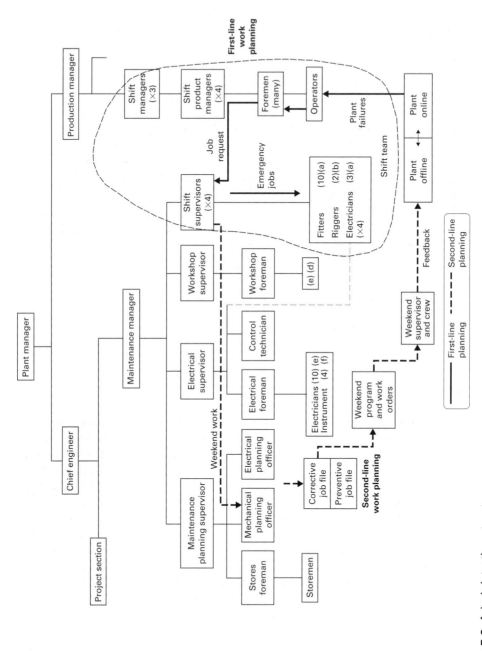

Figure 5.6 Administrative structure

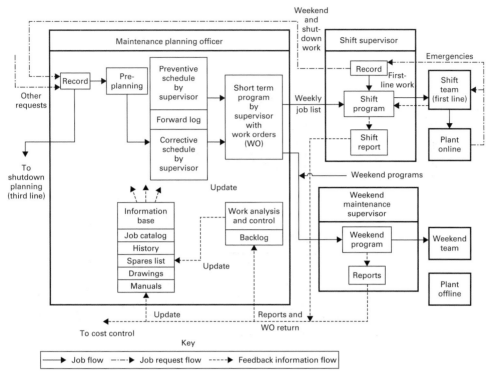

Figure 5.7 Work planning system

5.3.1 The shift work planning system

The function of the shift trade group is to carry out the emergency maintenance and some minor scheduled tasks during the normal weekly shifts. It requires what is essentially a reactive planning system centered around the shift supervisor. The main problem is to identify priorities, especially for those jobs that should be passed back to the planning office for weekend execution. A simple way of doing this is to define all jobs that need to be started within twenty four hours of their shift occurrence as first line and to prioritize them on safety and economic criteria into 1(a)s and 1(b)s. The shift crew will also deal with the minor preventive, 1(c), jobs. In general these will be sent through on a simple list from the planning office and fitted into the program as convenient. The major shift planning requirement is to quickly obtain information on spares, drawings, safety and job methods, hence the usefulness of a computerized maintenance information base.

The work request/work order (e.g. see Figure 5.8) is the main vehicle for conveying information/instructions through this system. In practice this function can be carried out in a number of ways:

- Separate documents for requesting work (the job request) and instigating work (the work order).
- A combined document for both requesting and ordering (see Figure 5.8).

- A master work order for larger jobs with numerous linked sub-work orders (linked via a common work order number).
- A standing work order per shift artisan to cover the numerous small first-line jobs that occur across a typical shift.

Maintenance request No. D 0353						Week no.	Classification		
Plant description			Date						
Plant location			Time	a.m. p.m.		Analysis	Plant No		
Requested by		Required By							
Defect/work required	Is production stopped?			Yes No	Tool BDN	1		Tick one box	
					M/c running	2			
					M/c breakdown	3			
					Not applicable	4			
Cause					Wear and tear	1			
					Accident and misuse	2		Tick one box	
					Component failure	3			
					Job report	4			
					Not applicable	5			

Action taken

Tradesman's signature	Date	Clock no.	Time on	Time off	Total hours		Rate	Amount	
					HRS	DEC		£	p

Maintenance foreman's signature					HRS	DEC
				Repair time		
For office use only				Down time		

Figure 5.8 Typical work order

The document can be hard copy or electronic or a combination of both.

One of the main difficulties on shifts is collecting good quality failure and repair data. At worst, it is totally lost and at best the more important events are captured on some form of individual or group shift log. Paperless computerized information systems are becoming increasingly used in these situations.

The author has observed that in many cases the work order is used mainly to provide costing data rather than to co-ordinate work and indicate job methods.

One of the planning difficulties in the case of shift-groups is the co-ordination of resources, across shifts, for emergency jobs which take longer than a single shift. One obvious way of facilitating this task is to allow the shift supervisors a short overlap for updating each other. Some companies frown on this practice, however, if it increases overtime.

5.3.2 The weekend work planning system

The link between the planning systems for shift work and for weekend work is the planning office. Any job which, in the shift supervisor's judgment, meets the priority and planning guidelines for second-line work – mainly weekend work – is referred back to that office. Modification and corrective work from other sources, e.g. from the production or engineering departments, that needs maintenance resources for its execution is similarly referred.

The usual procedure is that any incoming job has to be notified on a maintenance work request order (indicating such basic information as requester, job description, priority and so on). Such jobs can be requested by telephone with hard paper back up, via planning meetings or by direct input into a computer system. The information on preventive jobs will already be held by the planning office system as part of the previously agreed preventive schedule.

The main function of the weekend planning system is planning and scheduling the weekend work. Part of the initial job-recording activity is to identify those jobs that are best carried out within the shutdown plan and to enter them into the job list for this (see next section), all other work being entered into the weekend system. The main function of preplanning is to ensure that any long lead-time resources required, e.g. spares, are identified and ordered before the relevant job is entered into the schedule of outstanding tasks. This, in turn, requires an understanding of the job procedure – in outline at least. It is important, therefore, that the system identifies who is responsible for specifying the job method. In the case of the FPP this was done jointly by the planner and the supervisor, some procedures being already recorded in the job catalog (part of the plant information base).

> Identification of the job procedure is a key part of the planning process and can be accomplished in a number of ways:
>
> - In the case of standard jobs (jobs that occurred previously and the job method has been recorded in the job catalog) the procedure already exists.
> - The supervisor/planner may be familiar with the equipment and be able to specify the job method (this is the case in particular with simple jobs).
> - Where there is uncertainty as in the case of an equipment malfunction the initial job may go out as a 'trouble shoot'.
> - For modification work/construction work a separate planning group may be responsible for setting up the drawings, job procedures and spares, etc.

After pre-planning, the corrective jobs, with estimates of their durations and trade-force requirements, can be entered into the job schedule, where they are filed according to supervisor, plant unit and status (online, offline, etc.), priority and approximate week of execution.

It can be seen that Figure 5.7 separates the preventive from the corrective schedules. Modern software packages, however, are based on a combined job list and schedule – each job being identified, categorized and scheduled via a code. It will be appreciated that the job list is a record of all the outstanding work and that it can be presented as a histogram of future resource demand (categorized by job priority) and compared with the forecast of weekend completion of such work. *This is an essential part of maintenance work control.*

At each planning level there is a need for an appropriate work planning meeting. The shift maintenance system supervisors should, therefore, participate in the daily production meeting which, among its other activities, should review plant availability and any failures over the previous 24 hours. Similarly, there is a need for a weekly maintenance planning meeting (involving supervisors and manager) which liaises with the weekly production planning meeting (which should include a maintenance representative). The function of the weekly maintenance meeting is to review outstanding work and plant priorities and to decide on a weekend program.

In the FPP the designated weekend supervisor – responsible for the allocation, quality and control of the weekend work – would be a member of the weekly maintenance planning meeting, the weekend program having been agreed by the preceding Thursday. It would be his responsibility to carry out the secondary planning and job allocation, i.e. to check spares, drawings, work orders, methods, safety permits, co-ordination with other trades (electrical, production, cleaners), etc. – the necessary manpower, including contract labor, being agreed in conjunction with the planner.

> The point that is being made here is that the key function of the planner is to carry out all the planning tasks that are necessary but could not be carried out (easily) by the supervisor (who is on shifts). In particular this will involve the pre-weekend planning of multi-resource jobs (requiring different trades, cranes, spares, scaffolding, etc.). The supervisor is left to do the weekend planning (co-ordinating, of trades, allocation of jobs, etc.) and reporting.

5.3.3 Feedback of maintenance data for control

One of the responsibilities of the maintenance supervisor (shift and weekend) is the feedback of maintenance information. Such data can be captured on work orders, weekend or shift logs, or event reports – perhaps via direct computer input. The typical requirement might be for information on:

- additional work needed, or work not completed;
- resource usage (trades – with job times, spares usage, etc.);
- work carried out;
- causes of failures or potential failures, etc.

Some of this is needed for work control, some for updating the information base and some for other purposes such as control of maintenance cost, of plant reliability, of work planning effectiveness, etc. (see Chapter 4). *It is for these reasons that the author describes work planning as the key maintenance system.* This chapter will restrict itself to the use of such data for work planning and control purposes, *viz.*:

- *For the information base* (see Figure 5.7), an essential aid to work planning, the effectiveness of this database depending, however, on its continuous update – i.e. on the input of new standard jobs into the job catalog, plant history update, update of drawings and manuals after modifications have been carried out, etc.

- *For work control,* achieved via the feedback of information on jobs completed, time taken, jobs deferred, etc. This allows the main job lists/schedules to be updated, a view obtained of the outstanding work – forward log and backlog – compared to the completion rate (see Figure 5.9) and extra resources (contract or in-house) to be brought in if needed.

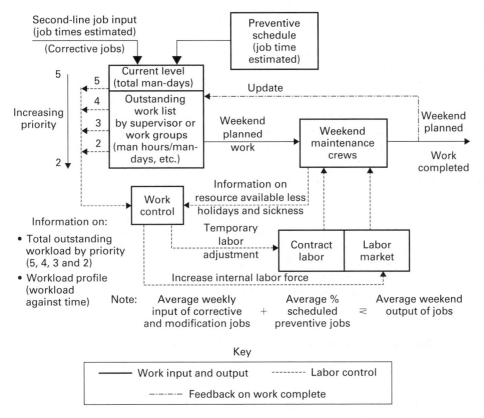

Figure 5.9 Principles of work control

Work control should also include the de-briefing procedure necessary after any unit overhaul, or even after the weekend program, the purpose being to ask 'Did we do it right?', 'Could we do it better?'

5.4 Comments on work planning and work control

The FPP was chosen to discuss maintenance work planning because it has several features that render the operation of its work planning system straightforward, *viz*.:

- The first-line work is done by shift teams, and the second-line work by weekend teams, so the chance of the first-line work interfering with the execution of the scheduled work is minimized. Where a single group carries out both categories of work, the planning becomes considerably more difficult. Questions arise concerning how much planned work should be committed into the weekly program. This is sometimes estimated as follows:

$$\begin{bmatrix} \text{Scheduled workload} \\ \text{for the next period} \end{bmatrix} = \begin{bmatrix} \text{Workload capacity} \\ \text{of trade group} \\ \text{for the next period} \end{bmatrix} - \begin{bmatrix} \text{Average level of non-} \\ \text{plannable work likely} \\ \text{in the next period} \end{bmatrix}$$

This might then allow the program to have both a *committed* and a *flexible* work element, in which case priority rules must be clearly stated.

> The author has also noted in such situations that it is usual for the preventive work not to be prioritized. On asking the reason for this he is often told 'it is because it must be carried out'. Unfortunately the pressure of the high-priority corrective work often means that it is not carried out (especially the routines). The comment then is 'we will make sure to do it next time' and sometimes 'the routine is not important anyway'. My response to this is 'if the routine is not important it should have been sorted out during the assessment of the life plan and should not be there'. If the routine is important it should have a priority and, if missed once should be top priority next time.

- The role of the planners can be clearly defined, and their use justified, as regards the weekend work. This is because the shift supervisors cannot carry out the planning role as part of their main responsibilities. They act as weekend supervisors on only once in 4 weeks – they need the ongoing planning back up. Situations do occur, however, where the supervisor acts as 'planner', the leading hand as 'supervisor' and the planner as 'clerk'. In other words, *there may be second-line situations, especially where good computerized maintenance systems are in use, where a specialized planner may not be required.*

Review Questions

R5.1   The work planning system used in the case study of Chapter 11 (ammonia plant) was not working well. List the main reasons for this and identify the key problem.

R5.2   Management are aware that the success of the maintenance control systems will depend, in part, on successful collection of data from the work planning systems. List some of the difficulties that may be encountered when trying to achieve this.

R5.3   A company operates an open computer controlled stores as part of their maintenance work planning. Artisans are expected to computer locate their own parts and computer record their withdrawal. Discuss the advantages and disadvantages of this system.

5.5 Guidelines for the design of work planning systems

Figure 5.10 shows a resource structure for an alumina refinery. Figure 5.10 shows three resource levels corresponding to the centralized shift crews (five crews in total,

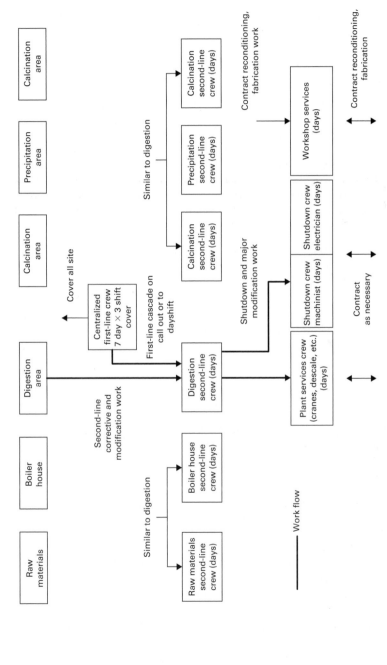

Figure 5.10 Simplified version of proposed resource structure for alumina refinery

one per shift covering 7 days first line), plant located decentralized day crews (six crews in total – second line) and centralized shutdown and plant service crews (third line).

Figure 5.11 shows a schematic work planning model which has been designed around this resource structure. The model includes the first-line planning, one area (digestion) to represent second- and third-line planning (shutdowns).

Each of the crews has its own area supervisor. Various decentralized plant-based planning offices, e.g. for the digestion plant, have been set up within an area planner to assist the area maintenance supervisors. There is also a shutdown planner centrally located in a shutdown planning office.

The planning system is fully computerized having a comprehensive maintenance information base and an information analysis and control module. The software is fully integrated with the other company functions, e.g. stores, general ledger, etc.

This example draws attention to several important aspects regarding the design of work planning systems, *viz.*:

(i)   The work planning system should be designed around the resource structure taking into consideration the levels of resource and the characteristics of the workload. If, as in the present example, there are three levels of resource then it is necessary to have three corresponding levels of work planning.

The scheduling lead time of the emergency work dealt with by the *shift crews* is short and planning centers around the supervisor and artisans. The main requirement from the documentation system is to provide the necessary information quickly.

With the *second-line crews* scheduling lead times vary from 24 hours to several weeks and the jobs are tackled by priority. Planning should center around the respective planners, e.g. the planner of Figure 5.11, who provides a weekly list of committed work taking into account the first-level spillover. His main function is to assist in the planning of individual jobs and to keep the schedules and work lists up to date. In addition he assists in the co-ordination of multi-trade jobs and provides general clerical back up. In Figure 5.11, example planning and scheduling is a joint planner–supervisor effort. It must be emphasized that with the most up-to-date computerized planning system the area planning is often carried out by the supervisor or team leader (i.e. no planner) especially if the areas have become self-empowered.

Shutdown planning for major parts of the refinery exploits the presence of redundancies, which enable plant (a boiler, kiln, etc.) or a process channel (e.g. a digester stream) to be taken offline – perhaps reducing capacity but never shutting down the complete refinery. The *centralized shutdown crews* and the *service crews* then go to the area concerned and supplement the local resource, the planning center of gravity being close to the shutdown planning office.

The function of the shutdown planner is to ensure that the shutdowns are scheduled so as to smooth the workload of the centralized resource. This requires close co-operation with the production planners. In addition, he ensures that the jobs are properly planned (in particular, long lead-time spares are identified) and the resources properly co-ordinated. The planning lead time for shutdown work is often in excess of 3 months (see the next chapter).

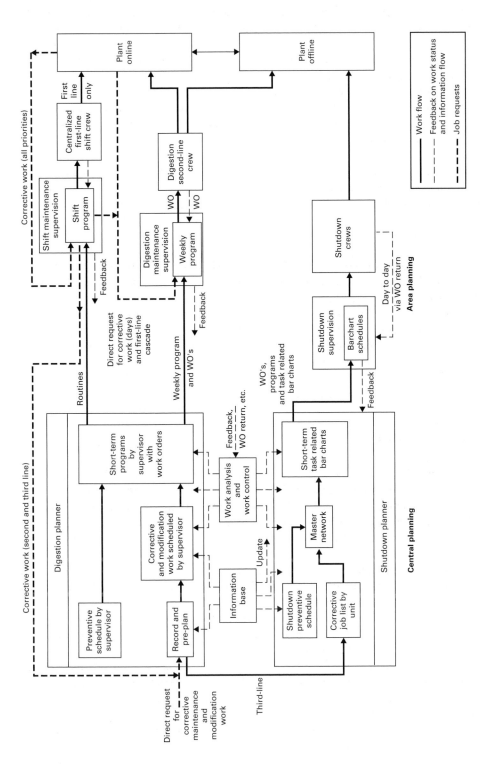

Figure 5.11 Work planning system for an alumina refinery

(ii) The design of the overall planning system should allow job requests to flow to the *best* level for planning, scheduling and controlling them, e.g. shift supervisor level for emergency work. In the example, jobs specific to the digestion stream that *do not* require the plant to be offline should be handled at the digestion planning level, those that *do* at shutdown level. By 'best' is meant where it is easiest to decide on priorities, plant status and job methods.

(iii) A set of job priority rules – which should indicate the initial planning level (e.g. emergency maintenance to be planned at first-line supervisor level) – should be defined and clearly understood by maintenance planning and supervision and by production.

(iv) The function, responsibility and lines of communication between each of the planning levels must be clearly defined.

(v) The right information about the workload and the resources must be available to the designated planner of the job at the right time.

(vi) The planner must have the authority (or access to it) to take the decisions (e.g. allocation of priorities) which affect the workload and resources.

Exercise

E5.1   Use Figure 5.7 and/or Figure 5.11 (which ever is the most appropriate) as a template to draw a work planning model for your own company. Remember that you will need to draw the resource structure and administrative structure before you draw the work planning system.

5.6 Safety aspects

There are many aspects of the maintenance work planning system that are important to the safety of personnel and of plant operation:

● Plant isolation procedures, including safety permits and the isolation tagging system, are essential in a hazardous area and must be incorporated into the work planning system.

● Standard job procedures, including methods, spares used, tools and *safety procedures*, should be mandatory in hazardous plants.

● All major overhauls should be preceded by a discussion of safety procedures and requirements.

● All contract labor coming on to site should be subject to job quality checks and should go through a safety induction program appropriate to the site and to each of its areas.

● All spare parts, whether new or reconditioned (internally or externally), should be subjected to a quality assurance program. This is, especially if they are destined for hazardous areas or functions.

● Formal procedures must be established for updating drawings and manuals after plant modification – and for communicating manufacturers' requirements or modifications to the holders of such information.

Review Questions

Answer the following review questions by referring to Figure 5.11.

R5.4　Explain why each of the following statements is probably correct:

(a) For the shift crews the center of gravity of maintenance work planning lies well toward the shift supervisor.

(b) Both for the shutdown crew and the workshop-based crews the center of gravity of work planning lies well towards the shutdown planning office.

R5.5　Some of the planning and scheduling for the second-line decentralized area crews is carried out by the area supervisors and some by the area planners:

(a) Identify the work that, on the one hand, is best planned and scheduled by the area supervisors and, on the other, by the area planner.

(b) Should jobs that go to the area supervisors via the area planners be planned and scheduled completely by the planners? Should this go so far as the allocation of jobs to specific artisans?

(c) Explain some of the key difficulties that an area planner might have in planning a multi-trade, multi-resource job for his area crew.

(d) Explain the importance, for the second-line area supervisors, of a job priority system.

(e) Why is it important to estimate job times before adding the jobs to the computerized job lists and schedules?

(f) Explain why it is important that all jobs are entered into the planning system (before their execution where possible, but perhaps afterwards in the case of emergency work).

R5.6　Describe what is required from the work planning system if it is to ensure that the plant will operate safely and that maintenance will be carried out safely.

Review Questions Guidelines

R5.1　• Software said to be user-unfriendly.
- Poor training in the use of the computerized work planning system.
- Pedantic isolation procedures that needed streamlining.

The key problem was that the shift operator–maintainer teams refused to carry out first-line maintenance. This work cascaded to the day teams and disrupted their scheduled work.

R5.2　• Artisans's resistance to providing data (habitual reluctance to co-operate, lack of time, dislike of writing, etc.).
- Poor quality of data (due to insufficient understanding of data needs, poor definition of requirement, etc.).
- Trade union insistence that data collection must be financially rewarded.
- Lack of training in the use of the documentation system.
- Poorly designed documentation systems which do not facilitate effective use of data and which, therefore, inhibit any enthusiasm for its collection.
- Lack of commitment on the part of supervisors and other managerial staff to data collection.

R5.3   Advantages – low cost of operating the stores. Disadvantages – includes the use of artisans's time, parts withdrawal not being recorded.

R5.4   First-level work planning deals with jobs that are of high priority (planning lead time less than 24 hours) or are small jobs that are not subject to planning input from outside (financial, the ordering of spares, etc.). The shift supervisor, therefore, plans and schedules such work.

In the case of shutdown work (and also of work undertaken by the workshop-based crews) the planning lead time may be as long as a year, so a great deal of financial and work planning is essential. Most of the planning and resourcing decisions can only be taken with information which is not readily available to the crew.

R5.5   (a) *Area supervisors*: jobs that do not require information or resources from outside, or are not subject to external financial constraints. As long as such jobs are entered into the system they are adequately visible to the area planner.

Area planner: jobs that call for co-ordination with other departments (including operations or production), that involve the use of a centralized, resource, or are subject to financial constraints.

(b) No. The area planner should always leave detailed and shorter-term planning and allocation to the area supervisors who are much more aware of the capability of their resources and of the short-term planning characteristics.

(c) Communication with other supervisors and contract resources. Co-ordination of resources to arrive at the right place at the right time.

(d) It ranks the jobs according to their importance to production and/or safety, which facilitates estimation of their scheduling horizons.

(e) Because it enables the workload to be profiled and compared with the available resources. *This is an essential part of work control. Estimates of job times also promotes better short-term planning.*

(f) In order to ensure the capture of data – on man-hours needed and expended, on cost of materials and on plant history.

R5.6   ● Plant isolation procedures.
● Standard procedures for hazardous jobs.
● Safety review meetings before major overhauls.
● Safety inductions for new workers and for contract.
● Quality assurance review of all new and reconditioned parts.
● Updates of drawings and manuals after a plant modification.
● Plant history recording and analysis to anticipate potential safety problems.

6 Management of plant turnarounds –
Part 1: Network analysis

*'If seven maids with seven mops
Swept it for half a year,
'Do you suppose,' the Walrus said,
'That they could get it clear?'
I doubt it,' said the Carpenter,
And shed a bitter tear.'*

Lewis Carrol

Chapter aims and outcomes

To explain the principles, concepts and procedure of network analysis.

On completion of this chapter you should be able to:

- draw a network for a small overhaul and identify the critical path and the task floats;
- convert the network into a bar chart and draw manpower loading histograms;
- appreciate how the network and bar charts can be used as the main planning and control vehicle for major shutdowns.

Chapter route map

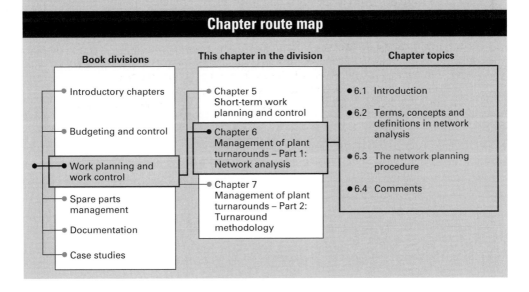

Book divisions	This chapter in the division	Chapter topics
Introductory chapters	Chapter 5 Short-term work planning and control	6.1 Introduction
Budgeting and control	Chapter 6 Management of plant turnarounds – Part 1: Network analysis	6.2 Terms, concepts and definitions in network analysis
Work planning and work control	Chapter 7 Management of plant turnarounds – Part 2: Turnaround methodology	6.3 The network planning procedure
Spare parts management		6.4 Comments
Documentation		
Case studies		

Key words

- Critical path analysis
- Network analysis
- Project planning
- Program evaluation and review techniques
- Turnaround planning
- Shutdown planning
- Task-on-arrow
- Task-on-node
- Bar chart

6.1 Introduction

Major plant turnarounds[1] pose problems of work planning and scheduling that are quite different from those presented by the ongoing work. The principal organizational characteristics of the typical third-line workload that they generate are as follows:

- A large peak in resource requirement, which has to be met by an influx of labor from elsewhere.
- A multiplicity of interrelated jobs, all of which have to be co-ordinated if the work is to be completed on time and to cost.
- A long lead time (often many months) for scheduling the work.
- Large cost penalties should, the planned duration of the shutdown[2] itself, be exceeded.

Planning and controlling the work for a major shutdown is therefore an exercise which is quite separate from the corresponding task for the ongoing work (although it relates to it). This can be seen from Figure 5.7, which models the complete work planning system for an alumina refinery. All jobs originating in the ongoing planning system (or from elsewhere) that can only be undertaken during the major shutdown are transferred into the shutdown corrective job list. The sum total of these (which can be many thousands for a large overhaul[3]) may require many months of planning and scheduling in order to build them into a shutdown program. Initially such a program is expressed as a master network (the master network is assembled using the ideas of network analysis). This network is then broken down into a series of short-time-frame bar charts (see Figure 6.1) with accompanying task specifications. It can be seen from Figure 5.7 that a number of

---

[1] *Turnaround*: An engineering event that takes place during a plant shutdown and involves the inspection, overhaul and, where necessary, the modification of existing equipment and the installation of new equipment.

[2] *Shutdown*: The period of time from the moment the plant is take offline to the moment it is brought back online.

[3] *Overhaul*: A comprehensive examination of a plant, or a major part of it, and its restoration to an acceptable (or desired) condition.

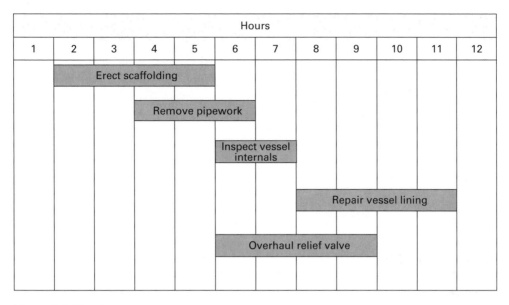

Figure 6.1 Bar chart

planning functions are common to both the ongoing and the shutdown work planning systems, *viz.* information base, work analysis, work order system, cost control.

Before discussing turnaround management in any detail it is necessary first to understand the concepts, principles and procedure of network analysis. Network analysis is a generic name given to graphic techniques, e.g. critical path analysis (CPA), program evaluation and review techniques (PERT), etc., used for studying the interrelationship between tasks/jobs in complex projects, e.g. a major plant overhaul. Computerized network analysis methods have long superceded the traditional bar chart, see Figure 6.1, for establishing the master networks for plant turnarounds. However, bar charts are still computer generated from the master network for monitoring and controlling the progress of the turnaround.

6.2 Terms, concepts and definitions in network analysis[4]

Task: An operation consuming time only, or time and resources. A task may be physical (such as the fabrication of an element of a structure) or it may be abstract (such as the accomplishment of a particular stage in a design calculation).

Event: A state of the project when all preceding activities have been completed and before any succeeding activity has started.

---

[4]This method of representation, which has been adopted throughout this section, is known as 'task-on-arrow (TOA)', as opposed to the alternative 'task-on-node (TON)' method. An explanation of TON, with worked examples, was given in Kelly, A., *Maintenance Planning and Control* (pp. 232 *et seq.*), Butterworths, 1984.

Figure 6.2 Two events linked by an activity

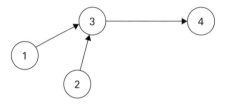

Figure 6.3 Interrelated activities

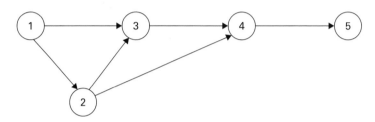

Figure 6.4 A network

Graphic representation of tasks and events: Each task in the project is represented by a directed line which forms a link in the network. The direction and length of the line has no particular significance in representing the flow of time. Events are represented by circles at each end of a task line. The arrowhead on the line identifies the events immediately preceding and following the task (see Figure 6.2). The identity of the task is given by a label inside each circle, and so the line shown in Figure 6.2 denotes the 'ij' task, linking the prior event 'i' with the following event 'j'.

Interrelationship between tasks: The interrelationship between tasks is embodied in the convention that a task may not begin until all preceding tasks in the same path are complete. Thus, in the example shown in Figure 6.3 the event 3 is not regarded as having been reached until both the tasks 1–3 and 2–3 have been completed, and until that stage has been reached the event 3–4 may not begin.

Start event: Is an event with succeeding but no preceding activities.

End event: Is an event with preceding but no succeeding activities.

Network: Is a graphic representation of the tasks necessary for achieving the objectives of a project and showing their interrelationships. The nodes of the network are formed by those events which are common to two or more tasks, and the terminals of the network are provided by the start event and the end event (see Figure 6.4).

A useful convention in the construction of networks is to treat time as flowing from left to right, and to number the events so that for each task the succeeding event has a higher number than the preceding event.

Figure 6.5 Parallel activities with the same terminal events

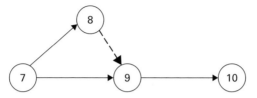

Figure 6.6 Introducing a dummy activity

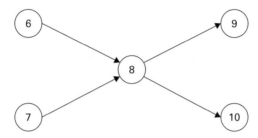

Figure 6.7(a) Valid network construction

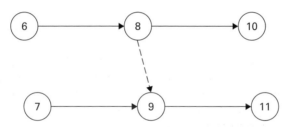

Figure 6.7(b) Additional dummy task

Dummy task: In the example of Figure 6.5, apart from the confusion of identity (both tasks would be identified as 7–8) there would be other difficulties in the analysis of the network. These can be overcome by introducing a *dummy* task into the network, as shown in Figure 6.6. A dummy is a logic link, a constraint which represents no specific operation. It is represented by a dotted line to distinguish it from a task and it carries an arrow to express the constraint. In Figure 6.6 this facilitates the expression of the relationship as '*task 9–10 may not begin until the parallel tasks 7–8 and 7–9 have been completed*' while giving separate identities to the parallel tasks.

The example shown in Figure 6.7(a) is a valid network construction only if the commencement of task 8–9 *and* the commencement of task 8–10 are dependent on the completion of task 6–8 *and* the completion of task 7–8. If the commencement of task

8–9 depended only on the completion of task 6–8, and not on the completion of task 7–8, an additional dummy task would have to be introduced (see Figure 6.7(b)).

6.3 The network planning procedure

The basic procedure for establishing a task network for a maintenance overhaul is shown in Figure 6.8. The procedure will be explained with reference to an example.

The procedure shown in Figure 6.8 is oriented toward network planning. A 'turn-around methodology' which includes data collection procedures is covered in Chapter 7.

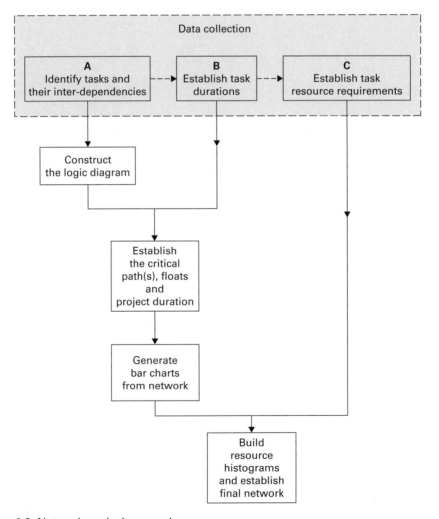

Figure 6.8 Network analysis procedure

6.3.1 Data collection

Step A: The initial step in data collection is to establish the complete list of tasks that are necessary to complete the overhaul and their interrelationships. It helps if the tasks are listed in the approximate chronological order of their execution. In a real project each task would be identified by a short descriptive title, but for the purpose of this illustration the tasks listed in Table 6.1 are identified alphabetically.

Table 6.1 Network relationships

Task	Interrelationships
A	Independent of all other tasks
B	Depends on completion of A
C	Depends on completion of A
D	Depends on completion of B and C
E	Depends on completion of A
F	Depends on completion of B, C and E
G	Depends on completion of (C), D and F
H	Depends on completion of (A) and C
I	Depends on completion of B
J	Depends on completion of (A), (C) and H

At this early stage it is often worth scrutinizing the interdependencies to see whether any redundant statements have crept in. For example, in Table 6.1 we were originally told that activity I depends on the completion of activities A, C and H, but we were also told that activity H depends on the completion of activities A and C and so it is sufficient to state that the commencement of I depends on the completion of H. In the table, such redundancies have all been shown bracketed.

Steps B and C: Having listed the tasks and their interrelationships it is necessary to establish the time and resource required for each task.

The time required to complete a task is termed its *duration*. In our example the resource is limited to manpower (in an actual overhaul resource would include numerous trades, spares, cranes, etc.). In the case of maintenance overhauls the duration and resource required for each task can be estimated in one or more of the following ways:

- Using the plant specific experience of the engineers, supervisors and artisans.
- Using previous history of identified or similar overhauls.
- From standard job procedures held in a job catalog.
- Using comparative estimating techniques (covered in the foundation module).

The estimated duration and manpower requirement for each of the tasks listed in Table 6.1 is given in Table 6.2.

6.3.2 Constructing the logic diagram

The work of constructing a logic diagram requires a large sheet of paper, a pencil and an eraser. Use as many dummies as necessary if this helps toward a simple layout of the diagram. The first attempt at drawing the logic diagram is shown in Figure 6.9.

Table 6.2 Task durations

Task	Duration (days)	Manpower requirement
A	9	3
B	9	2
C	7	2
D	5	4
E	5	1
F	3	3
G	7	2
H	8	2
I	7	1
J	1	4

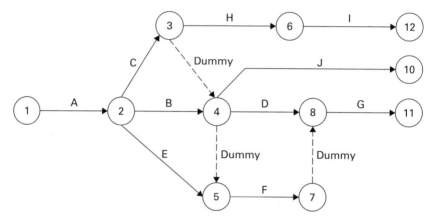

Figure 6.9 Logic diagram: first attempt

The network is started with event 1 (the start event) and then task A and event 2 (thus A is labeled as task 1–2). Tasks C, B and E can now be drawn coming out of event 2 (they are parallel tasks all depending on the completion of A – thus they cannot be started until A is complete and event 2 is reached). H can be drawn coming out of event 3 since it depends only on the completion of C (i.e. one task into B and one task out of C). Task D can be drawn coming out of event 4, but a dummy task needs to be drawn between events 3 and 4 because task D depends on both tasks B and C. Task F can be drawn coming out of event 5, but another dummy needs drawing between events 4 and 5 because task F depends on E, B (through the dummy) and C (through both the dummies). Task I can be drawn coming out of event 6 since it only depends directly on task H. Task G can be drawn coming out of event 7 since it depends on task D. However, it also depends on the completion of task F and a dummy is required between events 7 and 8. Task J is drawn coming out of event 4 since it depends on task B.

In order to complete the network the following checks are carried out:

- Are there any unnecessary dummies? Dummy 7–8 is unnecessary because task F could go straight into event 8 without causing task identification confusion. (Task F would be labeled as 5–8 and task D as 4–8.)

- Are there any tasks dangling? i.e. not connected to an end event. Tasks I, J and G are all dangling. This makes event 9 the end event and connects tasks J and G straight into it.
- Is the logic correct? This is checked by using Table 6.1 and starting at the end task.
  - Is task I dependent directly only on task H? The diagram is correct since only task H comes into event 6.
  - Is task J dependent directly only on task B? The logic is incorrect because the network shows task J dependent directly on task B and through the dummy on task C. The network diagram has to be redrawn to correct this. The rest of the logic is checked out correctly.

The completed logic diagram is shown in Figure 6.10.

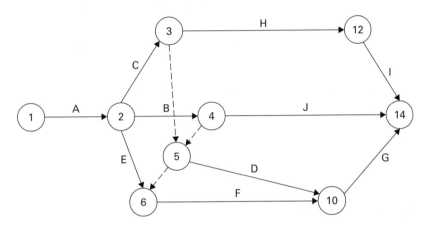

Figure 6.10 Completed logic diagram

6.3.3 Establishing the critical path, floats and overhaul time

Any uninterrupted sequence of events traced through a network, from the start event to the finish event, constitutes at path, e.g. A(1–2), B(2–4) and J(4–14) of Figure 6.10. In any network there is always one path, from the start event to the finish event, which is of particular interest, the total duration of it being not less than that of any other path between the same two events. This is termed the *critical path*. The total duration of the critical path is the duration of the overhaul, and the duration of the overhaul is governed by the critical tasks on this path.

To determine the critical path in a network it is necessary to examine the *earliest possible* and the *latest allowable* times for each event, after considering all possible routes through the network. The estimated durations, for the example whose network has already been drawn, are given in Table 6.2.

The earliest possible times are now calculated (see Figure 6.11). Within each event circle the event ordinal number is given at the top, the earliest possible time at bottom-left,

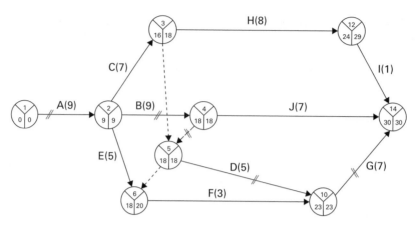

Figure 6.11 Completed representation of the network

and the latest allowable time at bottom-right. The time of the start (event 1) is set to zero, and the times for other events determined by addition of the task times. Thus:

Earliest time to event 2 = 0 + 9 = 9 days
Earliest time to event 3 = 9 + 7 = 16 days
Earliest time to event 4 = 9 + 9 = 18 days

There are two alternative routes to 5, i.e.:

Time to node 5 via event 3 = 16 + 0 = 16 days
Time to node 5 via event 4 = 18 + 0 = 18 days

Clearly the route via event 4 determines the earliest time at which event 5 can be reached, if both paths have to be completed (which, from the network definitions, they must), so the earliest time for event 5 is taken as 18 days. After working through the whole network in this way it is found that the earliest time for the end event (event 14) is 30 days. We now know that the duration of the overhaul will be 30 days, but the critical path has yet to be determined.

The latest allowable times for each event are found by taking the latest time for the end event (event 14) to be equal to the earliest time and then working back through the network to the other nodes, subtracting the task times. Thus:

Latest time to event 10 = 30 − 7 = 23 days
Latest time to event 6 = 23 − 3 = 20 days

There are two routes connecting event 10 with event 5:

By direct route, latest time for event 5 = 23 − 5 = 18 days
By route via event 6 latest time for event 5 = 20 − 0 = 20 days

Clearly, event 5 must be reached by the 18th day if the overhaul is not to be delayed. Working through the whole network in this way the latest allowable times of all the events are determined. The latest time for the start event should be found to be zero.

(If not, there is an error in the calculation.) An uninterrupted path can now be found through the network linking up event for which the earliest and latest times are equal. This is the *critical path* and the critical tasks are marked on the network diagram by a double bar across each line. These are the tasks which attract primary interest if the overhaul time is to be controlled or reduced.

A measure of the importance of non-critical tasks is given by the *float*, which is the time available for a task in addition to its normal duration. The *total float* available to a task is calculated from the earliest possible start time and the latest allowable finish time, and is the maximum additional time which can be absorbed by the task without delaying the overhaul. The *free float* available to an task is calculated from the earliest start time and the earliest finish time, and is the additional time which can be absorbed by a task without altering the floats available to other tasks. These quantities are calculated via the following relationships:

Total float = Latest finish – Earliest start – Duration
Free float = Earliest finish – Earliest start – Duration

Thus, the total float for task E is 6 days and the free float is 4 days. It can be seen that *all the tasks on the critical path have zero float.*

6.3.4 Deriving a bar chart from the network

The network has obvious advantages at the *planning and scheduling* stages of an overhaul. However, it lacks the bar chart's capacity to:

● represent the duration of a task by the length of a line;
● be the vehicle for recording the progress of work (and hence controlling it).

Translation of the network into a bar chart is therefore highly desirable. Essentially, this is done by using the *head and tail numbers* of the tasks to show the logic linkages between the tasks, the head number being the event number at the *end* of a task, the tail number that at the *start*. This procedure will now be illustrated, using the final network of the example, i.e. Figure 6.11.

List the tasks in order of increasing head numbers (see Table 6.3). Where two or more tasks have the same head number, arrange these in order of increasing tail numbers. The manpower requirement is also listed against each task – dummies require no resource.

The information of Table 6.3 is used to construct the bar chart shown in Figure 6.12.

> The bar chart framework is set up with the time scale along the top axis to cover 30 days. List of activities in the same order as Table 6.3 down the vertical axis. Task A is drawn onto the bar chart with the tail and head number marked at the beginning and end of the bar. Task C is then drawn on the chart, aligning its tail number with the head number A (providing these numbers are the same). These steps are repeated for all the tasks in turn using the rule – 'match the tail numbers with that same number which is farthest to the right'. Dummies are included as upright lines as shown.

The critical tasks are indicated as thick lines. An example of float is shown in task C.

Table 6.3 List of tasks by head and tail numbers

Task		Duration	Manpower
Reference	Tail no.–head no.	(days)	requirement
A	1–2	9	3
C	2–3	7	2
B	2–4	9	2
Du	3–5	–	–
Du	4–5	–	–
E	2–6	5	1
Du	5–6	–	–
D	5–10	5	4
F	6–10	3	3
H	3–12	8	2
J	4–14	7	1
G	10–14	7	2
I	12–14	1	4

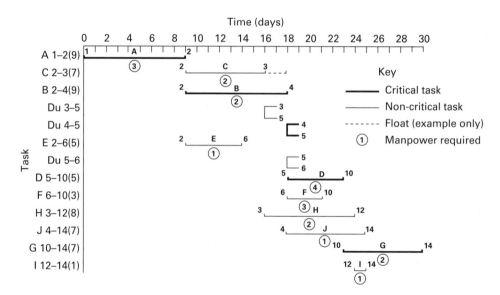

Figure 6.12 Bar chart

6.3.5 Resource histograms

The bar chart of Figure 6.12 is used to construct the manpower loading histogram of Figure 6.13. The manpower required on a day, say day 10, can be established by the addition of the tasks being carried out on that day, i.e.:

$$C(2) + B(2) + E(1) = 5$$

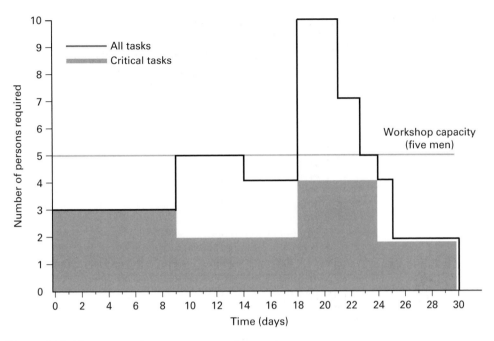

Figure 6.13 Histogram of manpower requirement

The histogram of critical task loading is shown superimposed on the main chart. Histograms of this kind in conjunction with float can be used to smooth the workload. In our example, the capacity of the workshop is indicated as five men – by floating the tasks it may be possible to bring the peak loading below this capacity level without affecting the overhaul duration.

6.4 Comments

This section has described the principles and procedure of network analysis. There are now numerous network analysis software packages available for assisting maintenance managers with the planning, scheduling and control of major shutdowns (e.g. microsoft project, Primavera, etc.). All that would be required is the information provided in Table 6.2 to be fed into a computer to enable the computer to provide completed networks/bar charts and also to carry out sophisticated analysis of the following kind:

- Multi-resource smoothing of type illustrated in Figure 6.13.
- Cost-effective reduction of project times (see Exercise E6.2).

A major advantage of computerized network analysis is the ability to control the progress and cost against budget via the feedback of task completion and actual task costs. The schedule/bar charts can be updated quickly (on a daily basis) and problem areas identified and corrected.

Exercise

E6.1   A maintenance overhaul consisting of 12 tasks shown in the table *has to be completed in not more than 30 days*. The restrictions on each task and provisional estimates of task duration are also shown in the table.

Task	Interrelations	Duration (days)
A	None	6
B	None	10
C	None	8
D	Not until C complete	10
E	Not until C complete	3
F	Not until D complete	9
G	Not until E complete	2
H	Not until A and D complete	8
I	Not until B and G complete	9
J	Not until H and I complete	3
K	Not until H and I complete	4
L	Not until K complete	2

Establish the following:

(a) The project time.
(b) The total float and free float of task G.
(c) The critical path.

Note: You will need to:

● complete the logic diagram,
● establish the earliest times and latest times,
● establish the critical path.

E6.2   The cost for each of the tasks is shown in the table below and additional information is given about ways of reducing the overhaul time. You are required to establish the most economical way of reducing the overhaul time by selecting the *best combination* of the listed actions.

Activity	Cost (£)
A	450
B	1200
C	2100
D	3500
E	1000
F	400
G	700
H	3000
I	2000
J	750
K	1000
L	900

Action 1: The duration of task D could be halved but this would double the cost.

Action 2: The duration of task F could be shortened by a third at a 50% cost increase.

Action 3: The duration of task H could be halved, but this would double the cost.

Action 4: The duration of task I could be reduced to 8, 7, 6 or 5 days at a cost increase of £250 for each day saved.

Note: For each day the overhaul time is reduced below 30 days £1000 is saved.

E6.3   Use the information from E5.2 to draw a modified network. Convert the modified network into a bar chart.

E6.4   The estimated manpower for each task is given in the table below. Construct a manpower loading histogram from this information and the bar chart. There are seven men in the workshop that can be used to complete this overhaul. Are these going to be sufficient? If not, suggest ways of improving the situation.

Activity	Men
A	4
B	2
C	2
D	6
E	3
F	4
G	5
H	2
I	4
J	3
K	4
L	5

Exercise Guideline Solutions

E6.1   The completed network is shown in Figure 6.14. The answers are as follows:
  (a) 32 days.
  (b) Total float on task G = LF – ES – D
$$= 17 - 11 - 2 = 4 \text{ days}$$
    Free float on task G = EF – ES – D
$$= 13 - 11 - 2 = 0 \text{ days}$$
  (c) Critical path is
    C(1–2), D(2–3), Dummy(3–4), H(4–7), K(7–8), L(8–9)

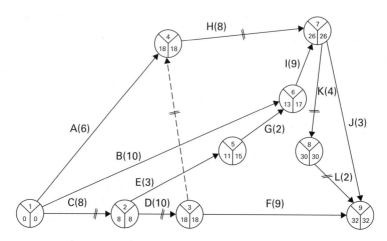

Figure 6.14 Completed network before modification

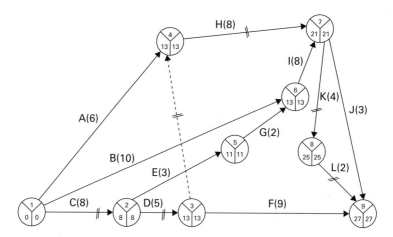

Figure 6.15 Network after modification

E6.2   The most economical method of reducing the project time is:
● Reduce D by 5 days in conjunction with reducing I by 1 day.
● This involves a total penalty of £750.
E6.3   The modified network is shown in Figure 6.15. It will be noticed that there are now two critical paths.
● C, D, dummy, H, K, L.
● C, E, G, I, K, L.
The bar chart for the modified network is shown in Figure 6.16.
E6.4   The histogram for the modified network/bar chart is shown in Figure 6.17. It can be seen that the area above the workshop capacity exceeds the area below the capacity line. Thus contract labor will have to be used.

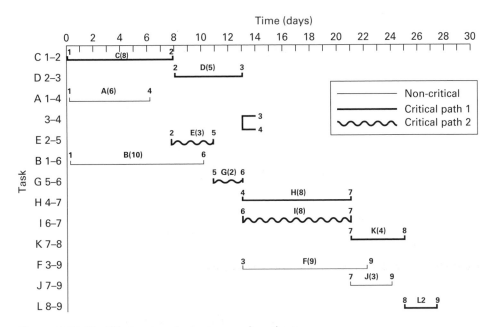

Figure 6.16 Modified network drawn as a bar chart

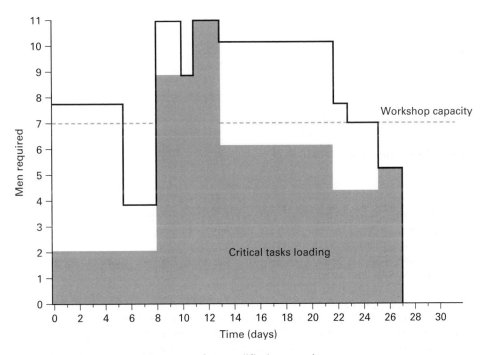

Figure 6.17 Manpower histogram for modified network

7 Management of plant turnarounds – Part 2: Turnaround methodology

'The six stages of a major turnaround:
Enthusiasm.
Disenchantment.
Panic.
Search for the guilty.
Punishment of the innocent.
Decoration of those who took no part.'
Comment by a disillusioned Shutdown Manager

Chapter aims and outcomes

To describe a methodology and associated procedures that can be followed to plan, schedule and control major plant turnarounds.

On completion of this chapter you should be able to:

- describe the four main phases of a generic turnaround methodology and understand the associated strategic issues involved;
- understand the sub-steps within each of the four phases and the key issues arising (e.g. you should be able to delineate a typical turnaround organization and understand the principles of its operation).

Chapter route map

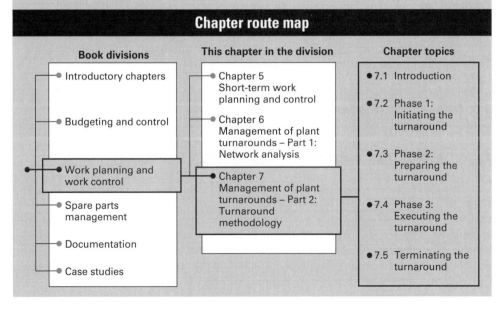

Book divisions	This chapter in the division	Chapter topics
Introductory chapters	Chapter 5 Short-term work planning and control	7.1 Introduction
Budgeting and control	Chapter 6 Management of plant turnarounds – Part 1: Network analysis	7.2 Phase 1: Initiating the turnaround
Work planning and work control	Chapter 7 Management of plant turnarounds – Part 2: Turnaround methodology	7.3 Phase 2: Preparing the turnaround
Spare parts management		7.4 Phase 3: Executing the turnaround
Documentation		7.5 Terminating the turnaround
Case studies		

Key words

- Turnaround methodology
- Turnaround organization
- Contractor work packages
- Shutdown duration
- Work scope
- Key data bar chart

7.1 Introduction

A general methodology for managing turnarounds is outlined in Figure 7.1 (contributed by T. Lenahan with additions by A. Kelly). The key strategic decisions and their timing relative to the four principal phases (each of which is divided into sub-steps) are indicated along the top of the figure.

Many variations of this methodology have been observed. For example, Figure 7.2, is a turnaround schedule for a small agro-chemical plant. In this case the planning lead time (i.e. the total planning time required up to the start of execution of the work) is about 2 months. A turnaround for a 500 MW boiler-turbo-generator might well demand a planning lead time of a year. The magnitude of the planning lead time and effort depend on the size and complexity of the turnaround and of the previous experience of similar or identical exercises. Major plant overhauls are usually much the same in 1 year as in another and this, therefore, makes the initiation and preparation phases that much more straightforward; this is the principal difference between turnarounds (where most of the work is maintenance) and major plant projects which involve the building and installation of new plant.

Exercise

E7.1   Use the turnaround methodology shown in Figure 7.1 as a template to map the turnaround procedures for your own company. Comment on any differences and make suggestions for improvement.

7.2 Phase 1: Initiating the turnaround

7.2.1 Forming a policy team and appointing a turnaround manager

It is the responsibility of the senior management of the company to form a policy team made up of the managers who have a stake in the turnaround and the ability to make decisions. This team must ensure that constraints, objectives and policy for the turnaround are well defined. Arguably, the most important decision made by the team will be the appointment of a turnaround manager to act as their agent because, once appointed, this individual will control all phases of the task, while the team will assume the tripartite role of facilitation, monitoring and endorsement.

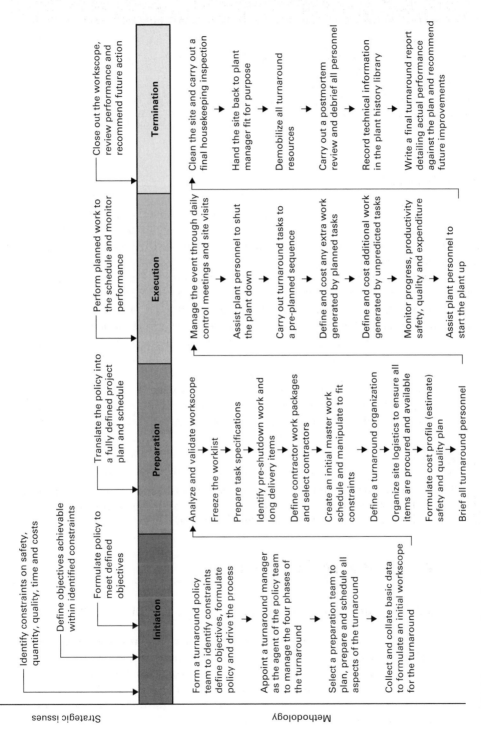

Figure 7.1 Turnaround methodology

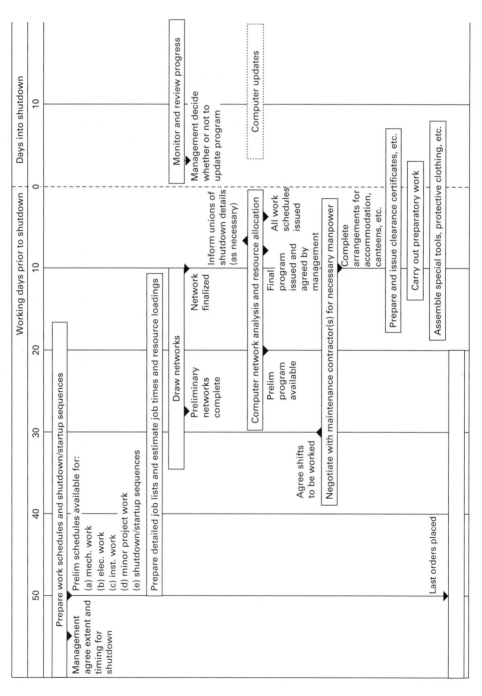

Figure 7.2 Overhaul program, agro-chemical plant

The turnaround manager should chair a regular meeting of the team at which progress will be reported and constraints, objectives and policy discussed on matters including timing, duration, workscope (including major tasks), materials, resources, contractor issues, pre- and post-shutdown work, costs, safety and quality.

7.2.2 Key policy decisions for the initiation phase

Two of the most important decisions that have to be made during the initiation phase involve the formulation of the turnaround objective and the timing of the plant shutdown. The objective needs to be compatible with the overall maintenance objective. For example, in the case of a base-load boiler-turbo-generator unit (see Figure 7.3) the maintenance objective might be:

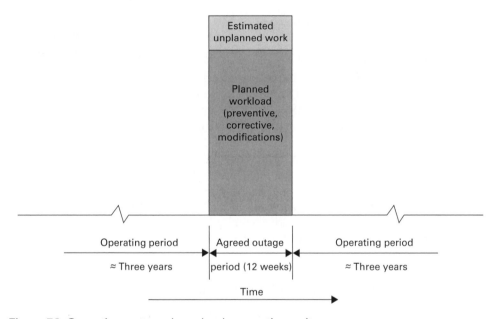

Figure 7.3 Operating pattern, base-load generating unit

> To minimise the sum of (i) the income lost due to planned outage, (ii) the income lost due to unplanned outage, and (iii) the direct cost of maintenance.

The turnaround objective might then be:

> To complete the agreed maintenance work within the agreed shutdown duration at minimum resource cost, and while meeting all relevant safety standards.

This general statement could also be supplemented by the setting of more detailed targets and standards for workload, work quality, plant condition, safety duration and cost. This objective is feasible because the generator would be shutdown during the annual period of low demand and there would be little to gain by reducing the shutdown duration. For production-limited chemical plant on the other hand the objective might be very different, putting the emphasis on the reduction of turnaround duration – at the expense of high maintenance cost. Clearly, the turnaround objective must be established at an early stage.

The timing of major plant shutdowns (e.g. whether they should occur at some fixed interval or should be usage or condition based) and their preventive work content are determined to a large extent by the maintenance strategy. Base-load boiler-turbo-generator plant, e.g. typically come off every 3 years or so as part of a station schedule with a 20-year planning horizon. The exact timing of the shutdown will be a function of the annual fluctuation in electricity demand, and other factors such as the need for grid maintenance. Although the frequency of the shutdown is time based (inevitably so in this extensive planning context) the preventive work content is determined in part via inspections, inspection history and previous shutdown history.

7.2.3 Selecting a preparation team

The turnaround manager is responsible for selecting a preparation team comprising:

- *A preparation engineer*: managing the team on a day-to-day basis, validating the workscope and delegating other work to the planners.
- *A planning officer*: supervising the planning team, assisting the preparation engineer to validate the workscope and creating the initial turnaround plan.
- *A planning group*: gathering basic data on the plant (e.g. drawings, specifications, plant standards), specifying tasks and providing all supporting documentation such as specifications of welding and pressure test procedures.
- *A site logistics officer*: organizing storage, supply and distribution of materials, equipment, carnage, transportation, services, utilities, accommodation and facilities.
- *A site logistics team*: of storemen, drivers and other semi-skilled personnel who work under the supervision of the logistics officer.

7.2.4 Collecting the job lists and other data

In order to prepare the turnaround work schedule the preparation team will need to gather a substantial amount of data from a number of sources – *the workscope*. To this end, the manager should set up a series of meetings, see Figure 7.4 which will run through the preparation phase until all relevant tasks and associated data has been obtained.

7.3 Phase 2: Preparing the turnaround

7.3.1 Analyzing and validating the workscope

The worklists supplied by the plant team will be raw data containing elements of unnecessary and duplicated work (which must be eliminated), incorrectly specified work (which must be corrected) and errors in material specification etc. During a series

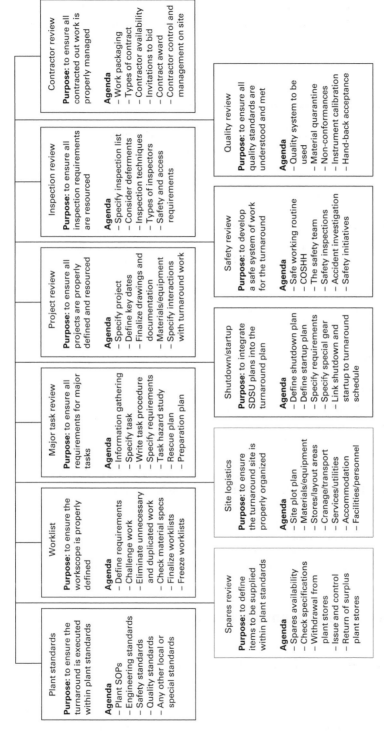

Plant standards

Purpose: to ensure the turnaround is executed within plant standards

Agenda
– Plant SOPs
– Engineering standards
– Safety standards
– Quality standards
– Any other local or special standards

Worklist

Purpose: to ensure the workscope is properly defined

Agenda
– Define requirements
– Challenge work
– Eliminate unnecessary and duplicated work
– Check material specs
– Finalize worklists
– Freeze worklists

Major task review

Purpose: to ensure all requirements for major tasks

Agenda
– Information gathering
– Specify task
– Write task procedure
– Specify requirements
– Task hazard study
– Rescue plan
– Preparation plan

Project review

Purpose: to ensure all projects are properly defined and resourced

Agenda
– Specify project
– Define key dates
– Finalize drawings and documentation
– Materials/equipment
– Specify interactions with turnaround work

Inspection review

Purpose: to ensure all inspection requirements are resourced

Agenda
– Specify inspection list
– Consider deferments
– Inspection techniques
– Types of inspectors
– Safety and access requirements

Contractor review

Purpose: to ensure all contracted out work is properly managed

Agenda
– Work packaging
– Types of contract
– Contractor availability
– Invitations to bid
– Contract award
– Contractor control and management on site

Spares review

Purpose: to define items to be supplied within plant standards

Agenda
– Spares availability
– Check specifications
– Withdrawal from plant stores
– Issue and control
– Return of surplus plant stores

Site logistics

Purpose: to ensure the turnaround site is properly organized

Agenda
– Site plot plan
– Materials/equipment
– Stores/layout areas
– Cranage/transport
– Services/utilities
– Accommodation
– Facilities/personnel

Shutdown/startup

Purpose: to integrate SDSU plans into the turnaround plan

Agenda
– Define shutdown plan
– Define startup plan
– Specify requirements
– Specify special gear
– Link shutdown and startup to turnaround schedule

Safety review

Purpose: to develop a safe system of work for the turnaround

Agenda
– Safe working routine
– COSHH
– The safety team
– Safety inspections
– Accident investigation
– Safety initiatives

Quality review

Purpose: to ensure all quality standards are understood and met

Agenda
– Quality system to be used
– Material quarantine
– Non-conformances
– Instrument calibration
– Hand-back acceptance

Figure 7.4 Meetings organized during preparation phase

of meetings (see Figure 7.4) the preparation team should set out to validate the workscope and define all requirements by analyzing every major, minor and bulkwork request on the worklist to ensure that it needs to be done, it is correctly specified, and that all requirements are specified.

7.3.2 Freezing the worklist

The validated workscope will be the foundation upon which every other aspect of the turnaround rests. Therefore, at a pre-determined date (normally between 2 and 6 months before the event) the worklist should be frozen and no further work accepted. The frozen worklist can then be transformed into the workscope that will be used to accurately calculate key indicators such as cost, duration and resourcing of the event. In reality, work will usually requested up to and even beyond the start date of the turnaround. If the worklist is not frozen it would be impossible to accurately calculate these key indicators. Any work requested after the freeze date should be handled by a 'late work' routine which should be costed and resourced separately.

7.3.3 Preparing task specifications

The raw worklist will consist basically of three categories of work, each of which will need to be treated differently as regards planning and specification, *viz.*:

- *Major tasks* (e.g. overhauling a switchboard): Large packages of work that are characterized by long-duration, high-technical content, unfamiliarity or high risk. The preparation engineer should be responsible for planning and specifying both the technical and safety content of these and for producing a critical path network (see Figure 7.5).
- *Minor tasks* (e.g. washing and inspecting a small heat exchanger): Small packages of work of medium duration which still require individual planning and specification. These tasks are planned and specified by a planner, on a task sheet (see Figure 7.6).
- *Bulkwork* (e.g. replacement of many similar valves): Numerous small jobs with identical or similar requirements that can be packaged by type and listed on a bulkwork route card (see Figure 7.7).

7.3.4 Identifying pre-shutdown work

During the analysis of the worklist some jobs, spares or materials will be identified which, because of their special nature, need to be dealt with as early as possible, namely:

- Long delivery spares and materials, which must be ordered at the earliest possible date if they are to be available when required (e.g. delivery of a replacement main-compressor rotor can take up to 18 months).

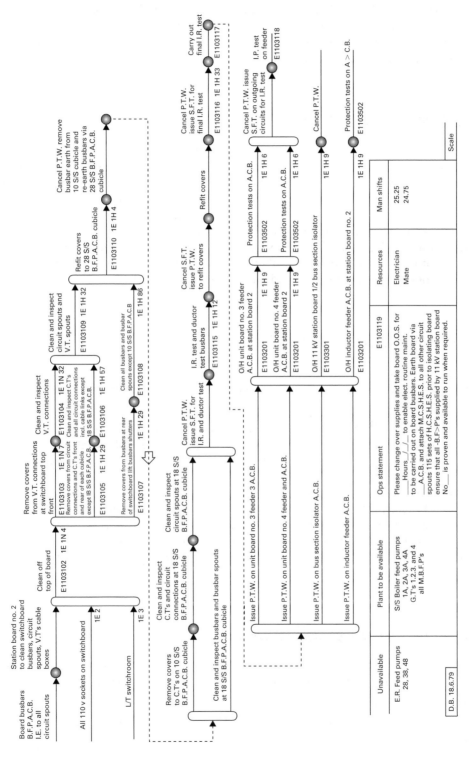

Figure 7.5 Critical path network, 11 kV switchboard overhaul

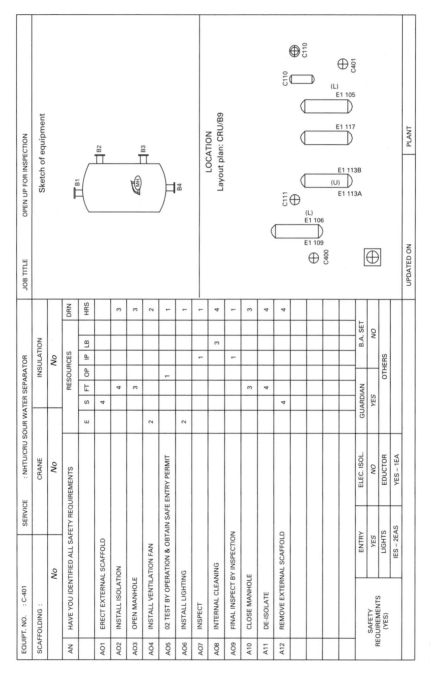

Figure 7.6 Sample task sheet

BULKWORK ROUTE CARD No ------------

YEAR ------------   PLANT ------------   UNIT/AREA ------------   ITEMS ------------

ITEM NUMBER	ASSOCIATED PLANT NUMBER	INST/ELEC DISCONNECTION (IF REQUIRED)	REMOVED	DECONTAM	SENT TO W/SHOP FOR OVERHAUL	RETURNED FROM WORKSHOP	OVERHAULED ITEM FITTED	SPARE ITEM FITTED	INST/ELEC RECONNECTED (IF REQUIRED)	TESTED AND COMMISSIONED

Figure 7.7 Bulkwork route card

- Spares which have to be prefabricated and tested before they can be installed in the plant.
- Specialist sub-contractors and equipment – the more specialized, the longer their waiting list, so their availability should be checked and orders placed on them early.
- General services and utilities – such as temporary electrical and telephone cables, water and gas pipelines, etc. – must be laid well in advance of the turnaround start date.

7.3.5 Defining contractor work packages and selecting contractors

The decision must be taken as to what work will be contracted out, how it will be packaged and what mix of contractors will be used.

7.3.6 Creating the work schedule

Once tasks have been specified (and, where necessary, networked) to the appropriate standard – and all necessary materials, equipment, resources and services identified – they must be assembled into a master schedule which will meet the current constraints on workload, money, time and resources. Figure 7.8 shows the elements of the master schedule and the steps that need to be taken to prepare and finalize it. The logic register referred to is simply the working patterns which are initially set up in the schedule, e.g.:

- bulkwork to be executed on an 8-hour shift, 5 days per week, only;
- minor tasks and some major tasks on 12-hour shifts, 7 days per week;
- nominated major tasks (including the critical path task) to be accomplished on a continuous 24 hour cycle).

The start date and time of any given task will be dependent on when the job is released by the plant shutdown program and the resources available at that time. All tasks that do not lie on the critical path will have a certain amount of float time and this will be translated into earliest and latest start and finish times for each significant element of the task. This allows a measure of flexibility in the plan.

If a turnaround is large and complex it is customary to produce networks at two levels. For example, Figure 7.9 is a 'key date network' for a boiler-turbo-generator overhaul. At the level of this network an arrow represents a major section of the overhaul. Such major sections of work can be themselves represented by a detailed computer-generated network (see Figure 7.5); at this level the arrow represent a single task. The master network can be regarded as a route map of the complete turnaround, showing how all the tasks are logically related. As already indicated, the networks are best converted to bar charts for the execution phase.

7.3.7 Techniques for creating a schedule

These have been covered in Chapter 6 and are as follows:

- For small overhauls it may be possible to use bar charted shuffle boards on which tasks can be moved back and forth along time lines.
- Using computerized network planning software such as microsoft project or Primavera.

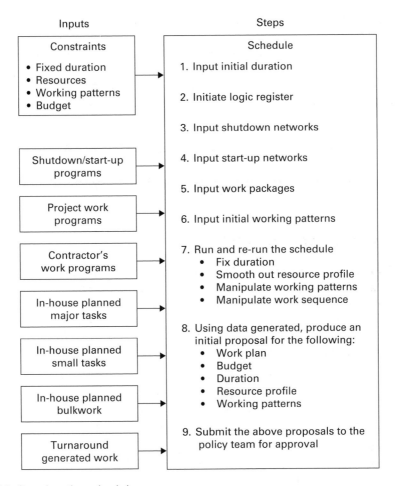

Figure 7.8 Creating the schedule

Two points should be noted:

- Most commercial software network packages are not ideal for turnarounds because they have been designed for project management (which tend to have long-duration tasks). In addition, they do not handle bulkwork in a satisfactory manner and often distribute it throughout the program to suit resource levels – so that, e.g. two valves at the same location may be scheduled to be removed on different days when common sense would dictate that they be removed at the same time. This case is not as trivial as it may at first seem because, on a major event there will be many hundreds, if not thousands, of such bulkwork items. This leads to a situation where a computer may used for scheduling tasks in general but bulkwork tasks will be scheduled manually.
- Manual planning (on a shuffle board or planning sheet) is only practical for small overhauls because the amount of detail required for a large one would swamp a manual planning format. Also, if there is a significant change of intent in the turnaround logic, the plan is difficult to change.

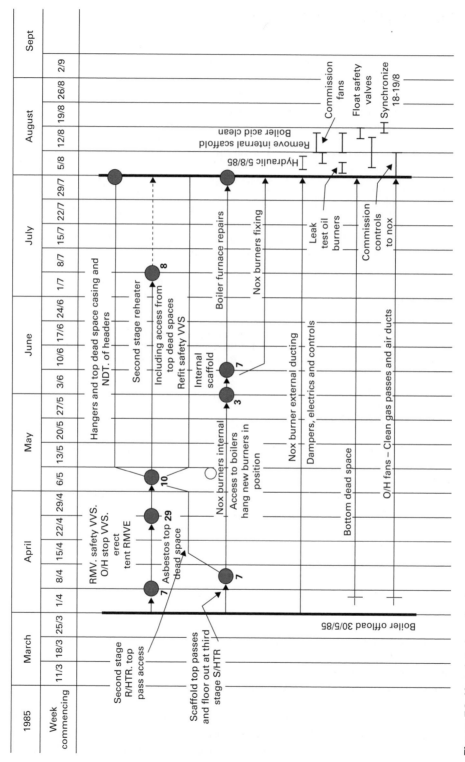

Figure 7.9 Key date bar chart

7.3.8 Optimizing the schedule

An optimum schedule balances out the constraints of workload, duration, cost and resources. The first run of the schedule will be based on raw data. For instance, it may be that the duration required by business needs is not realistic for the required workload and the available resources and if the resources were to be increased the cost would overrun the budget. A first-run schedule often exhibits an erratic manpower profile, i.e. a requirement for significantly different levels of resource on consecutive days (e.g. mechanical fitters required might number 189 on day 1, 66 on day 2, 12 on day 3, 82 on day 4, 29 on day 5 and so on). This would have to be evened out by reorganizing the work schedule.

The turnaround manager is responsible for optimizing the schedule and then presenting it to the policy team for discussion. It may well be that this process would have to be reiterated several times before the policy team's final approval is obtained and bar charts produced showing the sequence of tasks on a daily and weekly basis. These charts will need to be updated daily during the execution phase.

Review Question

R7.1   Outline the key differences between ongoing planning (for the first- and second-line workload) and the planning and scheduling of the major work (third line) – see, e.g. the complete work planning model of Figure 5.11.

7.3.9 Forming the turnaround organization

The form of the organization will be dictated by current constraints and policy team decisions. For example, Figure 7.10 outlines an organization, managed by a consultant turnaround manager, which dealt with three areas: one which involved a large project handled by the company's project department, another which was handled by a contractor and yet another which was handled by company personnel (both of the latter being covered by a single co-ordinator). The control electrical work was treated as a separate 'area'. The plant team handled the shutdown and startup phases and the company supplied a team to control work quality (and who signed off tasks when they were satisfactorily completed).

A typical organization would comprise the following:

- plant personnel with local knowledge;
- turnaround personnel with planning;
- co-ordination and management skills;
- technical personnel with engineering, design and project management skills;
- contractors with the skills and knowledge to carry out the work.

Throughout the organization, control would be maintained by the practice of single point responsibility, which requires that, at any given stage of every task there will be one person who has been nominated as responsible for accepting the task from the

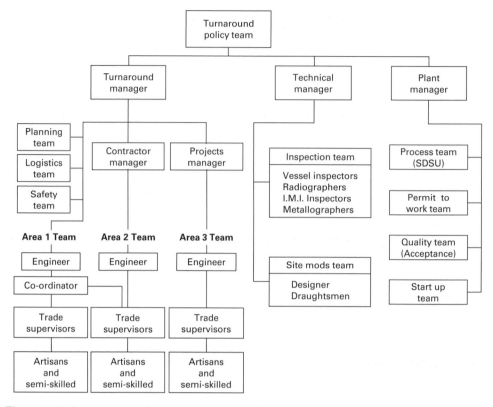

Figure 7.10 An example of a turnaround organization

previous stage, ensuring that the current stage of the task will be completed to the required standard and handing the task on to the next stage.

An organization that has been employed for carrying out turnarounds of certain power plants is shown in Figure 7.11. Plant-specialized core teams were set up for each major plant area (e.g. for the boilers). Supplementation of these, as necessary, from a centralized trade pool created an organization which was essentially an area (trade matrix).

Exercise

E7.2   Map the turnaround organization used in your own company. How does it compare to the organization shown in Figures 7.10 and 7.11. Make suggestions for improvement.

Review Question

R7.2   The matrix structure shown in Figure 7.11 is a typical structure used in carrying out major turnarounds.

List the main advantages of this structure for carrying out major turn-arounds.

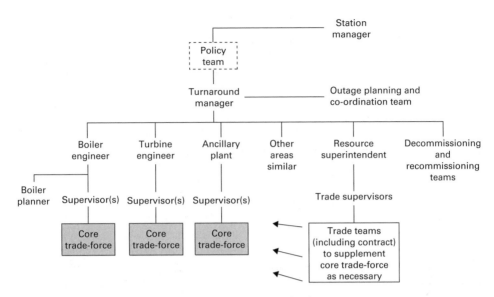

Figure 7.11 A typical power plant turnaround organization

7.3.10 Defining the site logistics

Turnaround logistics are concerned with the procurement, location and movement of all items and services required. The site logistics are concerned with identifying the turnaround resources and services and their current location and organizing their movement around the site. A team under the leadership of a logistics officer (e.g. see Figure 7.10) should be responsible for providing all turnaround requirements.

One method of displaying much of the information required for logistic decision-making is to draw up a plan of the site that shows the plant and its available surrounding land, and to overlay this with the locations of such things as stores, lay-down areas, water-washing bays, turnaround offices, accommodation, etc. Vital safety information can be recorded in the form of locations of non-load-bearing surfaces, prohibited or hazardous areas, fire assembly points, toxic refuges, emergency showers and eye baths. Such a plan ensures that everyone involved has a general understanding of the logistic arrangements.

7.3.11 Formulating a cost estimate

As soon as the main features of the workscope are known, an estimate of the cost – to within plus or minus 20% – could be generated by calculating the approximate number of man-hours required to carry out each major job, each minor job and all of the bulk-work, and then multiplying this figure by an average hourly rate. If this manpower cost were then taken to represent approximately 30–35% of the total cost, then trebling it would give the total cost of the turnaround, to within the tolerance stated. (Obviously, if any *accurate* cost information were to be available at this time it should be used in the calculations.) This figure (the *ball-park* estimate) should be calculated early on in order to give the policy team some confidence that the estimated costs are of the correct order, or to give them the opportunity to make changes if they are wildly different from the budgeted sum which has been set aside for the turnaround in the strategic budget. As harder information becomes available the estimate can be recalculated, its accuracy increasing until a stage is reached when all significant costs are either known or can be assessed very accurately (resulting in the *refined* estimate). This stage can be reached after the turnaround plan has been approved.

7.3.12 Formulating a safety plan

During a turnaround the normal routine of a plant is breached, many more people than usual will be concentrated in its limited area, many will be strangers to the plant and its hazards, and most will be working under pressures of time – all of which has the potential to make the plant a much more hazardous place than usual. A 'safe system of work' must, therefore, be implemented – to safeguard personnel, property and the environment – and should consist of five major elements, *viz.*:

The safety team: Led by a safety officer, the team is responsible for a number of safety functions including, but not limited to:

- developing a safety strategy for the turnaround;
- briefing all personnel on safety before the event commences;
- providing help, advice and assistance on safety to all personnel during the event;
- providing and controlling guardians for tasks requiring entry permits;
- co-ordinating emergency marshals and controllers.

Safe working routine: This should contain safety guidelines for ensuring that the workplace and surrounding environment are safe, materials used are not hazardous and that people are competent and well-briefed on the requirements and hazards of the tasks they are required to perform. The routine should be driven on a day-to-day basis by the supervisors.

Task hazard assessment: A process for analyzing and dealing with the hazards involved in performing a specific task, this has four stages:

(i) defining the main steps of the task,
(ii) for each step, identifying any hazards involved,
(iii) specifying what type of loss is attached to each hazard,
(iv) specifying action to either eliminate or guard against the hazard.

The assessment should be carried out on all major tasks and on a selection of minor and bulkwork tasks. Also, if any member of the team should have reservations about *any* task it is essential that it be subjected to a hazard assessment.

Safety inspections: The working site must be continuously monitored in order to ensure that the safe system of work is adequate and that personnel comply with it. Two formal inspection routines are vital elements in the monitoring program. The first is general safety inspection carried out on a daily basis by a team of managers who should be invited by the safety officer to take part; they should look for unsafe acts, unsafe conditions and instances of untidiness and bad housekeeping around the site in general. The second is recurrent spot checks carried out on randomly selected tasks by a team who should be invited by the safety officer to answer the following three questions:

1. Are the safety measures specified for the tasks adequate?
2. Are they understood by those performing the task?
3. Are they being complied with?

Information gathered via both routines should be fed back, for possible action, to the daily turnaround control meeting.

Accident investigation: If, in spite of the safety measures taken, an accident should occur it should be the responsibility of the turnaround manager to convene an investigation to ascertain the:

- type and extent of loss inflicted on people, property or the environment;
- nature of the specific incident that caused the loss;
- immediate reasons for the incident;
- root causes underlying the accident.

7.3.13 Formulation of the quality plan

Every task should be properly specified, and executed to specification. Critical tasks should be checked, on completion, by qualified and plant-based quality teams to ensure that the work has complied with plant quality standards. All tasks should be signed off by a plant-based person. The quality plan should define the critical tasks and identify the plant-based personnel who have the authority to sign off tasks.

7.3.14 Briefing of all turnaround personnel

The purposes of briefing are to:

- provide accurate general information;
- alert everyone to the rules governing the turnaround;
- create a common understanding among – and to gain commitment from – all those involved.

Typically, it will provide information about:

- timing, duration and work patterns;
- local manpower and contractors;
- workscope and schedule;
- the turnaround organization;
- accommodation and facilities;
- the safety system of work and the quality plan.

7.4 Phase 3: Executing the turnaround

Once preparation is complete and all personnel have been briefed, the turnaround manager should take charge of the event. Figure 7.12 outlines his daily routine.

- Check previous 24 hours progress with the planning officer
- Check cost control and forecast with the quantity surveyor
- Visit the safety cabin and check on safety issues
- Visit the stores and check on delivery and issue problems
- Visit the workshops and check on daily progress
- Tour the site to check on safety and housekeeping – talk to people
- Take part in any scheduled safety inspection or spot check
- Visit permit to work issues to discuss any issues
- Visit the quality team and discuss quality issues
- Vet overtime requests and approve/modify reject

- **Meet with the plant and engineering manager**
  - Resolve technical problems
  - Discuss and approve/reject request for extra/additional work
  - Formulate strategies to keep the turnaround on program
  - Resolve industrial relations problems
  - Resolve interface conflicts
  - Define consequences of any change of intent

- **Chair the turnaround control meeting**
  - Safety officer reports on safety issues and any incidents
  - Area engineers report on area work progress and problems
  - Project managers report on progress of projects
  - Plant manager reports on any plant issues
  - Maintenance manager reports on any engineering issue
  - Quality team leader reports on quality issues
  - Quantity surveyor reports on expenditure and cost issues
  - Chairman sums up/issues instructions/delegates tasks

- **Write a daily turnaround report and issue it**

Figure 7.12 Turnaround manager's daily routine

7.4.1 The shutdown of the plant

The shutdown of the plant should normally be controlled by the plant manager and his team. The turnaround manager should supply the resources to perform the civil, mechanical, electrical and instrumentation work of the shutdown. From 'product off' the plant would be taken through run down of stock, cleaning, cooling, sweetening of the atmosphere inside vessels and equipment, and isolation of all equipment – to the point when the safety team would carry out atmospheric tests in vessels and equipment to ensure the absence of noxious, toxic or volatile substances. The plant could said to be 'dead', i.e. safe to work on.

7.4.2 Carrying out the turnaround tasks

The first few days of this phase should be devoted to opening up large items of equipment (vessels, columns, rotating machinery, etc.) and stripping out small items (valves, small pumps, motors, etc.). After stripdown the main activities would be plant inspection, repair, refurbishment and equipment cleaning. At this point large specialized tasks, such as catalyst renewal, column re-traying and compressor overhaul would be started.

7.4.3 Defining and costing the extra work

Inspection of equipment will often reveal faults which were not predicted and which require the carrying out of work which is *extra* to that which has been planned.

> Inspections undertaken during previous shutdowns, inspections undertaken online, and effective planning should minimize the occurrence of this 'extra work'.

Such work should be specified, costed and submitted for approval to the plant and turnaround managers on a daily basis. If the work required is going to have a negative impact on any of the turnaround objectives it should be submitted to the policy team for action. Should the work be approved it should be entered on an extra worklist and added to the work schedule. Occasionally, a fault could be revealed which could have such a serious impact on turnaround objectives that it could require decisions to be made by management at the very highest level.

7.4.4 Defining and costing additional work

During the event, work may be exposed which was not on the worklist because it was either not considered necessary or was overlooked by the plant team. This *additional* work should be treated in exactly the same way as extra work except that it should be recorded on a separate worklist. After the turnaround this should be investigated to ascertain the reasons why it was not included in the original worklist.

Review Question

R7.3   A guideline for major shutdowns is that at least 80% of the completed shutdown workload should be preplanned. List some of the key actions that need to be taken to accomplish this guideline.

7.4.5 Monitoring progress, productivity, safety, quality and expenditure

The main monitoring vehicle should be the daily control meeting. Figures 7.13(a) and 7.13(b) is a comprehensive checklist of the subject matter that should be covered. This

- Open the meeting and control through the chair
- Ask for and note reports in pre-set order
- Ask specific questions to clarify points
- Do not allow detailed discussion of issues at this meeting – convene separate discussions
- Sum up general progress on key indicators
- Voice any concerns on trends or specific issues
- Make executive decisions and inform the meeting of them, their requirements and consequences
- Delegate specific actions to particular people
- Delegate responsibilities to convene further discussions on key issues outside of the control meeting
- Announce next day's quality initiative
- Announce next day's safety slogan
- Make any other announcements
- State, and ask for, any other business
- Close the meeting

Figure 7.13(a) Turnaround manager's control meeting agenda

formal tool should be supplemented by a process of continuous communication between members of the team. A 5 or 10 days window of the kind outlined in Figure 7.14 is often adopted for monitoring the progress of the turnaround.

7.4.6 Starting up the plant

A point will eventually be reached when most of the tasks will either have been completed or be nearing completion and the decision could be taken to disband the turnaround organization and replace it with a 'startup' team. This should be led by the plant manager with the turnaround manager assuming a support role. The daily control meetings should be replaced by regular startup meetings (often held twice a day). The startup phase will be a mixture of completing any remaining turnaround tasks and bringing plant systems back on line.

7.5 Phase 4: Terminating the turnaround

During the startup phase, and for approximately 4 weeks after, actions should be taken to demobilize all turnaround resources and to return the plant area to its former state. In addition to this, a formal debrief should be conducted while events are still fresh in people's minds, to record what happened and any lessons to be learned. The final action of the termination phase should be for the turnaround manager to compile and issue a report which should detail the work done, compare actual against planned performance and make recommendations for future events of the same kind.

Safety officer's report	Area engineer's report
• Details of accidents/incidents in last 24 hours • Details of any recurring accidents/incidents • Findings of daily site inspection and spot check • Summary of site safety level and details of any particular safety concerns • Recommendations for safety improvements • Details of any safety initiatives or awards • Tomorrow's safety slogan	• Progress on major tasks including any technical problems and solutions • Tasks completed, boxed up and handed back and percentage completion of other major tasks • Progress on small tasks and bulkwork • Any hold-ups or shortages on manpower, materials, equipment or services • Any conflicts with other areas of work • Whether the area is on schedule or behind – and, if behind, the strategy for getting back on target • Assessment of unavoidable overrun, how many hours or days, and why it is unavoidable
Project manager's report	**Plant manager's report**
• Progress to date on project including any technical problems and solutions • Progress on any 'break ins' • Any 'bad fit' problems due to poor design • Any hold-ups or shortages on manpower, materials, equipment or services • Any conflicts with other areas of work • Whether the area is on schedule or behind – and, if behind, the strategy for getting back on target • Assessment of unavoidable overrun, how many hour or days, and why it is unavoidable	• Current ability of permit to work issuers to issue permits on time and strategy to eliminate any delays • Any handover quality issues • General view of on site performance • General view of on site housekeeping • Any upcoming on site problems • Warning of any system coming back online early • Warning of any process activity that could impact turnaround progress or safety
Maintenance manager's report	**Quality team leader's report**
• Any concerns on turnaround progress • Any engineering concerns • Any quality performance concerns • Any upcoming engineering problems • Any questions on turnaround engineering work being done	• Quality trends in the last 24 hours • Any specific quality problems • Any recurring quality problems • Any recommendations for quality improvement
Quantity surveyor's report	
• Actual expenditure to date vs. planned expenditure • Expenditure trends in each area • Specific examples of cost overrun • General forecast on final turnaround cost • Any recommendations for tighter cost control or cost saving initiatives	

Figure 7.13(b) The daily control meeting: information and actions

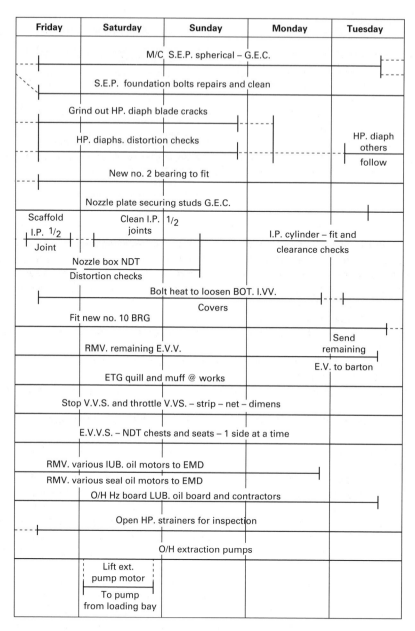

Figure 7.14 Bar chart for a 5-days window for shutdown control

Review Questions

R7.4   This question refers to the agricultural chemical plant of the case study in this book (see Chapter 11).

List the main reasons why Fertec carried out major work planning successfully.

List the main problems in major work planning that were identified during the audit.

R7.5   Explain why the planning and scheduling of a major overhaul of a 20-year-old petroleum refinery should be easier than the planning and scheduling of the installation of a new petroleum refinery.

Review Questions Guidelines

R7.1   The planning and scheduling of major shutdowns has a much longer planning horizon – in the case of power stations it is up to 1 year. A major shutdown involves a multitude of interrelated tasks requiring some form of network analysis. In addition it generates a major resource peak which can involve employing hundreds of contract trades.

R7.2   The main advantages are as follows:
- The turnaround manager provides single point control for the duration of the turnaround.
- There is a dedicated planning team the core of which came from the initiation phase preparation team.
- Each plant area, e.g. turbine has its own specialized engineer and specialized core trade-force.
- During the turnaround the demand for labor varies across each of the core teams and is supplied from the centralized resource pool.

R7.3   In order to ensure that at least 80% of the shutdown work is planned it is necessary to:
- have excellent plant and maintenance history from previous shutdowns, e.g. what was replaced? What was worn but left to the current shutdown? etc.
- have excellent offline condition monitoring (non-destructive testing during shutdowns) and online condition monitoring and condition monitoring history.

R7.4   Fertec suffered badly over a number of years as a result of poorly executed shutdowns. In order to overcome this problem they set up a permanent shutdown planning team with a shutdown manager. This group was responsible for planning the shutdown for the two sites. They were shutdown planning specialists and acquired state of the art shutdown planning knowledge and techniques. In general they followed the shutdown methodology outlined in Figure 7.12.

The main problems identified during the audit are listed in the case study and can be summarized as follows:
- Improvement needed in shutdown/startup plans, site logistics and shutdown history of the large machines.
- Lack of standard job procedures with inspection test plans.
- Software links required across the main maintenance software and Primavera to enable cost control.

R7.5   The petroleum refinery would have built up considerable planning and plant history from previous shutdowns. This information is invaluable when planning future shutdowns. Such information would not be available for a new installation.

PART 4

Spare parts management

8 Spare parts management

'A place for everything, everything in its place.'

Anon

Chapter aims and outcomes

To model and describe the operation of a maintenance stores system and to explain the techniques, principles and concepts necessary for its cost effective performance.

On completion of this chapter you should be able to:

- model and describe the operation of the stores system and the rotable system;
- define the stores function and objective;
- understand how to set inventory levels for fast moving parts, slow-moving parts and rotables;
- model a stores documentation system and explain its operation;
- understand the alternative ways, with advantages and disadvantages, of allocating the responsibility for stores management;
- identify the main stores and rotable performance indices.

Chapter route map

Book divisions

- Introductory chapters
- Budgeting and control
- Work planning and work control
- Spare parts management
- Documentation
- Case studies

This chapter in the division

- Chapter 8.0 Spare parts management

Chapter topics

- 8.1 Introduction
- 8.2 Outline of the stores operation
- 8.3 Inventory policy
- 8.4 Management of repairable equipment (rotables)
- 8.5 Inventory policy guidelines
- 8.6 Stores documentation
- 8.7 Stores organization
- 8.8 Stores and rotable performance indices
- 8.9 Summary

8.1 Introduction

Most companies tend to manage the purchasing, storage and supply of spare parts and materials as a separate department to the management of the maintenance department (see Figure 8.1). The management of spare parts and materials is a company level system (Level E of Figure 2.3), supplying the maintenance system with one of its essential resources. The maintenance department can be regarded as the main customer of the stores department that reports (with purchasing) to the commercial manager.

The theory and practice of stores management is a subject in its own right, quite a few textbooks having been solely devoted to stores management in general and stores

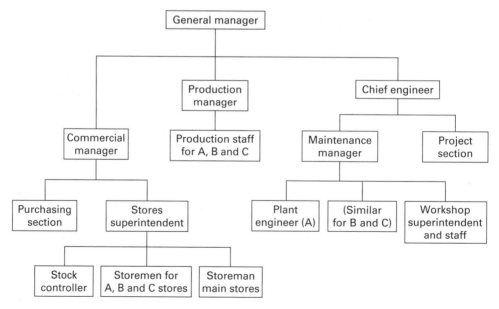

Figure 8.1 Administrative structure showing centralized responsibility for stores

inventory control in particular. This section will concentrate on those areas of stores management that are particular or unique to maintenance management (e.g. slow-moving spares).

8.2 Outline of the stores operation

A model that describes the operation of the stores system is shown in Figure 8.2. Spare parts and materials are one of the essential resources (the others being labor, tools and information) necessary to carry out maintenance work.

The basic *function* of the maintenance stores can be defined as:

> *to act as a buffer (or reservoir) between the uncertainties of the supply from the manufacturers (or from the reconditioning workshop – external or internal) and the inherent variability of the maintenance demand.*

The rational **objective** of running a spare stores and controlling its inventory is to minimize the sum of the associated direct costs (of obtaining and holding the spares) and the indirect costs (of loss of production or repair time due to waiting for spares).

In other words if large numbers of every conceivable spare were to be held the downtime would be minimal, but the costs of obtaining and holding the stock would be excessive and it is unlikely the stores objective would be achieved.

For ease of identification and retrieval maintenance parts are coded (e.g. by type, size, and type and make of bearing) and given a description/name, cataloged and given a stores locator. Each 'stores item' requires an *inventory policy*, a set of rules for deciding how the number of parts held in store is to be controlled so that the stores objective will be met, see Figure 8.2. For example one simple inventory policy for a stores item would be to determine a maximum number of parts to hold and a minimum level at which parts type should be re-ordered. (There are a number of different inventory policies suitable for different types of part usage rate.) *Stock control* monitors the usage (and delivery) of each stores item in conjunction with the designated inventory policy in order to control part replenishment, i.e. it uses the inventory policy to decide when the part should be re-ordered. This information is passed to *purchasing* which places an order with a *manufacturer*. It will be appreciated that it is essential that all parts crossing the stores boundary are recorded and entered into stock control.

Figure 8.2 shows that the stores system also has a major part to play in the storage and control of internal and external reconditioned parts, mainly complex replaceable items. An additional source of spare parts can come from 'cannibalizing' old and unwanted units, however these are unlikely to be controlled by stores.

If there were only one type of part in stores and the demand for it was high then stores management would be easy, although Figure 8.2 would still describe the operation of the system. The practice, however, is much more difficult – the main complicating factors are:

- *Multiplicity of parts and material types*: Stores in even a small plant might well hold over a thousand different 'stores item' – hence the need for cataloging. The onus

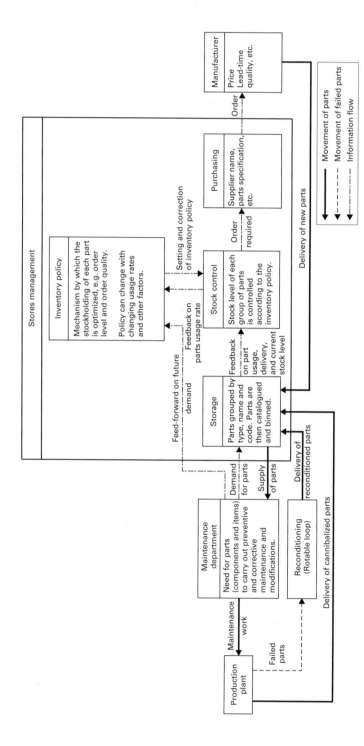

Figure 8.2 Maintenance spares management system

should be on the engineering and maintenance departments to reduce this multiplication via procurement policies based on rationalization and interchangeability. A complicating factor, however, is that in industrial companies the maintenance requirement accounts for only a part of the total stockholding; there will also be production stock, commercial stock and so on. The question then often arises as to whether maintenance should manage its own stores or whether stores management should be centralized under the commercial department (see later).

- *High total cost of the spare parts holding*: A medium-sized power station might well hold stock to the value of twenty million pounds (2000 values), a small company to the value of 5% of the capital replacement value. A typical analysis of such a stock-holding often reveals that some 80% of the total cost is accounted for by 20% of the stores items held (see Figure 8.3). More often that not these high cost items tend to be the slow- or very-slow-moving spares.

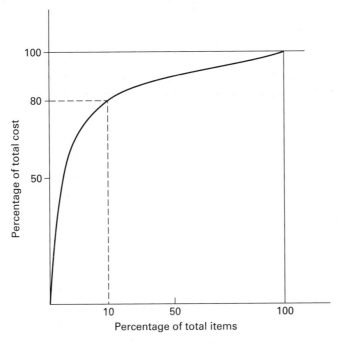

Figure 8.3 Pareto plot of probable spares cost distribution

- *Wide range of usage rates and lead times*: Each of the stores items requires an inventory policy which depends largely on usage rate and to a lesser extent on lead time. As explained, there are various well-validated quantitative techniques for determining the inventory policy for fast-moving parts. There are relatively few, however, when it comes to slow movers – and it is in this area that high costs are incurred.

Review Questions

R8.1   Define the objective associated with the storage of maintenance.

R8.2   A typical company administration is shown in Figure 8.1. The management of maintenance spares is the responsibility of the commercial manager. The maintenance manager has the responsibility for deciding on the spares to be held for new equipment. Explain how this division of responsibilities influences the achievement of the maintenance objective.

Exercise

E8.1   Carry out a Pareto analysis of your own company's spare parts stores in order to understand the spares/cost distribution (see Figure 8.3).

8.3 Inventory policy

To facilitate the setting of inventory control policies spare parts can be classified according to their usage rates into *fast moving* (where the demand is greater than, say, three items per year) and *slow moving* (demand less than that figure).

8.3.1 Inventory policy for fast-moving spares

Inventory control policies for fast-moving spares have been covered fairly extensively in various textbooks (including the authors') [1]. Just one such policy will therefore be presented here, and then only in sufficient outline to illustrate the basic principles, the main effort of this section being directed at the problem of slow-moving spares.

As already explained, the task is to balance the cost of holding stock against the cost of running out. In general, inventory control theory attempts to determine those procedures which will minimize the sum of the cost of:

- *running out* of stock (production loss due to stoppage, cost of temporary hire, etc.);
- *replenishing* stock (which in part depends on the quantity ordered);
- *holding* stock (interest on capital, depreciation, insurance, etc.).

There are two basic categories of control policy for fast movers, *viz.*:

1. *Re-order level*: replenishment prompted by stock falling to a pre-set re-order level;
2. *Re-order cycle*: stock reviewed, and replenishment decided, at regular intervals.

Lewis, in his concise and readable textbook [2] on this topic, further subdivides these categories into five policy types (a classification which, he states, is exhaustive, other types usually being further elaborations on one or more of these basic schemes). For illustration this section will describe a re-order level policy.

A re-order level policy – the so-called 'two-bin' system (see Figure 8.4): The inventory policy is set in terms of a re-order level M and a re-order quantity q. The stock is

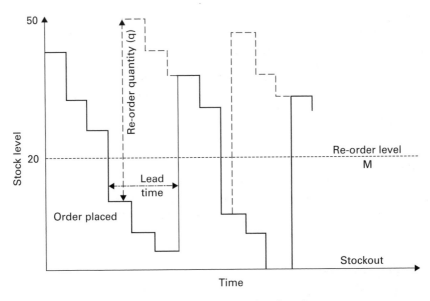

Figure 8.4 Variation of stock level under a re-order level regime

continuously monitored and a replenishment order for a fixed quantity q is placed when stock on-hand (stock held plus stock on order) falls to or below a pre-set re-order level M (i.e. storage in two bins, order placed when first bin empty, service from second bin until order received). The re-order level stock (i.e. the contents of the second bin) thus acts as a reservoir which diminishes the risk of running out of stock arising from the random variability of demand and the uncertainty of the lead time. The resulting pattern of stock holding is shown in Figure 8.4 where the solid line represents the stock held, and the broken line the stock on-hand (as defined above).

In the two-bin system a fixed quantity is ordered at variable intervals of time; in general to operate such a method needs continual monitoring of all stock transactions and it is only with the advent of the computer that it has become at all widely used.

The re-order quantity q can be evaluated from the expression

$$q = \left(\frac{2DC_O}{C_H}\right)^{1/2}$$

where
D is the mean demand for the part per unit time,
C_O is the cost of the replenishment order,
C_H is the cost, per item, of holding the part.

The re-order level M can be calculated from the expression:

$$M = DL + k\sigma_D L^{1/2}$$

where
L is the mean lead time,
σ_D is the standard deviation of demand per unit time,
k is the standard normal variate.

In this evaluation, the cost of stockout is incorporated in the idea of a required *level of service* – an acceptable value of the likelihood that, during any given lead time, demand *will* be met. It can readily be shown [3] that, if the rate of demand for the item can be assumed to be 'Normally' distributed, or approximately so, then the probability that, during a lead time, demand will *not* be met, i.e. a stockout *will* occur, is a function $F(k)$ of the 'standard normal variate' k, i.e.:

$$1 - (\text{Level of service}) = F(k)$$

Thus, if the desired level of service is, say, 99%, then $F(k)$ will be 1% or 0.01, and k is then readily found from the published tabulations of the standardized normal probability density function.

Current stores-control software uses models such as the above to automatically control inventory levels for fast-moving spares. In addition, it can monitor changes in demand, and in the other variables involved, and automatically adjust the control levels, i.e. the settings for M and q.

Example 8.1
Calculation of the re-order level M for a particular spare given the following data:

The average demand rate and its standard deviation are $D = 20$ *and* $S_D = 5$ demands per month, respectively.

The ordering lead time, $L = 4$ months and the desired level of service is 99%.

$$F(k) = 1 - (\text{level of service}) = 1 - 0.99 = 0.01$$

From Table 8.1 (an extract of the normal pdf), the standard variate $k = 2.326$, so

$$M = (20 \times 4) + (2.326 \times 5 \times 4^{1/2}) = 103 \text{ parts.}$$

Table 8.1 Extract from the normal pdf table

k	F(k)
3.0	0.001
2.50	0.006
2.0	0.023
1.50	0.067
1.0	0.157

Exercise

E8.2 Stores management have the following data on a particular type of pump.

Average demand rate	12 per year
Standard deviation	3 per year
Cost of ordering	£40 per order
Cost of holding	£60 per pump per year
Lead time	2 months
Desired level of services	96%

They want you to calculate the re-order level and the re-order quantity from this data.

8.3.2 Inventory policies for the control of slow-moving spares

It was noted earlier that the greater part of the value, and hence the dominant control problem, of a spares inventory lies in the expensive slow-moving parts, where over-stocking is not quickly corrected by subsequent consumption. The decision that is then required is whether to hold none, one or – at the very most – two of a given part. Mitchell, working for the National Coal Board of the UK, developed a technique for dealing with this problem [4]. The way the technique is used depends on whether the parts fail randomly or by wear-out.

Random failure parts: If demands for a part, although infrequent, occur quite ran-domly (*i.e. they are equally likely to occur at any time*) then the probability $P(n)$ of receiving n demands in any given lead time can be assumed to be given by the Poisson distribution, i.e.:

$$P(n) = \frac{m^n \exp(-m)}{n!}$$

where m is the mean demands per lead time(L_D)

For a re-order level system where only one item is ordered at a time (which would probably be the case with a very high-cost item) and *non-captive* demand (i.e. stock-out would be met from another source, egg by making – at known extra expense – the spare in the workshop; with *captive* demand stockout would be met by earlier delivery of a spare on order), Mitchell derived the decision chart shown in Figure 8.5. It indi-cates the value of N, the number of items *on hand* (i.e. in stock plus on order), which will minimize C_N, the average total cost per unit time (of holding and stockout, the cost of ordering being assumed negligible). For points on the line $C_0 = C_1$ equal cost arises if $N = 0$ *or* 1; along $C_1 = C_2$ equal cost arises if $N = 1$ *or* 2 (unlike the curve $C_0 = C_1$, the position of this latter curve is a function of L – and is therefore plotted for various val-ues of this).

So, for a given spare, for which L, D, C_H and C_S (the stockout cost) are known, the chart is used as follows. If C_S/C_H and D give a point lying:

(a) below $C_0 = C_1$ then no spare should be held,
(b) between C_0 and $C_1 = C_2$ then one spare should be held,
(c) above $C_1 = C_2$ then two spares should be held.

Example 8.2
Estimation of the optimum stockholding for an electric motor, given the following information:

1. Estimated cost of holding the motor, $C_H = £100$ per annum.
2. Estimated cost of not being able to replace from stock in the event of an unexpected failure, $C_S = £1000$.
3. Average lead time for re-ordering, $L = 12$ months.
4. Motor failures occur randomly with an average incidence, $D = 0.20$ failures per annum.
5. Thus, average interval between demands $= 1/D = 1/0.20 = 5$ years and $C_S/C_H = 1000/100 = 10$.

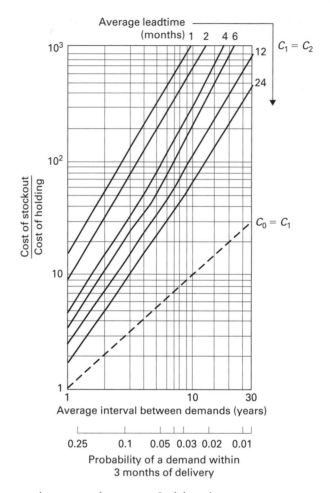

Figure 8.5 Slow-moving spares inventory decision chart

These are the co-ordinates of a point on Figure 8.5 that lies above the line:

$$C_0 = C_1 \text{ and below the line } C_1 = C_2 \text{ for } L = 12 \text{ months}$$

Note: The vertical and horizontal scales of the chart are logarithmic.
The decision is therefore to hold one spare motor.

Exercise

E8.3   A maintenance engineer carrying out the review of a life plan for a discharge system is concerned about the inventory policy for the main
pump. He has gathered the following information. The pump is not
repairable. On failure it is replaced with a new pump purchased from the
manufacturer – the lead time is 4 months. The pump fails randomly with
an average incidence of 0.5 failure per year. The estimated cost of holding

the pump is £200 per year. The estimated cost of not being able to replace the pump from stock is £4000.

Use the slow moving decision chart to recommend an inventory policy for the pump?

Wear-out failure parts: The same chart can be adapted for deciding stock levels for slow moving *wear-out* items. The chart's bottom scale is replaced by one showing the probability that, for a given part, a demand will occur *within* the first 3 months following its delivery (given that no demand has occurred while it has been on order). If, for a particular spare, the assessment of this probability, and of C_S/C_H, give a point on the chart:

(a) below $C_0 = C_1$ then ordering is deferred,
(b) above $C_0 = C_1$ then one spare is ordered immediately.

It is recommended that each such decision problem should be re-evaluated approximately every 3 months.

Example 8.3
Estimation of the optimal stockholding for a gearbox given the following information:

1. Estimated cost of holding the gearbox, $C_H = £100$ per annum.
2. Estimated cost of not being able to replace from stock in the event of an unexpected failure, $C_S = £500$.
3. Average lead time for re-ordering, $L = 6$ months.

Failure data have been extracted from the maintenance records of a user with many such gearboxes and are prepared as shown in the following table, for plotting on Weibull* probability paper:

Time t from new (weeks)	Cumulative percent f(t) of gearboxes failed
120	0.00
160	2.50
200	12.50
240	27.50
280	70.00
320	90.00
360	97.50
400	100.00

The straightest plot is produced (see Figure 8.6) if the guaranteed life t_0 is taken to be about 120 weeks and gives a gearbox mean life of about 260 weeks, *or* 5 years (i.e. this is a slow-moving item) and a *b*-value of about 3.2 (indicating a wear-out mechanism of failure).

For this sort of item the second of the decision chart (Figure 8.5) procedures – involving reference to the scale on the lower of the two horizontal axes – is followed,

---

* The Weibull probability distribution is outlined in Appendix 1.

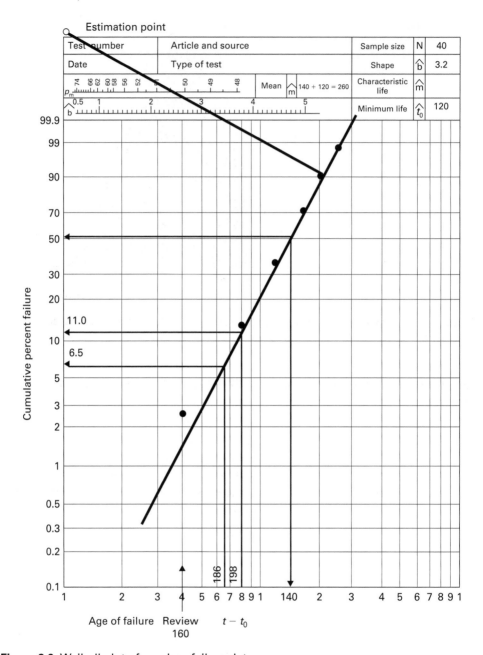

Figure 8.6 Weibull plot of gearbox failure data

the position being re-assessed every 3 months from when the gearbox is new. At each re-assessment it is necessary to re-calculate the probability that there will be a demand for a gearbox within 3 months of its delivery.

Review at 160 weeks into the gearbox's life:

If ordered now, delivery would be at $160 + 26 = 186$ weeks.

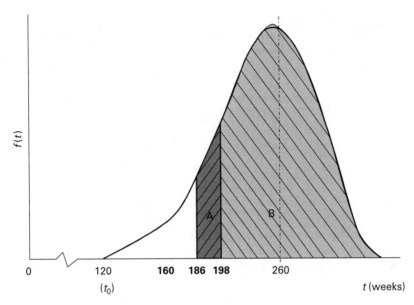

Figure 8.7 Gearbox failure distribution, illustrating derivation of data for review at 160 weeks

The lower scale requires assessment of the probability of a demand occurring within 3 months (12 weeks) of that delivery. This is given by the ratio of areas indicated on Figure 8.7, i.e. by

$$\frac{A}{A + B}$$

where the areas A *and* B represent probabilities. Their values can be derived from the Weibull plot of Figure 8.6, which indicates that the cumulative probabilities at 186 weeks and 198 weeks (i.e. the areas, under the failure probability density distribution, to the left of those points), respectively,

$$F(186) = 6.5\% \text{ and } F(198) = 11\%.$$

Thus

$$\frac{A}{A + B} = \frac{11 - 6.5}{100 - 6.5} = 0.05$$

Also

$$\frac{C_S}{C_H} = \frac{500}{100} = 5$$

These are the co-ordinates of a point lying just above the line $C_0 = C_1$ on the decision chart. Thus, at 160 weeks into the life of the gearbox the decision would be to buy a spare.

Mitchell further recommended that, for the purposes of his approach to their control, slow-moving spares should be classified as below:

● *Specials*: (Bought for use on a specified date, egg for a plant modification or over-haul.) Should be ordered so that delivery occurs as shortly as possible before their use. Clearly, the 'safe' prior interval will be a function of the confidence with which the date for the part's use and the lead time for its ordering are known.

- *Adequate warning items*: Condition monitoring (or some other indication of impending failure) can provide adequate notice, relative to the lead time of failure. The part is therefore not held in stock.
- *Inadequate warning items*: For technical or economic reasons no inspection or other technique is available for providing notice of failure. Such parts can be subdivided, as already discussed, into those that fail *randomly* (controlled via the first procedure for Figure 8.5 explained above) and those that *wear out* (controlled via the second).

The author has noted during his auditing experience that many companies identify what they call *insurance spares* (or sometimes strategic spares). These are high-cost spares that are not expected to fail during the life of the unit to which they belong (they have a very low failure rate). However the economic consequences of failure (if such a part was not available after a failure) is so high (C_S/C_H value would be off the scale of Figure 8.5) that the part is held and capitalized. A number of companies have entered into 'inter-company sharing arrangements' to spread the cost of holding such parts.

Review Question

R8.3   With reference to Figure 8.7 (which shows the failure distribution for a gearbox failing due to some form of wear-out mechanism) explain the procedure for establishing the inventory policy for such parts.

8.4 Management of repairable equipment (rotables)

8.4.1 Introduction

It is often more economic to repair or recondition certain types of equipment (mostly complex replaceable items, e.g. gearboxes, electric motors) within the company workshops (or via contractors) rather than purchase new equipment. Parts that are reconditioned in this way are sometimes called rotables. The 'rotable loop' was shown as one means of supplying parts on the stores model of Figure 8.2. The rotables go round the in 'use–reconditioning–in stores–maintenance–in use' loop until they are worn out, scrapped and replaced by a new part.

8.4.2 The rotable system

The rotable system is shown in more detail via the example of Figure 8.8. We are concerned with the management of the rotable loop and its linkage with the stores rather than the economies of repair vs replace.

Figure 8.8 shows that most functions within the loop are the responsibility of the maintenance department and Figure 8.1 shows how these have been allocated. The key function is the planning and scheduling of the workshop workload. The function of the stores is to provide a buffer between the maintenance demand and the workshop supply. It can be seen that stores holds both the rotables and the parts required for

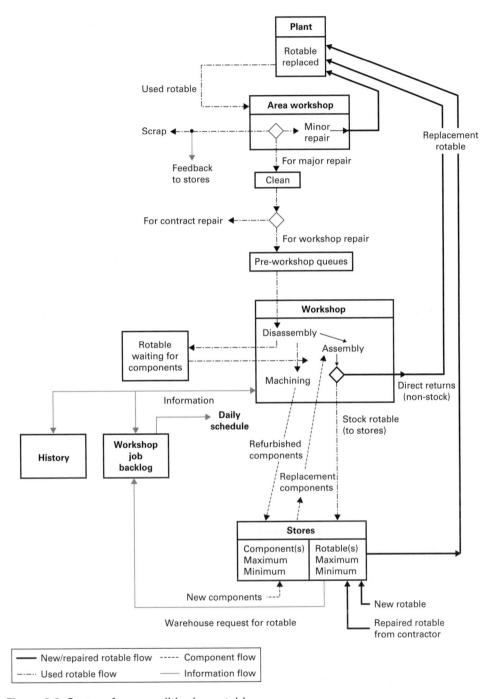

Figure 8.8 System for reconditioning rotables

internal rotable reconditioning and/or repair. Rotables need to be described and cataloged in the same way as other parts. An extension of the stores code can also be used
to give each rotable a unique identification number (some times referred to as its 'birth
certificate number'). This is illustrated in Figure 8.9 for the gearbox of a discharge unit:

- 03/F/002 is the location number of the discharge unit; it can be used to identify the
  unit on site; as well as in the maintenance management system.

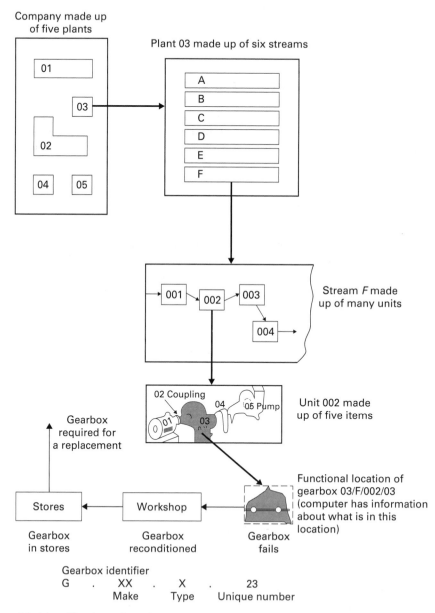

Figure 8.9 Identification of rotables

- 03/F/002/03 is the functional location of the discharge unit gearbox; it can be regarded as a 'pigeon hole' within the information system where information on the gearbox resides.
- G.XX.X.23 is the unique rotable identification number.

The gearbox identifier enables it to be tracked around the loop. It also provides workshop management with the means to collect failure, costs and repair history.

The cost of reconditioning a rotable is established from the workshop planning/costing system and is passed into the company costing system when the rotable is taken out of stores for maintenance (see Figure 4.4).

8.4.3 Rotable inventory policy: the theory

Most rotables in industrial plant tend to be slow movers. It is possible to use the ideas of Figure 8.5 to estimate the maximum/minimum rotable levels to be held in stores. In such a situation the lead time is a function of the workshop repair rate which in turn depends on:

- the number of rotables in the system,
- workshop planning efficiency,
- workshop job priority systems, etc.

An alternative technique that can be used for the determination of a rotable inventory policy has been described by Hodges [5]. He assumes that a rotable fails randomly with a failure rate of p per year. Thus if there are N assets using rotables the combined rotable failure rate is Np. He shows that if the mean time to repair is T years (equivalent of a lead time) then the savings in downtime D if *one* rotable is held in stores (max 1, min 0) is given by:

$$D = 1 - e^{-NpT} \text{ years per year}$$

If *two* rotables are held (the second rotable providing cover while the first rotable is being reconditioned – a policy of max 2, min 1) then

$$D = 1 - (1 + NpT)e^{-NpT} \text{ unit years per year}$$

And so on to x rotables:

$$D = 1 - e^{-NpT}\left[1 - NpT + \frac{1}{2}NpT^2 + \frac{1}{(x-1)!}(NpT)^{(x-1)}\right] \text{ unit years per year}$$

The relationship between the value of NpT and the annual downtime savings in unit years per year is shown in Figure 8.10.

Example 8.4
An underground copper mine has 20 identical front end loaders. Gearboxes have been causing a problem in as much as there has been a number of stockouts. The present inventory policy for this type of gearbox is to hold a maximum of 2.

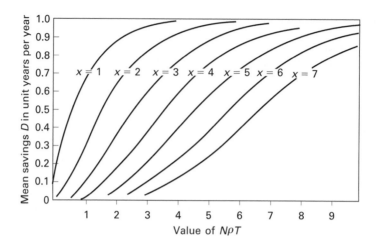

Figure 8.10 Rotable spares inventory decision chart

(a) Use the following information in conjunction with Figure 8.10 to calculate the average downtime cost of the loaders caused by gearbox stockouts.
  ● The average repair time for the gearbox is 10 weeks.
  ● The average life to the reconditioning of a gearbox is 4 years.
  ● Lost profit due to loader downtime averages £30 per hour.
  ● The loaders have an 80% usage factor.
(b) Calculate the reduction in downtime losses if management increases the stores gearbox holding to 4.
(c) Explain how you would establish which of (a) or (b) is the best policy. What additional information would you require?

Solution
(a) $N = 20$, $p = \dfrac{1}{4} = 0.25$ per year, $T = \dfrac{10}{52} \approx 0.20$ years
  $NpT = 1$
  Using Figure 8.10 with $x = 2$ gives an annual loader downtime D of 0.3 loader years. The annual cost of downtime is $365 \times 24 \times 30 \times 80\% = £210,240$.
  Thus the annual lost production cost $= £210,240 \times .3 = £63,072$.
(b) Using Figure 8.10 for $x = 4$ gives an annual average loader downtime of 0.02 loader years.
  The annual lost production cost is $£210,240 \times 0.02 = £4205$.
(c) The following additional information would be needed to compare the alternative policies:
  ● Average cost of reconditioning the gearboxes.
  ● The company's policy with regard to investment decisions, e.g. payback period or return on investment.
  ● The discount factor.

A representative time is selected to compare the alternative policies, say 6 years. Life cycle costing analysis could then be carried out to compare the extra investment in two gearboxes compared to the discounted saving over the 5 years.

Exercise

E8.4   In the worked Example 8.4 establish the downtime losses of the front end loader if 20 extra loaders were purchased and the stores inventory policy remained unchanged.

8.4.4 Rotable inventory policy: in practice

It is the authors' experience that in practice the rotable inventory policy tends to be guesstimated and subsequently adjusted via usage history and experience. It should be noted that the stores/workshop management have considerable flexibility in terms of supply. If the workshop becomes overloaded, i.e. excessive rotable waiting time in the pre-workshop queues (the *herding problem*) it is possible to use external reconditioning or purchase new rotables. The workshop priority rules can also be used to allow urgently required rotables (with nil stock) to jump the queue. If this happens as the rule rather than the exception it results in severe workshop disruption (the *bypass problem*).

It should be emphasized that when the rotable loop is operating normally new rotables are only purchased when a failed rotable is deemed non-repairable and scrapped. It is important that there is a linkage between the stores and maintenance information system to flag up scrapped rotables – failure to do this will allow 'the loop to run dry'! (The *loss problem*.)

8.5 Inventory policy guidelines

Gathering the information on inventory policy together from Sections 8.3 and 8.4 enables the categorization of inventory policy as shown in Figure 8.11.

Other actions/policies that can be carried out/adopted for optimizing the spares inventory are as follows:

- *Spares criticality analysis* – all new equipment should be subjected to a spares criticality analysis as a part of the establishment of a unit life plan.
- Establish where possible '*consignment stock agreements*' (suppliers maintains stock on behalf of the client which are only paid for when used).
- Establish *rationalization* procedures to reduce the number of different part types stocked. This can be achieved via *standardization* of equipment used, interchangeability and *modularization*.

Some time ago the author was involved in a research project concerning bus fleet maintenance. The maintenance strategy used for a bus fleet in a UK city was compared with that for a USA city. One of the major differences was that the UK fleet used many different kinds of buses and even a greater variety of engines and gearboxes, while the USA fleet had one type of bus and relatively few types of engines and gearboxes. This meant that the stockholding for spare parts and rotables was much smaller and far less complex in the USA city bus fleet than the UK city bus fleet.

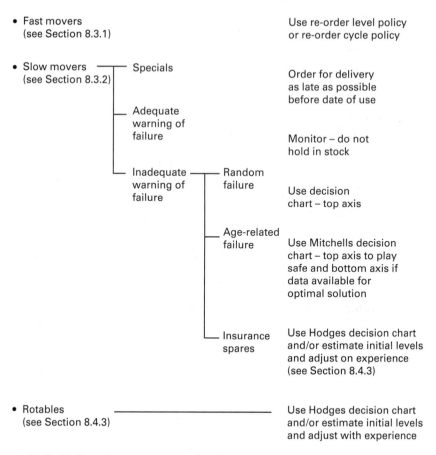

Figure 8.11 Guidelines for spares control policy

Review Questions

R8.4   One of the main difficulties of managing a maintenance stores is associated with the multiplicity of parts and the wide range of usage rates. List the *main* actions that can be taken to eliminate this problem.

R8.5   Draw a simple diagram to illustrate how spare parts inventory policy can be categorized by the parts usage rate.

8.6 Stores documentation

To manage a stores and rotable system of the kind outlined in Figures 8.1 and 8.9, some form of documentation system is essential. Although these are now almost always fully computerized, the principles underlying their operation can be most clearly explained by reviewing the various activities of a traditional paper-based system (see Figure 8.12).

All stores items must be given a description, a stores code number (see Table 8.2) and a 'bin' location number (see Table 8.3) – bin being used in a general sense for any

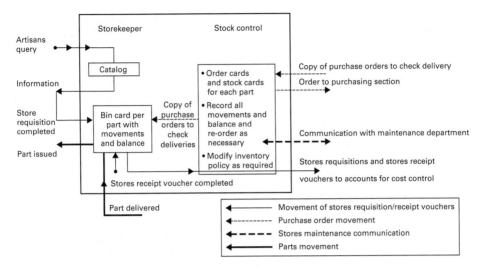

Figure 8.12 A paper-based stores documentation system

Table 8.2 Extract from a simple coding system for spare parts

Two digits to identify major groups, e.g.	
01	Abrasives
05	Bearings and accessories
06	Belting and accessories
09	Chain, rope and wire
14–17	Fasteners
19–20	Hose and fittings
34	Packing
36–38	Pump parts
50–53	Piping
56	Valves
60–79	Electrical and electronic
80–99	Plant-specific spares
Two digits to identify sub-groups, e.g.	
06-35	Belt – timing
06-40	Belt – transmission
06-45	Belt – variable speed
Three digits to assign unique part numbers, e.g.	
06-45-255	Belt – variable speed, Dayeo 46V26

Table 8.3 Extract from spare parts catalog

Valves, Group number	Unit of issue	Cost	Re-order point	Re-order level	Bin no.
56-01-150: 1/8 cock, Air BR 125 SE	each	2.26	2	4	2/04
56-01-166: 1/8 cock, Pet BR 125 SE	each	1.75	2	4	2/02

storage arrangement (shelf, drawer, pigeon hole, box, drum, sack, marked floor space or whatever) that isolates a stores item. These are basic essentials for the elimination of duplication, for simpler parts ordering and faster part location.

Figure 8.12 models a stores system in which no part can be delivered or withdrawn without the transaction being recorded. The issue of a part to the trade-force is covered by a *stores requisition* document (see Figure 8.13) on which data (plant or unit number, job number, work type, etc.) are also recorded for the maintenance costing system. All deliveries (which should be checked for conformity to specification) are covered by a *stores receipt voucher* (see Figure 8.14).

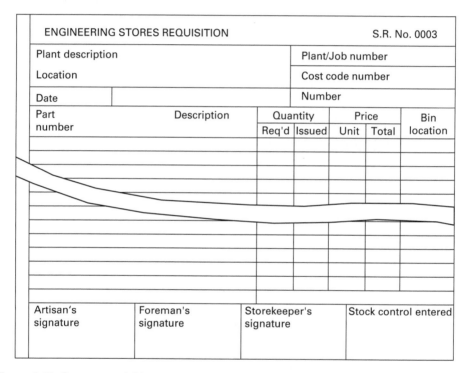

Figure 8.13 Stores requisition

For each 'stores item' the storeman keeps a *bin card* on which he records all transactions (receipts and issues) and the stock balance – many stores also attach a simple *part label* to atleast one part as an identification check. This is particularly important in the case of rotables – the label should include its identification number, when it was received in stores and the date reconditioned. All requisitions and receipts pass through stock control on their way to the accounts department and the stock controller records them, and also the various stock levels, on *stock control record cards*. This information is in turn required for the operation of the inventory control policy (see Figure 8.4) and for monitoring changes in demand rates, lead times and so on. Stock replenishment orders are handled by the purchasing department.

In most companies the computerized system for stores control is integrated with the systems for general purchasing, invoicing and maintenance activities. The store system

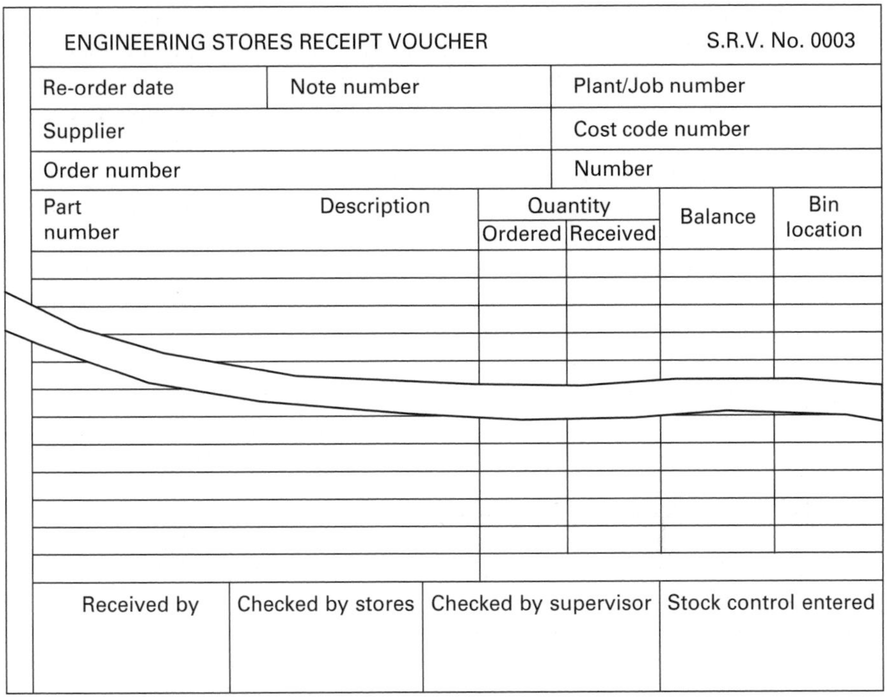

ENGINEERING STORES RECEIPT VOUCHER					S.R.V. No. 0003	
Re-order date	Note number		Plant/Job number			
Supplier			Cost code number			
Order number			Number			
Part number	Description	Quantity Ordered	Received	Balance	Bin location	
Received by	Checked by stores	Checked by supervisor		Stock control entered		

Figure 8.14 Stores receipt voucher

is 'paperless', even down to the use of bar-code readings for registering parts requests and issues. Most stores catalogs facilitate searching for parts under various standard codings and verbal descriptions; parts may also be identified and ordered by artisans operating from their own terminals.

Some of the common problems with stores documentation are as follows:

- The trade-force find difficulty in finding a part in the catalog because of poor part descriptions. This can be overcome by using colloquial names linked to standard descriptions.
- The computer system indicates the part is in stock but in fact it is found to be 'nil stock'. This is mostly caused by the trade-force (or somebody!!) taking parts out without booking – perhaps on nights when there is no storeman, or as a result of an open stores policy.

Case study 1 (see Chapter 11) involves two similar chemical plants, Fertec A and Fertec B, operated by the same company. Fertec A were experimenting with an 'open stores policy' – the trade-force could locate the part on the computer and then 'self-serve' signing off when the part was taken. In spite of system safe guards 'parts' were still 'going missing'. Fertec A used a strict 'closed-stores policy'. It seemed to the author the chief storeman 'rode shotgun' outside the stores door and the trade-force were not allowed to pass – certainly not if they were unaccompanied by a storeman. His view was that he had learned from long experience 'that artisans were not to be trusted in the stores'.

- Parts are not checked properly on receipt and it is not until they are withdrawn that it is discovered that they are the wrong specification (in particular a problem with electronic parts). It is important for quality assurance that a proper inspection procedure is set up for incoming parts – in particular for complex, expensive assemblies.
- Equipment can deteriorate in the stores. It is important to set up effective inspection and maintenance procedures for stored parts, e.g. motor shafts should be periodically turned.
- The inventory control policy for parts can be disrupted through the setting up of unofficial stores. Supervisors often distrust computerized stores and withdraw parts to hold in their own 'unofficial stores' – the '*magpieing problem*'.

An alumina refinery brought in a centralized computer controlled stores system. The decentralized stores were all brought within the closed boundaries of the new stores system. The 'unofficial stores' were also located and closed. In spite of this the area supervisors built up a number of new 'unofficial stores' because they said 'they could not rely on the new stores'. Their actions were contributing to the stores problems – I call this the 'magpieing problem'.

Review Question

R8.6   With reference to the rotable system of Figure 8.8 explain the following:
- Herding problem
- Bypass problem
- Loss problem
- Magpieing problem.

8.7 Stores organization

Figure 8.1 shows an example of a company administrative structure where the responsibility for stores management is a separate function to maintenance management. An outline of the corresponding company resource structure is shown in Figure 8.15.

Figure 8.15 shows the stores location within the maintenance resource structure, i.e. mainly centralized with a number of sub-stores to match the decentralized maintenance groups. Figure 8.1 indicates the commercial department's responsibility for stores management, i.e. for its budget, for part storage, cataloging, issuing, ordering and receipt, inventory policy and staffing. The maintenance department being responsible for the initial order quantities and for the specification. This tends to be the arrangement because of the advantages of centralization of stockholding, purchasing and invoicing. (Remember that maintenance stores accounts for only one part of the total company stockholding – albeit in most cases the dominant part.) The main problem with this arrangement is the tendency of all maintenance departments to play safe, overspecify and overstock – this is especially so with the slow moving and insurance parts. Periodically, the commercial department may attempt to correct overstocking and in doing so may over-react, leading to eventual stockouts.

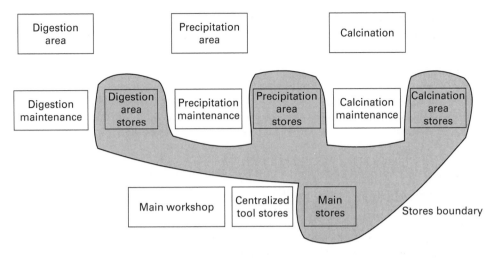

Figure 8.15 Resource structure, showing stores location

Where the responsibility for spares management is as shown in Figure 8.1 effort must be devoted to:

- clearly identifying the role of the commercial department;
- putting systems in place at the maintenance–stores interface which will ensure that decisions should *always* be referred back to maintenance regarding the changing of inventory policy of *insurance spares* and *high cost parts* (to ensure they are still wanted);
- ensuring that there are stores staff who are technically competent in the maintenance and engineering areas.

There are many possible variants of the structure of Figures 8.1 and 8.15. Some companies, e.g. make the maintenance department fully responsible for their own spares; others adopt the Figure 8.1 arrangements but also make maintenance responsible for the inventory policy.

8.8 Stores and rotable performance indices

It will be appreciated that there are many variations of the store system and rotable system shown in Figures 8.2 and 8.9. Modeling systems in this way allows an understanding of the way in which they operate and facilitate the establishment of performance indices. Some of the main performance indices are listed in Table 8.4.

Review Questions

R8.7 A artisans establishes that according to the stores computer system a part he wants is in stock. The storemen subsequently find the part is not in stock. List the possible reason for this situation.

R8.8 List the key performance indices for stores management and at least three key performance indices for the management of rotables.

Table 8.4 Stores and rotable performance indices

Spare parts performance indicators

Number of different 'stores items'.
Value of total parts in stock.
Turnover ratio = value of annual issues/value of total stores inventory.
Value of slow-moving parts as a percentage of total inventory value.
Value of insurance parts as a percentage of total inventory value.
Ratio of annual stores administrative cost vs inventory value.
Total stock outs per period.
Stock outs per period causing production loss.
Level of service index = stock outs per period/total requests per period.

Rotable performance indicators (see Figure 8.9)

Number of rotables 'store items'.
Number of rotables in stock.
Value of rotables in stock.
% of rotables externally reconditioned.
% of direct return rotables (non-stock).
% of rotable externally reconditioned by category (e.g. gearbox).
% of rotables replaced per annum by category.
Average waiting time for rotable repair.
Average waiting time for rotable repair caused by component stockout.
Rework index for internally reconditioned rotables.
Rework index for externally reconditioned rotables.

8.9 Summary

The authors auditing experience indicates that the maintenance stores function is often not well carried out. The maintenance department feel they do not get a good service (service slow, unable to find parts, stockouts) while the senior management consider there is high administrative costs due to overstocking, especially with the slow-moving category:

- The worst case the author has come across was a chemical company where each maintenance supervisor (four in total) was responsible for his own stores. There were 13 different storage areas, most were open. The parts were not categorized or cataloged.
- A recent audit of a power station revealed that the slow movers and insurance parts accounted for some 83% of the stockholding costs but there had never been a review of their usage.
- An audit of a cement plant established that while the slow movers/insurance parts accounted for the majority of stockholding costs a spares criticality analysis had never been carried out. Investigation revealed that some critical parts were not being held.

In order to overcome such problems the author believes that it is important to model the maintenance-stores system shown in Figures 8.2 and 8.8. This enables the management of a company to:

- understand the way in which the system operates;
- identify the stores objectives and procedures to ensure they are compatible with those of the maintenance department;

- use the techniques, models and procedures of this chapter (and references) to provide the necessary corrective action.

References

1. Kelly, A. and Harris, M.J. *The Management of Industrial Maintenance*, Butterworths, 1978.
2. Lewis, C.D. *Scientific Inventory Control*, Newnes-Butterworths, 1971.
3. Harris, M.J. An introduction to maintenance stores organization, *Terotechnica*, 1, 1979, pp. 47–57.
4. Mitchell, G.H. Problems of controlling slow-moving spares, *Operational Research Quarterly*, 13(1), 1962, pp. 23.
5. Hodges, N.W. *Strategic Spares and the Economies of Operations*, Mechanical Engineering Publications Ltd., London, 1994.

Exercise Guideline Solutions

E8.2   Re-order level $M = DL + K\sigma_D L^{1/2}$
$F(k) = 1 - \text{(level of service)} = 1 - 0.96 = 0.04$
From Table 7.1 the standard variate to $= 1.75$

$$M = 12\frac{2}{12} + 1.75 \times 3\left(\frac{2}{12}\right)^{1/2}$$

$$M = 2 + 2.14, \text{ say } 4$$

$$\text{Re-order quantity } q = \left[2.12 \times \frac{40}{60}\right]^{1/2}$$

$$= 4.$$

The recommended policy is to set the re-order level at 4 and the order quantity at 4.

E8.3   The pump failures randomly – use the top horizontal axis. Average incidence between demands is $(1/D) = (1/0.5) = 2$ years

$$\frac{C_S}{C_H} = \frac{4000}{200} = 20$$

These are the co-ordinates of a point on Figure 8.5 that lies above the line $C_1 = C_2$ for $L = 4$ months.
The recommended inventory policy for the pump is maximum two, minimum one.

E8.4 $N = 40, p = \frac{1}{4} = 0.25, T = \frac{10}{52} = 2.0$

$NpT = 2$
Using Figure 7.10 with $x = 4$ gives an annual loader downtime D of 0.16.
The annual lost production cost is £2,10,240 $\times$ 0.16 = \$33,638.

Review Questions Guidelines

R8.1   'To minimize Σ of holding costs + stockout costs'.

R8.2   Explained in Section 8.7. Maintenance engineers tend to play safe with initial orders for slow-moving parts. They over specify and overstock – they are concerned mainly with avoiding stockouts and unit unavailability. Periodically the commercial department may attempt to correct overstocking and in doing so may over-react, leading to stockouts – they are concerned mainly with the cost of holding.

R8.3   Figure 8.7 shows that no failure is likely before 120 weeks and the probability of failure then increases with time.

    The inventory procedure for such 'wear-out parts' is a 'dynamic procedure', i.e. the inventory controller/engineer is expected to check at 3 monthly intervals 'the probability of a demand within 3 months of delivery'. The bottom axis with C_S/C_H is then used to establish if a spare should be purchased.

    In practice there is little point in checking until, say, 100 weeks into the gearboxes life and thereafter at 130 weeks, 160 weeks, etc.

R8.4   Rationalization, standardization, modularization, interchangeability.

R8.5   See Figure 8.11 – but you should attempt to draw it without reference.

R8.6   The herding problem: Most of the rotables in the cycle end up on the preworkshop queues. Usually caused by maintenance workshop inefficiency and/or overloading/understaffing of the workshop.

    The bypass problem: The reconditioning of critical rotables jump the workshop queues.

    The loss problem: A rotable is scrapped without letting the stores know.

    The magpieing problem: A supervisor/engineer builds unofficial stores using official stores stock.

R8.7   ● Artisans/or others removing parts from stores without booking them out.
    ● Part is in stores but in the incorrect bin.
    ● Supplier sent the wrong part which was not checked on receipt.

R8.8   Listed in full in Table 8.4.

PART 5

Documentation

9 Maintenance documentation systems: what they are and how they work

'A page of history is worth a volume of logic.'

Oliver Wendell Holmes

Chapter aims and outcomes

To explain the structure and operation of maintenance documentation systems.

On completion of this chapter you should be able to:

- draw a functional model of a maintenance documentation system; identifying each of the seven modules and explaining how the system operates;
- take each of the seven modules in turn, explaining their maintenance documentation function, the information they need in order to perform their function, and the documents, files and reports they use or are generated by them.

Chapter route map

Book divisions	This chapter in the division	Chapter topics
• Introductory chapters	• Chapter 9 Maintenance documentation systems: what they are and how they work	• 9.1 Introduction
• Budgeting and control		• 9.2 A functional model
• Work planning and work control	• Chapter 10 Computerized maintenance information systems: their uses and problems	• 9.3 Plant inventory (Module 1)
• Spare parts management		• 9.4 Information base (Element 2)
• Documentation		• 9.5 Preventive maintenance schedule (Module 3)
• Case studies		• 9.6 Condition monitoring (Module 4)
		• 9.7 Short-term work planning (Module 5)
		• 9.8 Long-term work planning (Module 6)
		• 9.9 Maintenance control (Module 7)
		• 9.10 Summary

9.1 Introduction

The business-centered maintenance system paradigm that was outlined in Chapter 1 (see Figure 1.1) made clear that some form of documentation system, for recording and conveying information, is an essential operational requirement for all the elements of the maintenance management cycle.

Maintenance documentation can be defined as:

> *Any record, catalog, manual, drawing or computer file containing information that might be required to facilitate maintenance work.*

A maintenance information system (MIS) can be defined as:

> *The formal mechanism for collecting, storing, analyzing, interrogating and reporting maintenance information.*

Although almost all current systems are computerized, the basis of their mode of operation has evolved from that of the traditional paperwork system and can be most easily explained by discussing the various components and information flows of the latter.

9.2 A functional model

The way in which a MIS generally functions is outlined in Figure 9.1, a model which has evolved over a number of years through extensive studies of both paper-based and computerized systems, and which therefore illustrates the principal features of both types – features which, inevitably, they have in common.

The system can be considered to be made up of the following interrelated modules:

1. Plant inventory
2. Maintenance information base
3. Maintenance schedule

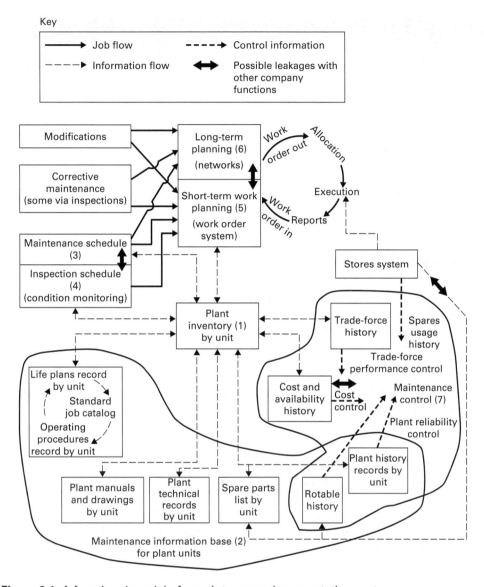

Figure 9.1 A functional model of a maintenance documentation system

4. Condition monitoring
5. Short-term work planning and control
6. Shutdown work planning and control
7. Maintenance control.

The plant inventory (1) (sometimes called the plant register) is a coded list of the plant units, e.g. a bauxite mill. This is the main way into the system. The maintenance information base (2) is a database of maintenance information, e.g. unit life plans, job catalog, etc. for each of the units. The maintenance schedule (3) is a schedule of the preventive maintenance jobs (over a year and longer) listed against each of the units in the life plans. The condition monitoring schedule (4) is a schedule of the condition monitoring tasks, e.g. vibration monitoring listed against each of the units in the life plans. The short-term work planning system (5) is the documentation/information system necessary to carry out the function outlined in the work-planning model of Figure 5.7. The system has to plan and schedule preventive jobs (arising from the maintenance schedule), corrective jobs (of all priorities) and where necessary modification jobs. The jobs are carried out by trade-force via hard copy or electronic work orders. Information coming back on the work orders (and other documents) is used to update the planning systems and provides information for maintenance control. The long-term planning system (6) uses the technique of critical path analysis and bar charting to plan and schedule the major work and then uses the short-term planning system (the work order system) to carry out the work. The maintenance control system (7) uses information coming from a number of sources, work orders, stores, shift record, etc. to provide various reports for cost control, plant reliability control, etc.

Up until about 10 years ago most MIS were stand alone, i.e. they had no electronic linkage with other company software. The most recent computerized maintenance systems are integrated electronically (they are in the same database) with stores, purchasing, invoicing, company costing, payroll and also can have electronic links to project management and condition monitoring software. This is discussed in more detail in Chapter 10.

Exercise

E9.1   Study your own MIS to see if you can identify each of the elements and sub-elements of Figure 9.1.

9.3 Plant inventory (Module 1)

The inventory can be regarded as 'the center of the documentation universe'. It is a list of the most basic information about every unit in the plant (e.g. see Table 9.1). Each unit is uniquely identified by a short description and a numeric or alpha-numeric code which flags up the main way into the system to obtain information on that unit. The inventory is complemented by a drawing reference (014C53) in order to locate the physical location of the unit. It should be noted that the unit number (03/F/002) is used for on-site identification of the unit as well as for documentation purposes – where there are a number of identical units it is essential for safety/planning reasons that there is a means of uniquely identifying each unit. It is essential that the site identification of units and other equipment is maintained. This includes the color coding of pipework to indicate the substance that is being conveyed.

A typical coding system was outlined in Figure 8.9 and an example is shown in Table 9.2. At unit level it is advantageous for the coding to indicate whether the unit mechanical (numbered, say, in the range 001 to 499), electrical (500 to 600) or instrument (700 to 999) and within each of these divisions the more straightforward numbering is probably in the order in which the units occur along the route of the process.

Table 9.1 Extract from a plant inventory

Plant inventory no.	Unit description	Location drawing	Manufacturer, type and year	Cost
03/F/002	Water discharge system	014C53	Smith Mark, IIB, 1986	£10,000

Table 9.2 A coding system

Plant serial no.	Plant stream letter	Unit serial no.	Assembly serial no.
03	F	002	03

Table 9.3 A coding system for rotables

	Type	Size	Serial no.
Gear box (G)	XX	XX	XXX
Electric motor (EM)	XX	XX	XXX

There are many variations of this simple unit coding procedure. For example the Ammonia Plant of the Case study 1 (see Chapter 11) used an alpha-numeric code at unit level, e.g. C06. The C representing compressors. There are a number of 'standard coding' systems that have been developed for process plant. Perhaps the best known and most widely used is the KKS system developed for the power industry but now used more generally for process plant.

As in the example of Figure 8.9 and Table 9.2, an assembly number may be added for accessing data from the information base or for history recording. Where a rotable resides in this location there are two codes involved *viz.*

1. 03/F/002/03 is a location code (sometimes called the functional location). The system has to be told what rotable is installed.
2. G/XX/X/23 is the rotable unique identifier – see Table 9.3 (sometimes called the birth certificate number). Manufacturers information/spares, etc. is held against the gearbox make and type while the history is held against the full number. This number also allows the tracking of the rotables around the rotable loop (see Figure 8.8). (In some industries the unit itself can be a rotable and needs a corresponding birth certificate number.)

Regarding coding systems in general, Idhammer [1] gives the following advice for ensuring system flexibility:

(a) Keep the plant inventory code separate from the spare part code. The former should facilitate access to the information base at the point where the coding of the relevant spares is listed.
(b) Keep the drawing code separate from the plant inventory code (but interconnected as in (a)).

(c) Keep the cost code separate from the plant inventory code. All jobs require a cost coding, but only site jobs need a plant coding for maintenance cost control.

(d) If there are several sites, do not over co-ordinate the coding system.

Review Questions

R9.1 Explain what you understand by a 'rotable tracking system'.

R9.2 With reference to Figure 8.9 explain the difference between a functional location number and a rotable birth certificate number.

Exercise

E9.2 Identify the plant inventory coding systems for your own company. These should include the functional location code and the rotable code.

9.4 Information base (Element 2)

For the efficient planning of work it is essential that maintenance-related information is held for each of the units in the inventory, the most important of this being:

- essential technical data,
- spares list,
- drawing records,
- maintenance instruction manuals,
- catalog of standard preventive and corrective jobs,
- life plan,
- operating instructions and safety information,
- rotable tracking.

The maintenance information base can be regarded as the sum total of all such data categorized by unit number.

Technical data: An expansion of the basic information in the plant inventory, see Table 9.4. It is usually divided into electrical, mechanical and instrumentation files. It holds essential information needed by the planner, e.g. outside service engineers, manufacturers details, guarantee period, specification details.

Spare parts list (SPL):* A list, for each unit, of all spares held in stores, the stores codings being listed against the units/items plant inventory number and/or against the items birth certificate number (see Table 9.5). Some systems add to this the spares available from the manufacturer and call the full list the bill of materials (BOM).* Other information, useful in an emergency, could also be included such as the location, on other units, of identical or similar parts.

Rotable inventory: A categorized list of rotables (see also Chapter 8.4.2). This can be accessed continually through the plant inventory or directly using the rotable description/

---

* Definitions vary – this is my terminology.

Table 9.4 Technical data records

Manufacturer		Description		Date purchased
Type	Specification no.	Size		Model
Capacity	Speed	Weight		Connection details
Foundation details			Service Engineer contact details	
Dimensions			Interchangeable with	

Table 9.5 Extract from a spares list

Plant inventory locator	Description	Location	Rotable identification no.	
03/F/002/05	Water pump	Wood handling	P/46/02/25	
Part name	Quantity	Price (£)	Stores code	Stores location
Pump assembly	2	300	123456	Shelf 1 (main)
Pump housing	1	25	123457	Shelf 2 (main)
Bearing	1	1	123452	Shelf 25 (main)

Table 9.6 Extract from an index of drawings

Plant inventory no.	Own drawing no.	Drawing description	Manufacturer's drawing no.	Date prepared	Date revised
Unit 03/F/002	0363943	Assembly drawing	2941/1973/350	73.01.06	
	3373735	Pulley drawing	2951/1973/387	73.04.06	

birth certificate number. This sub-module also holds the rotable history and when computerized allows the tracking of the rotable around the reconditioning loop.

Drawing records: The drawing records should include the users and manufacturers drawings suitably filed with an index against the unit number (see Table 9.6). Drawings can be held in drop-leaf files, on micro-fiche or more recently via computer document imaging. The drawing records are often an engineering responsibility. Nevertheless the important point here is that there should be a system for updating drawings and for maintaining the filing system and the index.

Manufacturers manuals library: Same comments as for drawing records but with an even greater emphasis for the need for a properly maintained master library and a system for updating workshop based sub-libraries or manual storage.

Life plans, job catalog and operating procedures: Life plans for units of plant were discussed in outline in Chapter 1.

Table 9.7 Life plan for a crane

	Maintenance life plan	
		Unit no.: 05/0/Z
Unit description	Five ton crane	Location: Workshop
	Mechanical	Electrical
Weekly inspection	*General* Check long travel drive motor for noise vibration and abnormal temperature. Check cross travel drive motor for noise vibration and abnormal temperature. *Hoist* Check motor for noise, vibration and abnormal temperature. Closely examine rope sheave and hook for damage. Establish correct operation of top and bottom limits. Check security and condition of pendant control.	None
3 monthly inspection	*Long travel* Check security of motor mountings. Test track for correct operation and check lining wear. Check security of drive shaft bearings. Inspect condition of reduction gears. *Cross travel* Check security of motor mountings. Test brake for correct adjustment and check lining wear. *Hoist unit* Test brake underload for correct adjustment and check lining wear. Check gear case for oil leaks. Inspect rope for wear and fraying. *General* Report on condition of lubrication. Report on general cleanliness of machine.	*Long travel* Check security and condition of motor leads and earthing. Inspect downshop leads for correct tension and slippers for wear. *Cross travel* Check security and condition of motor leads and earthing. Inspect catenary assembly for damage and check free operation. *Hoist unit* Check security of motor leads and earthing. Check condition of wiring to top and bottom limits. Check wiring and push buttons on pendant control. *Controller* Check condition of all wiring and security of connections. Check for correct and free operation of all relays. Check setting of overloads at 10.8 amps.

A simple inspection based life plan for a crane is shown in Table 9.7. This subsystem holds the list of life plans and is linked to the job catalog.

The job catalog lists the preventive and standard corrective jobs for each unit of equipment. Each of the jobs listed are written up in the form of a specification (e.g. see Figure 9.2) which specifies one of the preventive jobs from the crane life plan. Each of the tasks listed in the specification could, if necessary, refer via a code number to the kind of detailed task shown in Figure 9.3.

Although not shown, it is usual for such job specifications to contain estimates of duration and manpower and a list of spares needed for job completion – such a list sometimes referred to as the *application parts list* (APL). For the larger jobs these are often held as 'kits of parts' in the stores. It should be noted that whereas SPL's are important in the process industry, APL's are equally important where fleets of vehicles are used. In addition, these descriptions often indicate the plant status required if they are to be carried out (e.g. major overhaul, weekend shutdown, or online) and other jobs that could be carried out at the same time (opportunity scheduling). In the case of major shutdowns the catalog may include job descriptions linked to bar-charts.

Recurring corrective jobs (sometimes called standard jobs) are specified in a similar way and entered into the catalog against the relevant units. Because they do not have a frequency of execution their specifications are called up via the unit number when the need for the work arises.

Job specification	Unit no.		05/012			
Plant description	Maintenance code		11			
Five ton crane	Job code		Mech/3 monthly (M3)			
Location Workshop	Week nos.	8	24	37	1	
Spares required						
Drawings and manual refs.						
Special tools						

Long travel
1. Check security of motor mountings.
2. Test brake for correct operation and check lining wear.
3. Check security of drive shaft bearings.
4. Inspect condition of reduction gears.

Cross travel
5. Check security of motor mountings.
6. Test brake for correct adjustment and check lining wear.
    Etc.

Figure 9.2 Job specification

Couplings, type LB, ASEA, BEK etc.

Inspect for *wear* on the rubber bushings as follows. Turn the coupling halves away from each other. Make a mark straight across the halves in this position and then turn the halves in the opposite direction to the first turn. Measure distance between marks.

Job specification no. 0255
page 1 of 2

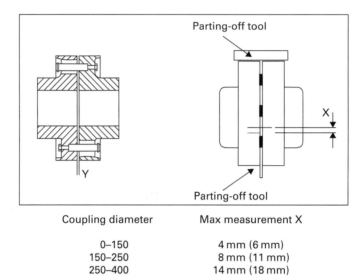

Coupling diameter	Max measurement X
0–150	4 mm (6 mm)
150–250	8 mm (11 mm)
250–400	14 mm (18 mm)

(The values in parentheses relate to stroboscope measurement)

Measure the distance Y at four points on the periphery without turning the coupling. Maximum permissible difference 0.1 mm for a medium sized coupling.

Figure 9.3 A detailed procedure

Review Question

R9.3   Define SPL, APL and 'BOM. Explain why a SPL is more likely to be used extensively in a process plant compared to an APL.

Plant history: It can be seen from Figure 9.1 that the plant history record for a unit has a dual function, contributing both to the maintenance information base (e.g. regarding when and how it was last repaired) and also to the plant reliability control system (e.g. facilitating identification of recurrent failures and their causes, see Section). The former function assists the planning of work and for this the history is best held in narrative form. Typically, for each job it should include as a minimum:

- date carried out,
- unit involved,
- duration and resources used,
- condition of unit and details of work performed,
- parts replaced and materials used.

R9.4   The 'plant history' function is in the information base module (2) and the maintenance control module (7). How would you differentiate between these functions? What sort of information do you need to collect for the information base function? What sort of information do you need to collect for the control function?

9.5 Preventive maintenance schedule (Module 3)

Maintenance scheduling was discussed in outline in Chapter 1.

The preventive schedule is formulated from the recommendations of the unit life plans and their job specifications (see Figure 9.4). The life plan for the crane shown in Table 9.7, e.g. is made up of four preventive jobs of different frequencies (see the 3-monthly mechanical service listed in Figure 9.2) and the schedule would program all such jobs taking into consideration plant and resource availability (see Figure 9.5 in which it can be seen, e.g. that the 3-monthly preventive work for the Crane is scheduled for Week 8, Week 21 and so on). The life plan for the Crane can be read off the horizontal line. The workload for any work is the addition of the work involved in each of the jobs in that week (the addition of the vertical columns).

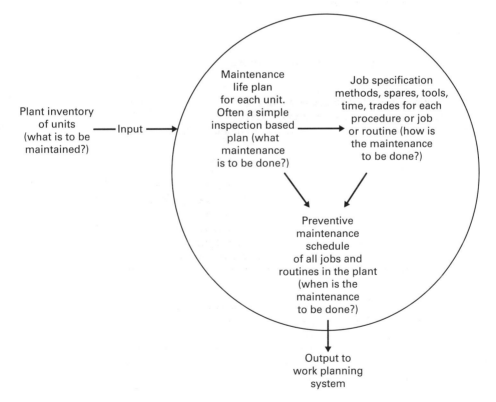

Figure 9.4 Outline of a traditional preventive maintenance documentation system

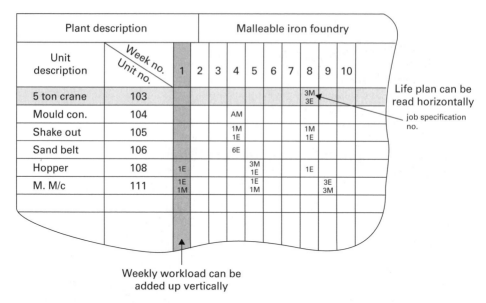

Plant description		Malleable iron foundry										
Unit description	Week no. / Unit no.	1	2	3	4	5	6	7	8	9	10	
5 ton crane	103								3M 3E			
Mould con.	104				AM							
Shake out	105				1M 1E				1M 1E			
Sand belt	106				6E							
Hopper	108	1E				3M 1E			1E			
M. M/c	111	1E 1M				1E 1M				3E 3M		

Life plan can be read horizontally

job specification no.

Weekly workload can be added up vertically

Figure 9.5 Preventive maintenance schedule for crane

This is an example of 'calendar time scheduling'. A preventive maintenance schedule should also have the facility for scheduling on usage, e.g. elapsed hours, tonnage through put, cycles of operation.

In the old paper-based documentation system, a schedule as in Figure 9.5, is used mainly for organizing the job specifications into some form of card index, see Figure 9.6. Comprising of 52 slots, this can then be used directly for the triggering and control of preventive work, i.e. each week it feeds a tranche of job specifications into the work planning system (each of which is accompanied by a work order on its way to the shop floor). The index can be updated and re-scheduled as necessary on the return of the job specification cards. Resulting corrective work is noted on the completed work order and is entered into the work planning system. Simple systems of this kind operated satisfactorily for small plants involved in the 'calender time scheduling' of routine preventive jobs i.e. services and inspections. They were much less successful for scheduling maintenance work in the large continuously operating plants e.g. alumina refineries.

Such plant requires more sophisticated scheduling to include:

- The facility for scheduling on usage, e.g. elapsed hours, tonnage, throughput, cycles of operation.
- The facility to integrate jobs from many units of plant into a single plant shutdown.
- Opportunity scheduling, the facility to schedule preventive jobs and standard corrective jobs into unscheduled windows.

Modern computerized systems have evolved from the ideas of the 'card index' but have the power and flexibility (if properly designed) to carry out all of the requirements of the maintenance scheduling function (see Chapter 10.3 for a discussion on the advantages of computerized work planning).

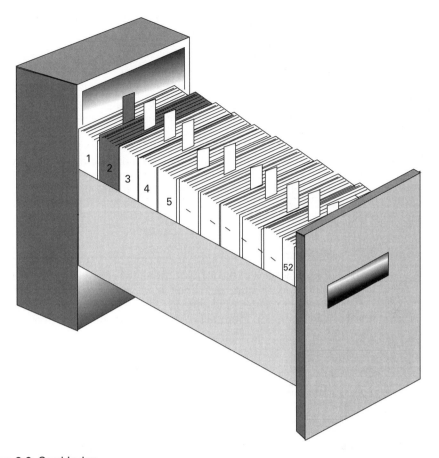

Figure 9.6 Card index

Review Question

R9.5   Companies do not often keep a record of life plans at unit level. The work is integrated into computerized preventive maintenance schedules. Explain why you think it is important to keep a record of unit life plans.

9.6 Condition monitoring (Module 4)

A life plan for a unit may well include inspections that need to be carried out and hence scheduled, independently of the main maintenance jobs. They can include:

(a) condition checks and readings carried out by operators,
(b) inspection routines undertaken by artisans,
(c) condition monitoring routines carried out by technicians using specialist instrumentation.

With the old paper-based systems inspection of the kind listed in (a) and (b) tended to be carried out on simple tick cards which might be sent to the responsible supervisor so that he could 'fit it in' to the schedule. Such inspections were subjective and relied on their efficiency on the experience and motivation of the trade-force/operators. Inspections of the kind listed in (c) tended to be scheduled by the technique involved, e.g. vibration monitoring. Inspection history was also stored/monitored separately by technique. When corrective work was triggered by the inspection a work order was raised and fed into the work planning system.

Minor inspections still tend to be carried out in the way indicated above. However specialist software has been available for many years to schedule condition monitoring routines, record, store and analyze the resulting data (see Case study 1, Chapter 11).

Review Questions

R9.6   Explain the function of each of the following: the inspection history of module (4), the plant history of module (7) and the rotable history of module (7).
R9.7   Explain why most companies (and software suppliers) keep the condition monitoring documentation module (4) separate from the main documentation system.

9.7 Short-term work planning (Module 5)

The principles of short-term work planning, scheduling and control were discussed in Chapter 5, the work planning system being modeled in Figures 5.7 and 5.11. As has been explained, the work order, see Figures 5.8 and 9.7, can be regarded as the vital operational vehicle for this system. The flow of this documentation – the main components of (and aids to) which are listed in Tables 9.8 and 9.9 – is shown in Figures 9.8(a) and (b).

Requests for *emergency* work are made verbally to area supervision who raise work orders. Requests for *deferred corrective* work and for *modifications* are made to the planner on work request forms. A work order is raised directly or, if appropriate, by reference to the job catalog. Priorities of such work are decided at a weekly planning meeting and the various jobs entered into the corrective job list.

Preventive work is planned and scheduled as explained in the previous section. Each week, the preventive maintenance system enters a list of jobs into the work planning system where they are considered for the weekly program alongside the corrective and modification work. Work orders are raised (by reference to the job catalog) and work that is *not* to be carried out is rescheduled using the planning board and job list.

The complete weekly program for each area or each plant is formulated in terms of resources, plant availability, and the opportunities known to be arising. This, along with the relevant work orders and any other necessary information (such as manual and drawing references, job specification codes, spares requirements) is then sent to the area supervisor who uses a short-term planning board or a simple allocation board to schedule and allocate the planned and the emergency jobs that come to him direct. Work orders are raised in triplicate, one copy remaining in the planning office, one with

Table 9.8 Work planning documentation

Work order	*A written instruction detailing work to be carried out.* The information this might carry is summarized in Table 9.9. When used to its fullest extent it can act as a work request, a planning document, a work allocation document, a history record (if filed) and as a notification of modification work completed. A typical work order (raised in triplicate in hard paper system and in this case not acting as a work request) is shown in Figure 9.7.
Work request	*A document requesting work to be carried out.* It usually carries such information as person requesting, plant number, plant description, work description, defect, priority, date requested.
Job catalog	A file of job specifications (preventive and corrective) as previously described.
Planning board	For preventive work, a scheduling chart as already described. For corrective work, a work order loading board covering a horizon of up to 12 weeks, in units of a week and having pockets to allow the work orders to be scheduled into the appropriate week.
Allocation board	A short-term planning showing men available on each day of 1 week. Allows jobs to be allocated to men.
Other	Safety permit, stores and tool note, weekly work program, stores requisition, top-ten report, cost report, history record.

Table 9.9 Information carried on a work order

Planning information
Unit number, unit description and site
Person requesting job
Job description and estimated time
Job specification and code number
Date required and priority
Trades required and co-ordinating foreman
Spares required with stores number and location ⎫
Special tools and lifting tackle required   ⎬ *Usually carried on*
Safety procedure number   ⎪ *job specification*
Drawing and manual numbers   ⎭

Control information
Cost code for work type and trade
Downtime
Actual time taken
Cause and consequence of failure
Action taken

the supervisor and one sent as the order to the artisans. As the work order is returned through the system the copies can be filed or destroyed. An important point is that *for effective cost control the execution of all work should be covered by a work order and a copy of all completed orders should return to the planning office.*

Plant description					Work order number			
Plant number		Plant location			**Permits**			
					P.T.W.	S.F.T.	L.O.A.	S.F.S.
Maintenance cost code		Job specification number			M	L.V.	H.V.	None
					Place of issue			
Coordinating supervisor and extension		Requested by and extension						
					Support and services			
Job/defect description					M	R	C	L	E	HP	W
					Stores check			
					Special tools			
					Transport			
					Check list no.			
					Action by scheduler			
					Stores	Work programme		
					Check initiated			
					Available	Permits requested		
					Note issued			
Priority		Date issued		Date required	Tools requested	Transport arranged		
Action taken (parts replaced)					Work allocated to			
					Job	Time	Date	
Cause					Started			
					Finished			
					Multi-trades involved			
Downtime (if any)		Foreman's signature and comments						

Figure 9.7 A typical work order

Exercise

E9.3   Use Figures 9.8(a) and (b) to map the work request/order (or whatever these documents are called) flow for your own work planning system. How does this tie up with the work planning model you drew in Exercise E5.1.

9.8 Long-term work planning (Module 6)

Turnaround planning was discussed in Chapters 6 and 7. This deals with the jobs (modification work, preventive work and those corrective tasks that can be held over) that need the plant to be offline for an extended period.

Thus, if the shutdown was to be undertaken under a paper-based documentation regime a simple file to identify and note all such jobs would be needed, which could be categorized according to the units, they were to be carried out on. Shutdown work tends to be different from ongoing maintenance in that the overhaul of even a small unit might consist of hundreds of interrelated jobs. A wall-mounted bar-chart could be used for the

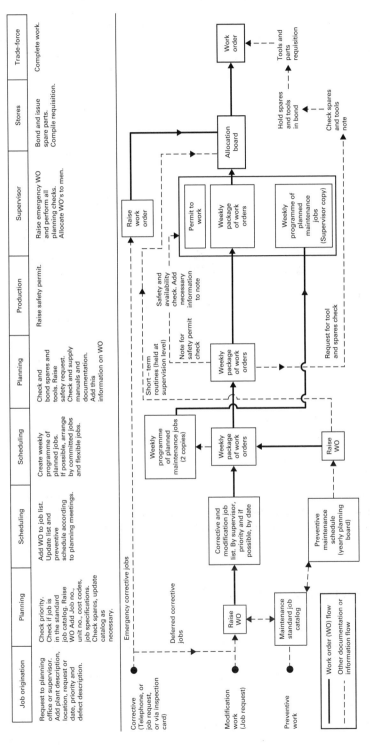

Figure 9.8(a) Maintenance work planning system (work order flow from origination to trade-force)

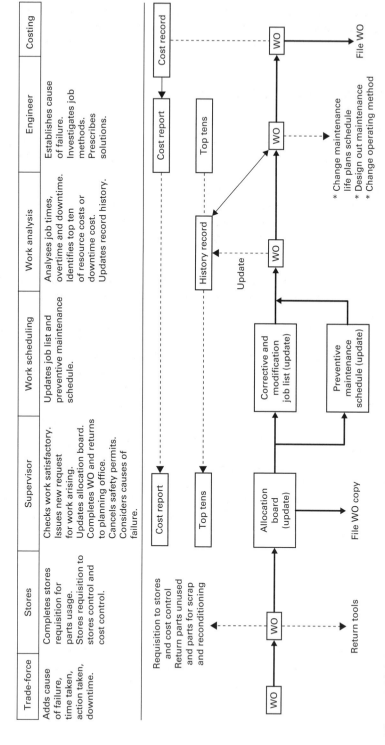

Figure 9.8(b) Maintenance work control system (work order flow from trade-force to completion)

scheduling of a small overhaul. In a large plant where there are many such interrelated overhauls the scheduling would need to be undertaken via a computerized critical path analysis. The execution and control of the shutdown, however, should still exploit the work order system so that day-to-day cost control and history recording may be sustained.

9.9 Maintenance control (Module 7)

This topic was discussed in terms of its principles of operation in Chapter 4. Much information transfer, storage and analysis is needed to facilitate the various maintenance control systems that were outlined. It will be instructive to identify the information that is critical for each of the main control systems.

Maintenance cost and availability control: The function and operation of this system was explained in Chapter 4. Put simply, it depends for its effectiveness on a true history being accumulated of maintenance costs and plant availabilities (and other parameters of maintenance output) for each unit of plant. The main documents used to collect this information are:

- work orders or time cards (which provide data on the manhours spent on each unit),
- stores requisitions and material purchase documents (for data on the parts and materials used on each unit),
- downtime record cards (for data on downtime, availability and output for each unit).

The information can be held in a costing record *for each unit* and can facilitate the production of *reports* on, e.g. total maintenance cost and achieved availability per production period per unit. Such data can then be built up to enable figures on total maintenance cost to be set against figures on total output, *per production line or per plant.*

Additional *reports* can be generated by dividing the total costs into preventive, corrective, mechanical, electrical, instrumentation, manpower, material and so on, figures which can be compared with target values or ranked to highlight problem areas.

Plant reliability control: The key document here is the *unit history*. As well as providing information base function, see Figure 9.1 and Section 9.4, it also has a maintenance control function, i.e. it facilitates the identification of problem units and the diagnosis of the causes of failures. The history record for each unit should therefore contain, as a minimum, the following information:

- Failure date and/or hours operated to failure.
- Duration of failure.
- Production/quality losses.
- Item/component affected.
- Probable cause of failure.

This can be provided via completed work orders, shift reports, defect reports or downtime records. Even with information as limited as this the reliability control system could generate lists of items ranked according to, say, mean time to failure, mean time to repair, or repair hours. For the more troublesome items thus identified, information on item defects and probable causes could then be interrogated to assist the prescription of corrective action.

The simplest form of history record is shown in Figure 9.9 and would operate with the type of system that was modeled in Figure 9.8.

History record mechanical					
Date	Item	Defect	Cause	Action	Downtime
4.10.84	0536 Coolant system	Flexible pipe	Rubbing on casting	Pipe rep. Bracket required	2 Hours

Plant description

Rhodes press

Plant no.

02.003

Figure 9.9 Extract from history record

Organizational efficiency: Reports generated to record the following indices:

- Trade-force performance.
- Trade-force utilization.
- Intertrade flexibility index.
- Absenteeism.
- Overtime.
- Trade-force turnover.
- Trades to non-trades index.
- Contractors to internal labor index.
- Spans of management.
- Levels of management.
- Ratio of staff to shop floor.
- Ratio of first level management to shop floor.
- Ratio of professional engineers to trade-force.
- Training cost per artisans.
- Job delay ratio.

Short-term work planning: Reports generated to record the following indices:

- Ratio of planned to unplanned work.
- Percentage of planned work deferred each week.
- Total outstanding workload in man days.

- Outstanding workload by priority in man days.
- Percentage of preventive routines completed per period.
- Rework as a percentage of all work.

Shutdown planning: Reports generated to record the following indices:

- Percentage of planned work actually completed.
- Actual cost as a percentage of budget.
- Ratios of actual shutdown time to planned duration.

Stores and rotables: Reports generated to record the indices outlined in Table 8.4.

Review Question

R9.8   The maintenance control module relies mainly on data collection during the work execution/reporting phase. The authors auditing experience indicates that in spite of sophisticated and expensive systems maintenance control is not carried out well. Explain why you think this is so.

9.10 Summary

The main aim of this chapter has been to develop a general functional model of the maintenance documentation system, to enable the reader to better understand his own documentation system.

The functional model, see Figure 9.1 has been used by the author in the following ways:

- As part of his technique for auditing a company's maintenance documentation system.
- As the basic model upon which to structure a company's *user specification* if it wishes to update its computerized documentation system.
- To guide the construction of a questionnaire for evaluating maintenance documentation software.

Exercises

E9.4(a)   Use the functional model of Figure 9.1 and the information of Section 9.3, 9.4 and Case study 1 in order to audit the maintenance information base of your own company. Select a typical unit of plant and check the following:
- The functional location code.
- Rotables used and their code.
- Manuals and drawings.
- The life plan and standard jobs and APLs.
- The operating procedure.
- Parts list.
- Unit plant history, cost history and essential spares usage history.

(b) Ask the personnel listed below to obtain a drawing, spare part, history record (for a period designated by you) for a particular unit. In each case time how long this takes:
- A planner.
- A supervisor.
- A tradesperson.

Reference

1. Idhammer, C., *'Maintenance Course Notes for Developing Countries'*, M. Gruppen Fack 1213, Lidingo, Sweden (*c.* 1980).

Review Questions Guidelines

R9.1   The birth certificate number of a rotable is used to track where the rotable is in the rotable loop at any time (see Figure 8.8).

R9.2   A functional location number can be regarded a plant location (or pigeon hole) where a rotable resides. It is necessary to tell the system what rotable is residing in the functional location. The birth certificate number is the unique identification number for the rotable. Maintenance information is stored against this number.

R9.3   A SPL is a list of parts held in stores against a plant unit. An APL is a list of parts for a particular job (sometimes held in stores as a kit). A BOM is a list of parts held by the manufacturer for a unit of plant. Every unit needs a SPL. It is likely only the larger or more frequent jobs will have an APL.

R9.4   The information base history is collected to provide information on 'what was done last time' (repairs, replacement, symptoms, etc.) before carrying out the next job (see Section 9.4 for typical information). The 'control history' is collected to identify recurring problems and to provide information on root causes (see Section 9.9 for typical information).

R9.5   The life plan for a unit is a complete record of the work you have deemed necessary over its life to control its reliability. If the unit causes reliability problems the life plan should be reviewed. The life plan is much easier to review when the jobs that are being carried out on a unit are written up against that unit.

R9.6   The condition monitoring history (4) is used to decide when to carry maintenance out on a particular item. The plant history of module (7) provides the records of major preventive and corrective work carried out on the unit. The rotable history provides the record of repair and reconditioning of the rotable.

R9.7   The function of the condition monitoring documentation is different and separate from the main maintenance documentation function. In addition condition monitoring technology and software has developed at a different rate than the main documentation system. In general the condition monitoring software is sold as a separate package and where necessary interfaced with the main system.

R9.8   The main reason is associated with poor quality of data collection at the artisan–supervisor–computer interface (see Table 4.1).

10 Computerized maintenance information systems: their uses and problems

'The newest computer can merely compound, at speed, the oldest problems.'
Edward Murrow

Chapter aims and outcomes

The benefits to be derived from the use of computerized maintenance documentation systems will be reviewed, as will the problems that may be encountered in their use.

On completion of this chapter you should be able to:

- understand how computerized maintenance documentation systems have evolved over the last 30 years;
- appreciate the benefits that 'state of art' computerized maintenance documentation systems can bring to the maintenance department;
- appreciate the problems that have to be overcome in order to use computerized maintenance documentation systems effectively.

Chapter route map

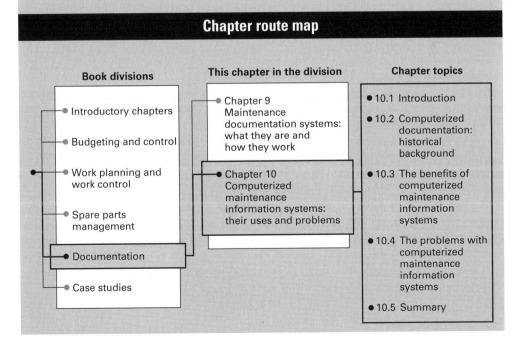

Book divisions

- Introductory chapters
- Budgeting and control
- Work planning and work control
- Spare parts management
- Documentation
- Case studies

This chapter in the division

- Chapter 9
  Maintenance documentation systems: what they are and how they work
- Chapter 10
  Computerized maintenance information systems: their uses and problems

Chapter topics

- 10.1 Introduction
- 10.2 Computerized documentation: historical background
- 10.3 The benefits of computerized maintenance information systems
- 10.4 The problems with computerized maintenance information systems
- 10.5 Summary

Key words

- Computerized maintenance information systems
- User requirement
- Application software
- Integrated systems
- Best of breed

10.1 Introduction

Figure 9.1 described the functionality of maintenance documentation systems. The author developed this model over a number of years as a result of investigating numerous documentation systems, of both the earlier, manually operated, 'hard-paper (HP)' type and the later, computer-based, variety. Although some small companies still use HP systems the vast majority have now used computer-based systems for many years. Nevertheless, the generic functionality model of Figure 9.1 describes adequately the overall (top level) architecture of computerized maintenance documentation systems.

10.2 Computerized documentation: historical background

Computer-operated systems* began to be used in the 1970s [1]. The early ones were Batch-operated on large centralized mainframe machines that were used company wide. The batch operation (perhaps only at weekends in the case of maintenance) limited the use of the computer for maintenance documentation to the more straightforward tasks, such as the scheduling of preventive maintenance.

The first online computerized maintenance systems made an appearance in the late 1970s. Initially these also used main frames in conjunction with an operating system that allowed for the application software (e.g. for maintenance documentation, stores control, etc.) to be operated in parallel – i.e. time sharing. Such multi-user systems, i.e. with numerous terminals connected to the mainframe, would dedicate several of these terminals for maintenance use. The early operating systems, however, were such that use of these machines was slow and inflexible.

The next (probably concurrent) advance was the use of dedicated computers (at this time they were called mini-computers) to run the maintenance application software. Such machines had multi-terminal access but, by modern standards, RAM (0.5 MB) and hard disk storage were severely limited. For this reason, for large systems the mini-computer was linked online to the company mainframe (distributed processing).

---

*A basic knowledge of computer systems has been assumed when writing this section. However, those who wish to update their basic computer knowledge should refer to reference [1].

The mini-computer operated the work planning function and the mainframe used state-of-the-art databases for maintenance history, spares lists, etc., i.e. for those documentation functions that required storage of large quantities of information.

Throughout the 1980s and into the 1990s there were considerable advances in the power of hardware, to the point that the PC came to have the processing power and hard disk storage of the mainframe of a decade earlier. In addition software and other technology improvement allowed for local networking (client-server arrangements) and wide area networking of PCs. Application software had become more portable due to the greater standardization of operating systems. In spite of these advances, up until the mid-1990s most maintenance documentation systems remained 'stand-alone', with at most an electronic linkage between the maintenance and stores software. During this period there were many maintenance documentation packages on the market, for all sizes of company and for use on systems varying from the single PC to the multi-user network.

One of the main consultancy tasks the author was involved in during this period was helping companies to establish their maintenance user requirement and then to help them select the best package to match that requirement and their existing hardware [2].

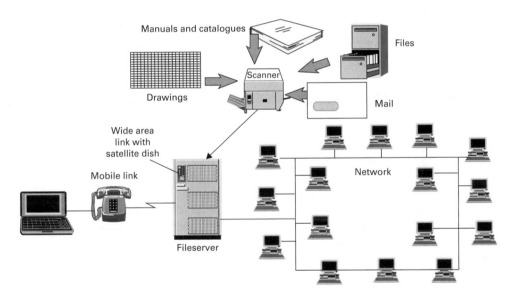

Figure 10.1 A document management system

Over the last 10 years the processing power and storage capacity of hardware has continued to increase and its cost to decrease. A typical modern hardware configuration – which includes the use of mobile computers (via digital telephony), Internet connection and e-mail facilities – is shown in Figure 10.1. In addition, software improvements and the development of scanners have facilitated the storage and transmission of drawings and pictures, etc. (document imaging). However, the most important introduction over this period has been that of electronic inter-connection of the company software functions (production control, stores control, maintenance control, etc.) into a company wide system (CWS) (see Figure 10.2). This electronic linking was achieved in the early CWSs through the introduction of interfacing software. This was expensive where the existing software was on a mainframe. In addition, movement of data across the interfaces could be slow.

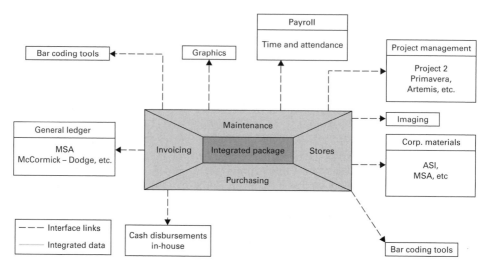

Figure 10.2 Part integrated, part interfaced company-wide software

In the mid-1990s a number of packages came onto the market with maintenance control, stores control, purchasing and invoicing on the same relational database, i.e. these functions were integrated. Such packages were then interfaced as necessary with other company functions (see Figure 10.2).

At about the same time, fully integrated CWSs also became available (see Figure 10.3). These provided many advantages, e.g. fast, seamless exchange of information between the different company functions. This was particularly important for the financial operation of a company and the strength of most of these integrated CWSs was in the financial software. However, some of the other company functions, including maintenance control, were often poor. Thus, one of the management questions of the time was:

Should we buy a fully integrated CWS or should we go for 'best of breed' and interface?

More recently the fully integrated CWSs have become more flexible and will allow linkages to other software.

With the most recent systems an effort has also been made to improve the interface between the user and the machine. For example, the traditional menu and keyboard input has largely been replaced (or partly replaced) by graphical user interfaces (GUIs)* (e.g. in PC Windows format). There are also many examples of bar code readers for stores management and pen computers.

---

*A basic knowledge of computer systems has been assumed when writing this section. However, those who wish to update their basic computer knowledge should refer to reference [1].

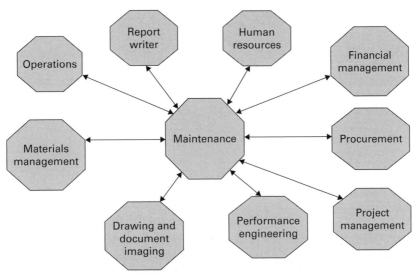

Note: All functions on the same
relational dates base as maintenance

Figure 10.3 An integrated information system

The authors consultancy problem in this area has changed and is no longer involved in selecting the best maintenance package. It is now involved in ensuring (as far as possible) that the CWS chosen by the company senior and financial management will satisfy the maintenance management user requirement.

Review Question

R10.1   Briefly describe the two main computer technology advances (in hardware and software) that have enabled company-wide software systems to be used.

Exercises

E10.1   Use Figure 10.1 as a guide to draw a schematic model of the hardware system in your own company.

E10.2   Use Figure 9.1 as a means of identifying the main modules of the maintenance package in your own company and then identify the electronic linkages (integrated or interfaced) with other company software.

10.3 The benefits of computerized maintenance information systems

Chapter 10.2 has explained how a typical state-of-art computerized information system for an industrial company is made up of a hardware configuration (as shown in

Figure 10.1) operating company-wide integrated software. The maintenance documentation software can be considered as one of a number of functional application packages hung-off the financial package (the General Ledger) (see Figure 10.3). The maintenance software can be considered as a number of structured and coded files (information base, history, etc.) held as a part of a common company relational database, and a series of programs (covering work planning, history analysis, etc.) that manipulates the data files in order to carry out the functions shown in the generic functional model of Figure 9.1.

The use of computerized maintenance information systems no longer has to be justified, any more than having to justify using a telephone system. It is almost inconceivable that a company information system would operate in any other way.

Some of the main benefits that have resulted from the computerization of maintenance documentation are:

- Systems of the kind outlined in Figures 10.1 and 10.3 allow all levels of maintenance personnel, from manager to artisans, to have quick access to the maintenance information (drawings, life plans, history, etc.) that is essential for cost-effective decision-making and job execution.
- The integration of the company information software within a common database allows information to be electronically communicated and shared company-wide, e.g. maintenance spare parts lists and rotable tracking are linked to the stores system; maintenance costs flow automatically from the maintenance department to the financial system.
- Communication within and between companies has been enhanced via e-mails. Access to the Internet has provided major advances in accessing the databases of equipment manufacturers. It has also provided opportunities for (a) setting up alliances for the holding of strategic spare parts and (b) 'spares-finder' access to Internet companies specializing in spares management.
- The use of PCs as part of the network has allowed maintenance personnel a wide range of generic analysis and planning tools, e.g. spread sheets.
- Computerized maintenance systems are *excellent* at storing, interrogating and retrieving information from the maintenance information base (see Figure 9.1). The main way into the maintenance information system has been via the plant inventory, Module 1. This traditionally requires the unit description or code to be known. In the most recent systems utilizing document imaging software (DIS) the inventory data can be held in the form of a coded process flow diagram which can be put on screen and used to trace downwards to identify the plant unit and then the component parts. The plant drawings, manuals and other information base data can also be held in the DIS and can be brought onto the screen. It must be emphasized, however, that DIS is expensive.
- The short-term work planning system (see Figures 9.1 and 5.7) has become much more dynamic and flexible and in many cases paperless. Computerized work planning systems give visibility of outstanding/completed work across the complete organization. They facilitate the cascading and balancing of the workloads of large complex organizations (see Figures 5.9 and 5.10) and provide the possibility of scheduling work flexibly over time horizons of from hours to weeks. They enable trade teams and artisans to do much of their own planning. They reduce the cost of

administrating the operation of a work planning system. They are sufficiently flexible to facilitate the operation of opportunity scheduling or of a strategy driven by condition based maintenance. The most recent software facilitates linkage between production scheduling and maintenance scheduling, i.e. via the computer, maintenance work can be scheduled into the production windows indicated in the production schedule (supply chain planning). Computerized work control systems (see Figures 5.7 and 5.9), in conjunction with work control indices, provide the necessary means of prioritizing and controlling the flow of work through the maintenance departments.

- The shutdown planning system can be electronically linked to the maintenance information system (see Figures 9.1 and 5.11), which facilitates the planning and scheduling of the shutdown on the network planning software, and the execution of the work via the ongoing work-planning work-order system. This also enables the shutdown costs to be collected, monitored and controlled (via S curves).
- Perhaps the greatest benefit (or potential benefit) of all is the computerized maintenance information system's ability to store, analyze and report on large quantities of control data (see Figure 9.1, Module 3). This includes the storing and analysis of history on costs, plant behavior, spares usage and labor usage – providing a variety of KPIs, control reports (Pareto, or Top Ten, analysis), etc. Such reports can be on-request, automatic, by exception, etc.

10.4 The problems with computerized maintenance information systems

Some 5 years ago the author was provided with the information that one in every two maintenance information systems was either scrapped within 2 years of its commissioning [2], or operated well below its designated capability. The main reasons given for this were:

- Underestimation of the time and money necessary to up-rate the life plans, spares lists, documentation, etc. and to transfer existing data into the new system.
- Underestimation of the time and money needed to provide the initial and ongoing training of the maintenance personnel in the use of the system.
- Poor quality of the maintenance information collected (descriptions of work undertaken, parts replaced, cause of failure, symptoms, etc.). This resulted from:
  - poor training in the use of the system, resulting in a reluctance to input data;
  - poor training in understanding the need for data, e.g. to establish the root cause of failure, etc.;
  - user-unfriendliness of the system, in spite of GUIs and improved software;
  - negative trade-force human factors.

While not wishing to be pessimistic, the author feels (as a result of his own auditing experience over the last few years) that in spite of the advances in hardware and software these basic problems still persist. The ammonia plant case study of Chapter 11 is an example of a large company using a 'state-of-the-art' company-wide integrated CWS, but with all of these listed problems. The author has found this to be typical of companies investigated. The following is a list of his main criticisms of the maintenance information systems of this company:

- The effort and cost of revising and improving life plans and the information base (spare parts lists, standard jobs, etc.) had been underestimated. Most of this information in the new systems was either poor or non-existent.
- The effort and cost of training the artisans in the use of the systems had been underestimated. Training courses had been set up, but had not been well attended and had not been followed through.
- The artisans regarded the new maintenance system (part of the recently installed company-wide integrated system) as inferior to the stand-alone maintenance system it replaced (which it was, in terms of maintenance functionality).
- The artisans considered that the new system was user-unfriendly and for this, and the reasons above, a resistance to the use of the new system had built up.
- It appeared that the main use of the new computerized maintenance system was to collect costs for the financial department.
- The auditor's over-riding impression was that the new company-wide information system was acquired because it was strong on the financial side, giving company-wide coverage of cost usage and control. The maintenance department was expected to go along with this decision. This, in conjunction with an incomplete and poorly specified *user requirement* for the maintenance information system resulted in a functional mismatch in a number of important areas, *viz.*:
  - The maintenance information base of the new CWS was not suitable for storing and interrogating the life plans and history for its large plant (pressure vessels and large machines). It was only suitable for ancillary equipment. Separate databases for large plant were set up and interfaced with the CWS.
  - The CWS maintenance software did not interface with the shutdown scheduler (Primavera) and did not produce S curves for financial control.
  - The ongoing work planning system of the CWS was not sufficiently dynamic to meet the company's workload and priorities.

10.5 Summary

The author has been involved in computerized information systems since 1975. Many of the problems raised in Chapter 10.4 were evident in those early years. In spite of the improvement in hardware and software these problems are even more evident today. If company and maintenance management are going to realize the full potential of information systems a lot more effort is going to be required to improve:

- the quantity and quality of data capture;
- the user-friendliness of the man–machine interface;
- the quality of systems training for artisans and operators.

In addition (and perhaps this is the most important point) it is essential that, before the purchase of new or upgraded information systems software, maintenance management should establish a comprehensive and detailed '*maintenance and information systems user requirement'*. They will then be able to compare this with the capabilities of what is on offer and negotiate the necessary changes.

Review Question

R10.2   List the main problems encountered by the users of maintenance information systems.

Exercise

E10.3   Carry out a survey, or an on-site investigation, in your own company to establish:
   (a) the extent to which the trade-force regards the maintenance information system as 'user-friendly';
   (b) whether there are problems in collecting and inputting maintenance data (list them);
   (c) those modules of the maintenance information system that are used most and those that are used least.

References

1. Bulger, P.M.J., *Large-Scale Software Projects – World-Class Success or Failure?*, Bulger Associates, 2000.
2. Kelly, A., *Maintenance and its Management*, Conference Communication, 1991.

Review Questions Guidelines

R10.1   Software that allowed the integration of different company functions on a common relational database coupled with the networking of PCs.

R10.2   These are listed in Section 10.4.

PART 6

Case study

11 Case study: Maintenance audit of an agricultural chemical plant

*'When problems mount so high that you cannot see anything else,
it pays to step back from your work so you can see the bigger picture.'*

Anon

Chapter aims and outcomes

The main purpose of this case study is to show how the business-centered maintenance methodology can be used to audit the maintenance management systems of a
large complex chemical plant. The full audit is presented, including that of the strategy
and organization as well as that of the systems, but its criticisms and recommendations focus largely on the systems. The study is also used as a vehicle for review questions relating to the preceding chapters.

Chapter route map

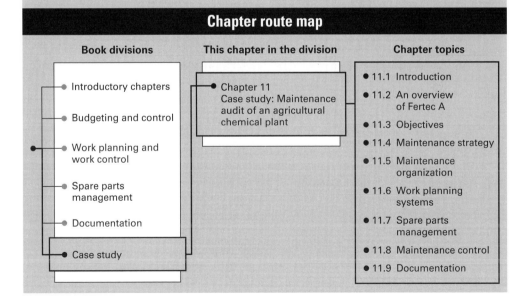

11.1 Introduction

This case study concerns a full audit of Fertec A a company manufacturing fertilizers for the agricultural industry. Fertec is made up of two plants: Plant A and Plant B located in different cities. This audit was carried out on the maintenance department of Plant A. Fertec is owned by a parent company Cario.

11.2 An overview of Fertec A

The plant layout of Fertec A is shown in Figure 11.1 indicating the location of the main process areas and the maintenance resources (labor and parts store). The labor resources are identified by a letter code that carried through to the organizational models.

An outline process flow diagram is shown in Figure 11.2. The ammonia plant is production critical since it supplies the other plants with ammonia and CO_2. There is some inter-stage ammonia storage. The plant can also be supplied with imported ammonia, which is much more expensive than that produced internally.

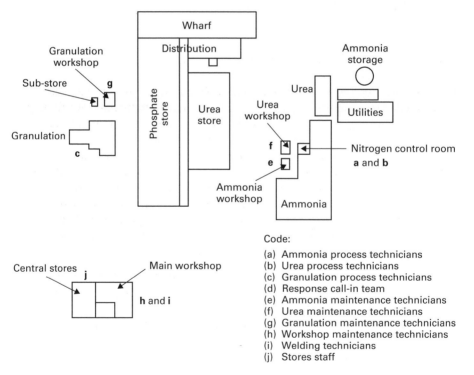

Code:
(a) Ammonia process technicians
(b) Urea process technicians
(c) Granulation process technicians
(d) Response call-in team
(e) Ammonia maintenance technicians
(f) Urea maintenance technicians
(g) Granulation maintenance technicians
(h) Workshop maintenance technicians
(i) Welding technicians
(j) Stores staff

Figure 11.1 Plant layout showing locations of technician resource

The complex is some 30 years old but has been up-rated, especially in the areas of instrumentation and control systems. The urea plant is currently being up-rated. The cost of energy (natural gas) is a very high percentage of the ammonia-plant-operating cost. The energy efficiency of the ammonia plant is low compared to the worlds best

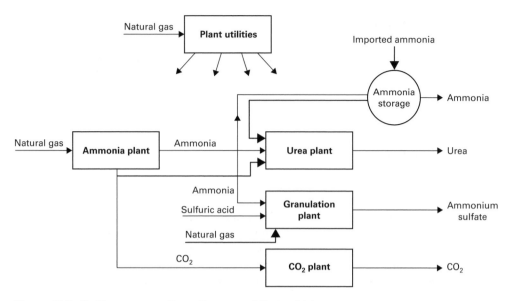

Figure 11.2 Outline process flow diagram of Fertec Ltd

because it has 'old technology'. The reliability of the plant has a major influence on energy efficiency and needs to be improved.

Fertec is one of a number of companies that belong to the parent group Cario. The senior management structure of Fertec A and its relationship with Fertec B and its parent group is shown in Figure 11.3. It should be noted that the Reliability Manager has responsibilities that cover both Fertec Plant A and Fertec Plant B.

A number of the senior positions in Fertec A had recently changed and had been filled with a young forward-looking team. The new team commissioned the audit because they felt that in order to remain competitive they needed to improve plant reliability and at the same time reduce maintenance costs. In addition they considered that there were 'attitude issues' that needed resolving both with respect to 'trade-force performance' and 'maintenance management standards'. The new management of Fertec A wanted answers to the following fundamental questions:

- Taking into consideration the ageing nature of the plant 'How effective is the maintenance strategy' (life plans, preventive schedule, etc.) in giving Fertec what they want in terms of reliability and output?
- How organizationally efficient is the maintenance department in providing this service at 'best cost'?
- How good are the maintenance systems?

11.3 Objectives

An outline of the process of setting objectives and business plans is shown in Figure 11.4. This is a form of management-by-objectives (MBO) closely allied to the authors business-centered maintenance approach.

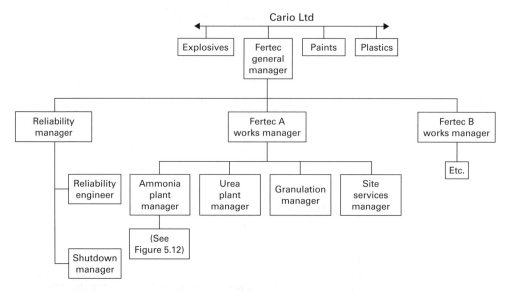

Figure 11.3 Senior management administrative structure of Fertec Ltd

The Fertec A senior management group (to include the group Reliability Manager) establish a 'works objectives and performance statement'. Objectives at this level are concerned with manufacturing performance. Maintenance objectives are set for those areas that directly affect manufacturing. For example, an objective is set to improve the availability of the ammonia plant from its current level of 88% to match the world best at 96%. Objectives are also set to improve energy efficiency.

At plant manager level the works objectives are translated into local plant objectives through three separate but linked objective/action statements *viz.* the people plan (concerns organizational efficiency objectives), the performance plan (concerns effectiveness objectives) and the safety plans. For example, in the case of the performance plan reliability improvement objectives are set for the critical units of the ammonia plant, e.g. the syn-gas compressor (SGC). In addition a series of tasks are identified to achieve these improvements, e.g. introduce the use of 'reliability centered maintenance'. These actions are allocated to specific engineers and supervisors.

The actions are reviewed by the plant manager at 3-monthly intervals. Similarly the works objectives and actions are reviewed by the senior management group at 3-monthly intervals.

In addition to this procedure each of the managers, engineers and supervisors are set annual objectives within which are included many of the objectives/actions of Figure 11.4.

11.3.1 Comments on objectives

The auditors were impressed with the objectives and the objective setting procedure. It had only recently been set up and required time to 'bed in'. The main criticism was that

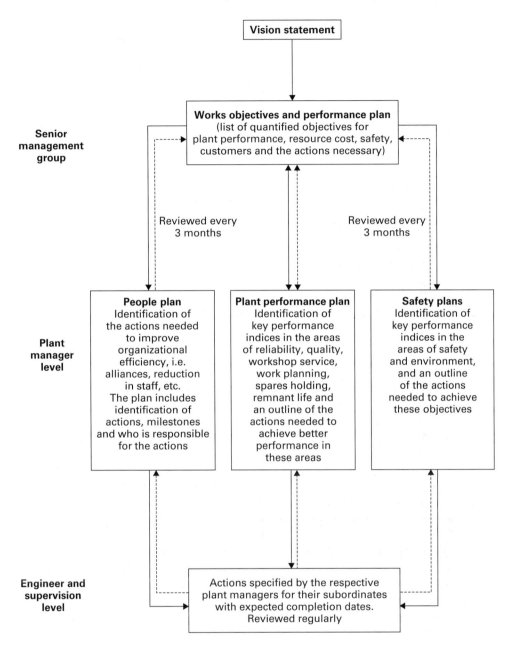

Figure 11.4 MBO at Fertec Ltd

the procedure had not been brought down to the 'self-empowered teams'. The auditors were told that this would have to wait until the 'negative human factors' of the process teams improved.

11.4 Maintenance strategy

11.4.1 Plant-operating characteristics

The outline process flow diagram for the Fertec A complex was shown in Figure 11.2. The ammonia plant is the rate-determining process – it is production limited. Ammonia plant failures can only be made up via imported ammonia (which is costly). The auditors were given the figure that a 1% loss of annual availability translates into many hundreds of thousands of pounds. The ammonia storage tank gives some protection (days) to the ammonia plant in the case of urea plant downtime. Failure of the ammonia plant also brings out the urea and CO_2 plants. The Granulation Plant is largely independent of the rest of the complex. In terms of downtime cost the following is the rule of thumb:

$$\text{Ammonia plant downtime costs} \quad >> \quad \text{Urea plant downtime costs} \quad >> \quad \text{Granulation plant downtime costs}$$

This section of the audit will be limited to the ammonia plant (the audit covered the strategy for the full complex).

An outline process flow diagram for the ammonia plant is shown in Figure 11.5. At unit level it can be seen that plant is a series process with limited redundancy. There are many units whose failure can affect the output of the ammonia plant and those that present the highest risk of failure are regarded as *critical*, e.g. the SGC.

11.4.2 Ammonia plant maintenance strategy

The current strategy is to operate the ammonia–urea–CO_2 complex for a 4-year period before a 4-week shutdown. This operating period is a function of statutory inspection of the pressure vessels (now self-regulating) and the need to inspect/repair/replace other plant units whose reliability falls off after 4 years. The timing of the shutdown is set to coincide with low annual urea demand.

The 4-year operating period has been determined by the reliability group based mainly on an empirical study of the 'risk of failure factor' vs the period of operation of pressure vessels before inspection (i.e. how long can we operate the plant for without affecting safety integrity?). They have established that the critical 20% of units carry 80% of the 'risk factor'.

Continuous vibration monitoring is used on the large machines mainly for operational safety but also for maintenance prediction. A number of other online monitoring techniques are used both on the large machines and the pressure vessels to aid condition-based maintenance.

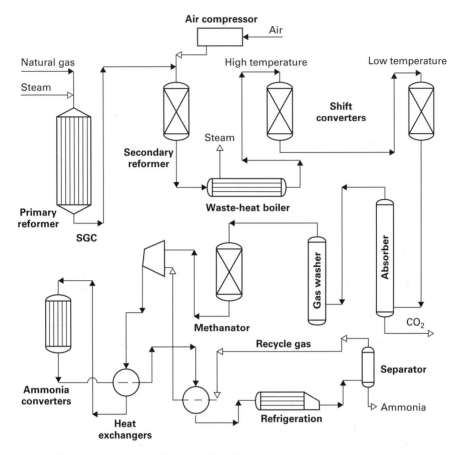

Figure 11.5 Outline of process flow model of the ammonia plant

The ammonia plant strategy has its center of gravity well toward condition-based maintenance. While the plant is operated for a 4-year period the shutdown workscope is mainly based on the work predicted from:

- online inspections;
- offline inspections from previous shutdowns;
- history from previous shutdowns.

The duration of the shutdown is normally 4 weeks which includes a 'dead-week' needed for shutdown and startup. The critical path during the shutdown is the reformer inspection (pressure vessel) and the SGC (large machine).

In terms of maintenance characteristics the plant can be categorized into large machines, pressure vessels, ancillary equipment, e.g. duplicate pumps and electrical/instrumentation (E/I) equipment.

Life plan for the SGC

A schematic diagram of the SGC is shown in Figure 11.6, which includes details on spare parts holding. The condition-based maintenance carried out on the machine is shown in

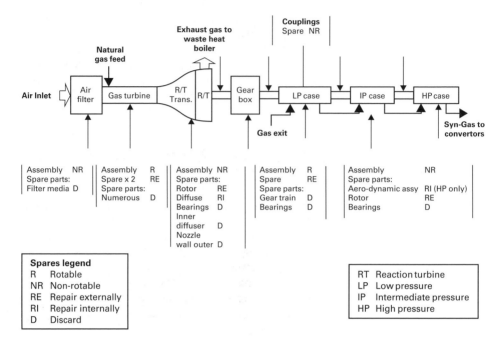

Figure 11.6 Schematic diagram of an SGC

Table 11.1 SGC condition-based maintenance

Bently Nevada system
- This sophisticated system records various data and has the ability to combine inputs to produce multidimensional displays.
- It produces data in real time plus long and short trend patterns.
- Items measured include:
  - Radial shaft displacement
  - Axial shaft displacement
  - Bearing temperatures: radial and thrust
  - Accelerometer readings (gearbox and gas turbine only)
  - Shaft orbit readings (multidimensional)
  - Shaft phase angle (multidimensional)
- In addition to the above approximately 200 process variables are monitored.
- All the above have alarm points and key items have shutdown settings.

Oil analysis
- Routine oil analysis.

Seal bypass test (compressor only)
- Routine seal accumulator drop test.

Oil debris analysis (gas turbine only)
- Online continuous monitoring.

Table 11.1. The machine is expected to operate continuously for 4 years. The shutdown workscope is established from previous shutdown history, deferred corrective maintenance, and the online monitoring information. Additional work is identified as a result of the offline inspection during the shutdown (unplanned).

Standard job procedures are in use, e.g. inspection-overhauls of the high-pressure case. These are comprehensive and detailed. The machine history records have not been formalized, are hard copy and reside in a number of locations looked after by a number of different people. The life plan has not been formally documented.

Although not shown in Figure 11.6 there is an automatic lubrication system for the SGC. There are simple documented service routines associated with this system which have been computerized.

Life plan for pressure vessels

The generic life plan for pressure vessels is based on condition-based maintenance. The maintenance carried out during the shutdown is based on condition prediction from previous shutdown history and on any online non-destructive testing (NDT) monitoring performed between the shutdowns. Additional work is identified from inspections carried out (open and closed) during the shutdown.

There are variations on the life plans to suit specific vessels. Those that are high on the 'risk factor analysis', see Table 11.2 for the basis of the calculations, are subjected to an in-depth analysis to up-rate the life plan. Every pipe, weld and hot support that might give rise to failure is examined to develop the most appropriate NDT technique and inspection methodology (e.g. see Figure 11.7).

This inspection-based life plan is backed up with a comprehensive computerized information base, the pressure systems database which includes for each vessel the following information:

- Process and mechanical data sheets.
- Inspection history.
- Inspection procedures and test plans (see Figure 11.7).
- The vessel life plan (which has involved risk assessment and remnant life analysis).
- Hard copy reports of previous shutdown case studies.

This computerized database is independent of the recently purchased company wide computerized enterprise system.

Ancillary equipment*

The life plans of such equipment is based on 'service routines' which are embedded in the main computerized maintenance system (linked to other company systems). A typical routine would be as follows:

Pump preventive routine: 3-monthly frequency:

- Oil change
- General inspection
  - Check coupling
  - Lift bearing cap, etc.

---

*For example, pumps, pressure relief valves, control valves, etc. – equipment that can be maintained outside of the main shutdowns.

Table 11.2 Assessment of criticality ranking for a pressure vessel

Pressure vessel CF601 sulfur drum		
Likelihood of failure		
Is there a known active metallurgic damage mechanism?	No known damage mechanism	0
Is there a known active mechanical damage mechanism?	Vibration fatigue	2
Have the inspections been effective?	Ineffective – no confidence	5
What is the frequency of inspections?	More than 30 years	4
How reliable are the control systems + operating parameters?	Poor	1
Are the vessel limits exceeded in plant upsets?	Yes	1
Are the vessel's limits exceeded in normal operation?	No	0
Have process conditions changed (but still within design)?	Yes	1
Are the vessel limits exceeded in plant startups or shutdowns?	Yes	1
Are the vessel's protective systems effective?	No	1
As detection of damage previously warranted further investigation?	Yes	1
Have repairs been required in the past?	Yes	1
How old is the vessel?	Over 30 years	3
Is the vessel original design to current standards?	No	1
Is the vessel material specification to currently acceptable?	No	1
Total		23
Consequence of failure		
Is the vessel contents . . . ?	A lethal gas?	7
What is the temp of the vessel contents?	Above 500°C	3
Are the contents flammable if they leak?	Auto ignites	3
Would a failure promote consequential damage elsewhere in plant?	Yes	5
Would emergency services help be required to contain a situation?	Yes	3
What is the vessel pressure?	Above 10 MPa	3
What is the volume of worst rating contents in the vessel?	Over 1000 m^3	8
Will a leak cause secondary damage to other equipment?	Yes	1
What is the distance to internal personnel?	Less than 10 m	2
What is the distance to the general public?	Less than 10 m	4
What is the business impact of a vessel failure?	Over £10,000,000	11
Total		50
Criticality risk ranking number = 23 × 50 = 1150		

These routines were established some 20 years ago and are in need of review. Many of the routines have been put into the new computer system without review. Vibration monitoring is also used for the rotating equipment in this category (mainly portable instruments but some periodic permanently wired systems).

In general the monitoring procedures have not been tied into the routines.

EQUIPMENT NUMBER: T503   PRESENT CLOSED FREQUENCY: 4 years   PRESENT OPEN FREQUENCY: Yearly   INSTALLATION DATE: 01-01-1968

DESCRIPTION: Ion Exchanger   VOLUME:

OPEN INSPECTIONS

Equipment item	Visual	Ultrasonic	Radiography	Mag/part	Dye/pen	Thermovision	Vibration	AE	Attenuation	Metallographic	Other
2RK65 to Tray Ring Weld	Yes				x						
Alignment	Yes										
Associated piping	Yes		O/head line only								
Davita/Lifting devices	Yes	Prior to S/D		Prior to S/D							
Earth connection	Yes										
Heads	Yes	Bottom									
Instrumentation	Yes	Evidence of bulging									
Insulation	Yes										
Internal liner	Yes	4 per petal			To Bot Tray						
Manway and bolting	Yes	Manway plant									
Nozzles	Yes	Manway liners		Internal							
Platforms/handrails	Yes										
Pressure relief devices	Yes										
Protective coating	Yes										
Shell	Yes	Lower 1.5/m			Liner welds						
Supports and bolting	Yes										
Thermowells and sockets	Yes				x						
Vessel bolting	Yes										
Vibration	Yes										
Welded joints	Yes										

Figure 11.7 Open inspection test plans for exchanger

In addition to the routines a 'contract lubrication system' has been introduced operated by one of the large oil companies.

The auditors noted that the operating procedure for units with duplicated drives was as follows:

- Electric motors: change over weekly
- Electric motors and steam turbine: use the electric motor and proof test the turbine weekly.

E/I equipment

The life plans are based on clean, inspect and calibrate where necessary. These preventive routines were set up many years ago and need review. It was noted that much of the more recent equipment, e.g. PLCs were not included on the routines and had not been reviewed. The large electrical machines had no documented life plan. More importantly the whole of the E/I equipment had not been reviewed in terms of 'spares criticality'. The information base data (job specification, modification and plant history, etc.) was either on hard copy (in a number of different locations) or held in people's memory.

11.5 Maintenance organization

11.5.1 Introduction

The methodology model (see Figure 1.1) showed that the maintenance organization is best understood by analyzing it into its resource structure and administrative structure.

11.5.2 The maintenance resource structure

A model of the resource structure for Fertec A is shown in Figure 11.8 and the inventory of resources is shown in Table 11.3. See also the plant layout of Figure 11.1 which indicates the location of the trade groups. The following are the main characteristics of the structure:

- Each of the maintenance and process group, e.g. the ammonia maintenance group, are intended to be self-managed and co-ordinated by their facilitator.
- The process groups include 25% artisans and are expected to carryout some first-line maintenance. In fact these groups carryout little or no maintenance.
- The out of hours priority maintenance is carried out by the response group (d) supplied on rota by all engineering technicians on site. These maintenance technicians are on an annualized hours agreement and do not get paid for callouts. The average overtime is about 5%. In order to enable all maintenance technicians to support the response group they are rotated across plants on a 2-yearly periodicity.
- The plant located maintenance day-groups, e.g. the ammonia maintenance group carry out most of the first- and second-line maintenance work in their own areas. They are supplemented by an average 25% contract labor to ensure the higher priority second-line work is complete. In spite of the use of contract labor the lower priority corrective and the preventive routines are neglected.

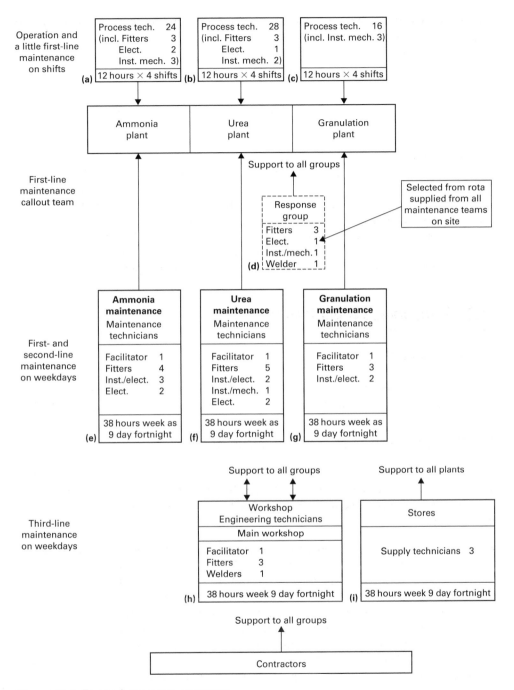

Figure 11.8 Fertec A resource structure

Table 11.3 Maintenance resource inventory

Resource categories	
Technicians	
Maintenance facilitator	4
Fitter	15
E/I	7
Instrumentation machinist	1
Electrician	4
Welder	2
Semi-skilled	
Stores technicians	3
Sub-totals	
Total maintenance facilitators	5
Total technicians (less facilitators)	29
Total semi-skilled resources	3
Total skilled and semi-skilled resources	32
Total maintenance resources	37
Total process technicians	68
Ratios	
Operators per maintenance employee	1.85
Percent semi-skilled of maintenance resource	8%
Total skilled and semi-skilled resource facilitators	6.5
Total skilled technicians/facilitators	5.8

- Inter-plant flexibility is encouraged by the management to cover the smaller overhauls. In general such sideways movement is resisted by the technicians.
- The area maintenance groups are supported in terms of fabrication, machining, reconditioning and spares by the workshop facilities, stores and external contract workshops, see Figure 11.9 for the reconditioning cycle.
- The workshop technicians also provide a maintenance service to non-manufacturing facilities.
- The 4-yearly shutdown (third-line work) involves an influx of many hundreds of artisans for a 4-week period to supplement the internal labor. The resource structure changes to a 'shutdown structure' for this period.
- The management has recently recognized the need for 'engineering skills training' and introduced a comprehensive list of 'goal-oriented learning' units.
- A number of surveys were carried out to include the following:
  - Production perceptions of maintenance service, in general the maintenance service was regarded as just satisfactory.
- Maintenance technicians' – 'human factors' – moral and goodwill toward management was low and equipment ownership less than satisfactory. There was a feeling of strong vertical polarization.
- An alliance between the company and an internationally known contractor has been proposed to carry out all non-core maintenance activities. This will include all workshop services, spare parts management and other non-maintenance activities.

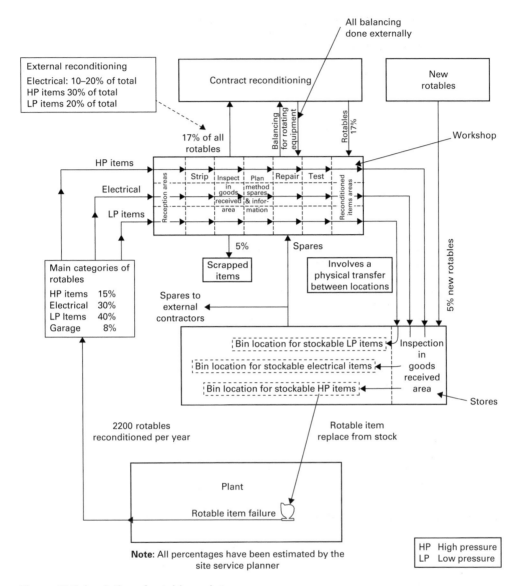

Figure 11.9 Logistics of rotable maintenance

- There is little or no skills flexibility between the mechanical trades and the E/I trades in spite of the two groups having a common facilitator and planner.

11.5.3 The maintenance administrative structure

The senior management administrative structure for Fertec A was shown in Figure 11.3. The administrative structure for the ammonia plant is shown in Figure 11.10 (the urea and granulation structures are similar), site services is shown in Figure 11.11 and the reliability group is shown in Figure 11.12. An inventory of the staff is shown in Table 11.4. These structures should be looked at in conjunction with the resource structure of Figure 11.8, the plant layout of Figure 11.1 and the trade-force inventory of Table 11.3.

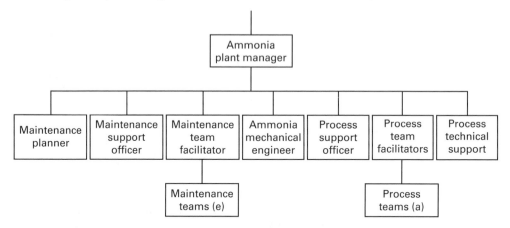

Figure 11.10 Ammonia plant administrative structure

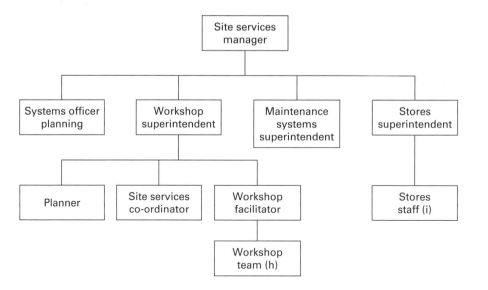

Figure 11.11 Site services administrative structure

The following are the main characteristics of the structure:

- The structure is built around the idea of semi-autonomous manufacturing units, e.g. the ammonia manufacturing unit (see Figure 11.10). Each of the plant managers report to the Fertec A Works Manager who is solely accountable for all operational activities on site.
- The manufacturing units are supported (in both Fertec sites) by the Reliability department via a matrix structure (see Figure 11.13). In general the auditors found the co-ordinating mechanisms across this matrix to be satisfactory.

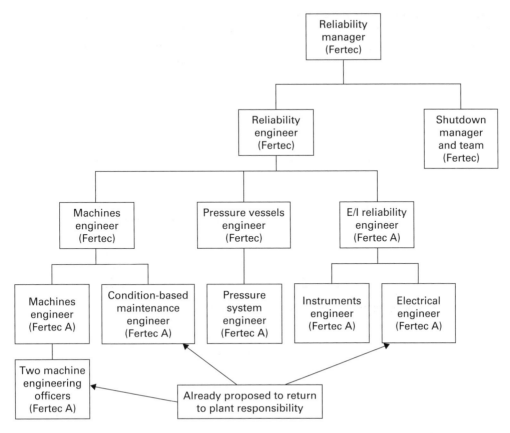

Figure 11.12 Reliability group administrative structure

- Within the manufacturing units, e.g. see Figure 11.10, the process technicians (to include 25% artisans) report via their Facilitator to the Plant Manager.
- The maintenance technicians also report via their Facilitator to the Plant Manager. In the case of the ammonia plant the team is made up of 10 artisans. The operation of the teams has reverted to the traditional structure with the facilitator acting as the supervisor and the planner carrying out the clerical duties. In addition technical support comes via the mechanical engineer and mechanical support officers. The E/I technicians feel vulnerable since no electrical engineer is employed within the works structure.
- The site services were only looked at in outline because a decision had already been taken to carry this function out via a contractor alliance.

11.6 Work planning systems

11.6.1 Short-term work planning, scheduling and control (see Chapter 5)

An outline model of the short-term work planning system for the ammonia plant is shown in Figure 11.14. This should be looked at in conjunction with the administrative

Table 11.4 Maintenance staff inventory

Staff categories	
Plant or site services manager	4
Mechanical engineer	4
Maintenance support officer	2
Maintenance planner	4
Maintenance team facilitator (in team)	4
Workshop superintendent	1
Maintenance systems superintendent	1
Systems officer planning	1
Site services co-facilitator	1
QA officer	1
Total maintenance staff	23
Sub-totals	
Total managerial staff	4
Total planning staff	5
Total engineers (non-managing)	4
Total special duties	5
Ratios	
Supervisors per manager	1.5
Supervised per planner	7.4
Engineering technicians (skilled) per planner	5.8
Engineering technicians (skilled) per engineer	7.2
Engineering technicians (skilled) per maintenance staff	1.3
Maintenance resources per maintenance staff	1.6

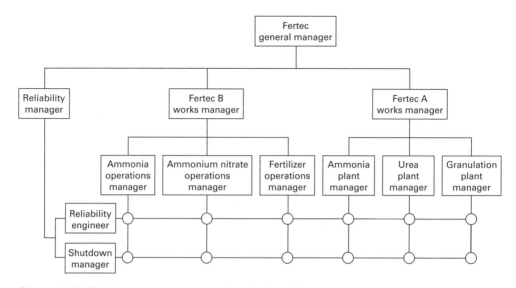

Figure 11.13 Senior management matrix relationships

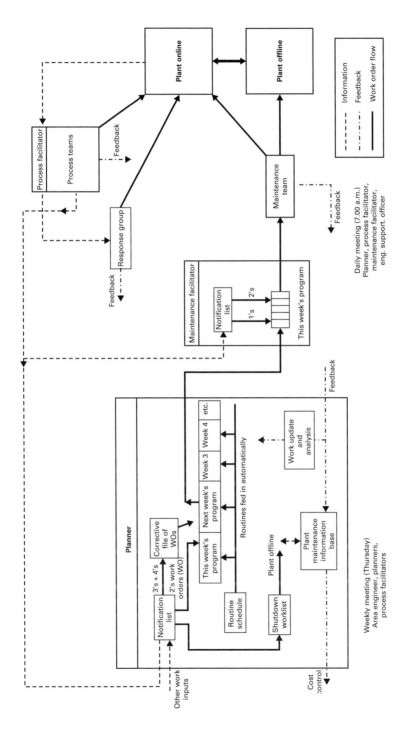

Figure 11.14 Ammonia plant work planning model

structure of Figure 11.10 and the resource structure of Figure 11.8. The ammonia system can be regarded as typical of the other plant-based systems.

This planning model is built around the resource structure of Figure 11.8. The shift process teams carry out little or no maintenance work. The response team handles 'out of hours' emergency work. The day 'maintenance team' handles the first- and second-line work.

The priority system is as follows:

1. Now, or as soon as possible.
2. This week, interrupt schedule.
3. Next week.
4. Shutdown, product change, opportunity.

Preventive routines are not prioritized and are 'fitted in'. The system is computer operated using a maintenance package which is part of an enterprise wide software package (EWSP).

A notification (a request for work) can be raised from a number of sources. Figure 11.14 shows a notification being raised by the process facilitator. The notification carries most of the history that is later transferred to the history record. In theory, resources cannot be used (labor, spares, etc.) until the notification has been raised to a work order (WO).

In theory, on shifts, if the process team is available and the job is within their capability the WO is raised against them. In practice the process team rarely carries out maintenance work. In the case of an 'out of hours' emergency the 'response group' is summoned and the WO raised.

In most cases the notification (1–4) goes directly into the facilitators and planners in-tray (notification list). In total about 10 WOs per day are received of which only one would be priority 1 – most WOs require one technician and a few might require up to five technicians. The facilitator/planer reassesses the priorities.

In general (across Fertec) the facilitator deals with the 1's and 2's (if necessary with assistance from the planner) and the planner with the 3's and 4's.

It was agreed that 'job instructions' are limited to the large machines. The planner and facilitator felt that opportunity windows are used in a satisfactory manner.

The actual labor hours go into the system at a later date (on occasions a very much later date) via the technicians updating the computer.

The permit to work (PTW) system operates via the facilitator. For the non-emergency jobs he takes the WOs and PTW over to the process facilitator at the end of the day. The tagging is carried out overnight and is checked by the day process facilitator before handing over to the maintenance facilitator. The maintenance facilitator starts work at 6.30 a.m. to cover the PTW and overspill jobs from the night shift. A daily meeting takes place at 7.00 a.m. to include the maintenance facilitator/day process facilitator/planner/technical support. The main purpose of the meeting is to establish the days program.

The main function of the planner (in all of the planning systems audited) was to plan next weeks work program. In this he is helped by the weekly meeting on a Thursday afternoon. The meeting involves the planner, facilitator, plant engineer and process people. The function of the meeting is to provide the planner with the information necessary for him to set up next weeks program (outstanding work by priority, production requirements for next week, routines outstanding, etc.). The planner establishes next weeks program to commit 75% of the existing manpower – some jobs are scheduled to the day/hour to match plant requirements and some jobs are 'flexible', i.e. they can be moved to different time/day. The most difficult jobs to plan are the multi-trade jobs – the planner deals with these. Multi-trade jobs can be handled via single WO or as is more often the case a master WO and sub-WOs tied up to the master.

The auditor was told that about 70% of the planned work is completed – this means that approximately 50% of the work is planned (goes via the planner) and 50% is unplanned (goes direct to the facilitator). This varies across the different plants and the unplanned percentage can be higher – resulting in a considerable level of the planned work (mostly routines) being dropped. The computer system can produce outstanding work by priority vs available resource. A backlog report has recently been introduced.

Comments

In spite of a low planner plus facilitator/technician ratio the users and customers of the work planning system consider it is not working satisfactorily. The following are some of the contributing factors:

● The maintenance technicians and facilitator find the computer system difficult to use. They consider it user-unfriendly and they say they have not been properly trained to use it.
● An incomplete or user-unfriendly maintenance database, e.g. lack of standard job procedures, poor descriptions of the spares in the stores system, etc. (these problems are being addressed).
● A high level of reactive work (in some plants) caused by the age of the plant and by the previous poor maintenance regimes (routines, etc.).
● A pedantic PTW/tagging system (this problem is being addressed to ensure compliance and to streamline).

In the authors' opinion the main problem is the unsatisfactory resource structure of Figure 11.8. The process teams are not carrying out any first-line maintenance work. All the maintenance work is cascading into six small plant trade groups. The priority 1's and 2's going direct to the maintenance facilitator is disrupting the weekly program set up by the planner. This means that in many areas up to 50% of the total workload is unplanned. (To operate an effective weekly forward planning system the unplanned element of the workload should be less than 15%.)

Recommendations

The auditors consider that the main problem is with the resource structure rather than the planning system. They proposed that the modified structure shown in Figure 11.15 be adopted. This would overcome the disruption outlined above. The 1's and a proportion of the less complex 2's would be carried out by the process technicians on shifts and the plant dedicated maintenance technicians on days (the auditors envisage these maintenance technicians working closely with the process technicians). The remainder of the work would be carried out by the nitrogen team. This should have a 90% planned

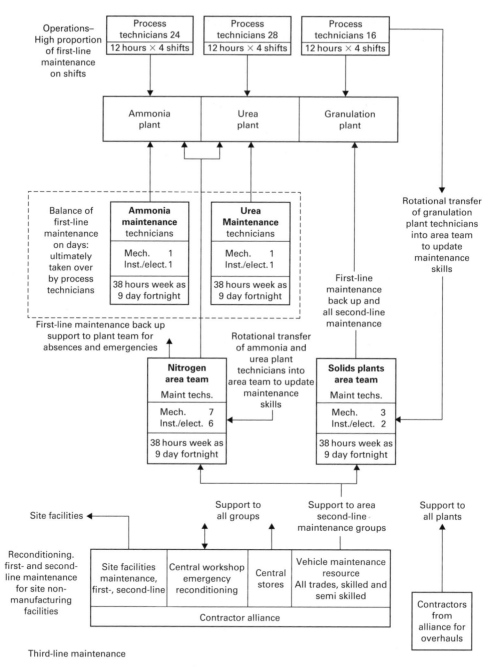

Figure 11.15 Proposal for modified resource structure

content. The auditors further recommend the facilitators should receive increased training to enable them to carry out the planning role.

11.6.2 The planning of the major shutdowns (see Chapters 6 and 7)

This was not a full audit of the shutdown planning procedure. Such an audit would need the presence of the auditors during the actual shutdown period. This exercise was limited to a review of the Fertec shutdown planning procedure by comparing it with the standard procedure of Figure 11.16.

Over the years, Fertec have had some poorly planned and executed shutdowns and as a result of this experience have set up a shutdown planning team reporting to the Reliability Manager (see Figures 11.3 and 11.12). The team is permanent and includes a shutdown manager and Shutdown Planners located at Fertec 1 and Fertec 2. This team is supplemented by key personnel immediately before and during the shutdown. The ongoing administrative structure of Figures 11.3 and 11.10, etc. is modified during the period of the shutdown (not shown). The resource structure of Figure 11.8 is also modified to include an influx of personnel (not shown). The scheduling and resourcing of the shutdown is carried out with the use of Primavera (a network planning package). The identified tasks off the main network are carried out using the main computerized work planning system.

Comments and recommendations

As a result of a history of poorly executed shutdowns Fertec have made major efforts to improve the planning, organization and execution of their major shutdowns. The auditors consider that Fertec have a shutdown planning procedure that approaches international best practice. The following are the main recommendations for further improvement:

- More thought should be given to the development of the plant shutdown and startup plans.
- A more rigorous approach to site logistics should be developed to ensure that 'the right thing is in the right place at the right time'.
- In order to be able to establish a comprehensive and detailed shutdown workscope it will be necessary for Fertec to improve their recording and storage or previous shutdown history. (Pressure vessel history is satisfactory.) In addition the history recording of online condition monitoring needs to be improved – at the moment there is no connection between this data and the plant information base history.
- One of the main reasons for poor quality work during shutdowns is the lack of standard job procedures with inspection test plans. The auditors are aware that improvements in this area are in hand but it is necessary to re-emphasize the considerable effort/resource that this requires.
- The computer software systems being used to carry out the shutdown planning require some improvement (perhaps interfacing). At the moment Primavera is going to be used to produce the schedule. This then needs to be fed into the computerized work

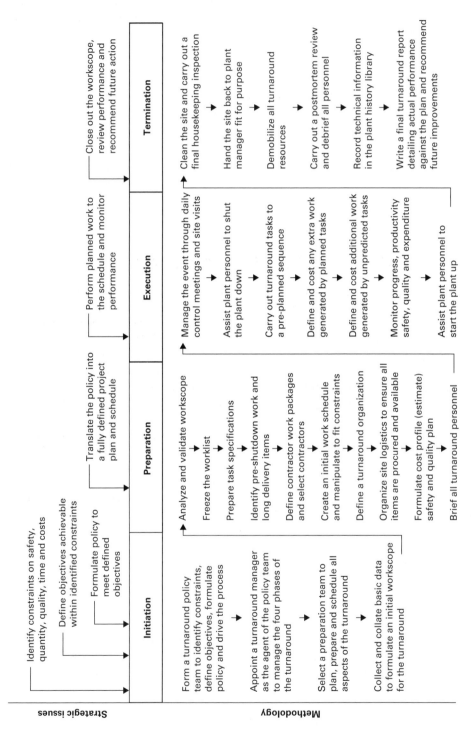

Strategic issues

Identify constraints on safety, quantity, quality, time and costs

Define objectives achievable within identified constraints

Formulate policy to meet defined objectives

Translate the policy into a fully defined project plan and schedule

Perform planned work to the schedule and monitor performance

Close out the workscope, review performance and recommend future action

Methodology

Initiation

Form a turnaround policy team to identify constraints, define objectives, formulate policy and drive the process

Appoint a turnaround manager as the agent of the policy team to manage the four phases of the turnaround

Select a preparation team to plan, prepare and schedule all aspects of the turnaround

Collect and collate basic data to formulate an initial workscope for the turnaround

Preparation

Analyze and validate workscope

Freeze the worklist

Prepare task specifications

Identify pre-shutdown work and long delivery items

Define contractor work packages and select contractors

Create an initial work schedule and manipulate to fit constraints

Define a turnaround organization

Organize site logistics to ensure all items are procured and available

Formulate cost profile (estimate) safety and quality plan

Brief all turnaround personnel

Execution

Manage the event through daily control meetings and site visits

Assist plant personnel to shut the plant down

Carry out turnaround tasks to a pre-planned sequence

Define and cost any extra work generated by planned tasks

Define and cost additional work generated by unpredicted tasks

Monitor progress, productivity safety, quality and expenditure

Assist plant personnel to start the plant up

Termination

Clean the site and carry out a final housekeeping inspection

Hand the site back to plant manager fit for purpose

Demobilize all turnaround resources

Carry out a postmortem review and debrief all personnel

Record technical information in the plant history library

Write a final turnaround report detailing actual performance against the plan and recommend future improvements

Figure 11.16 Generic major plant shutdown, planning methodology

planning system (at the moment manually) in order to collect and control costs. And since neither of these systems produces satisfactory S curves XCEL is used to carry out this function.

11.7 Spare parts management (see Chapter 8)

11.7.1 Introduction

This project was not concerned with auditing the stores management system – this is a major audit in its own right. The purpose of this section of a maintenance audit is to establish 'how good is the stores system in giving the maintenance people the service they need'.

11.7.2 Outline of the stores organization and systems

The plant layout diagram of Figure 11.1 shows the location of the main stores, sub-stores and the maintenance workshop.

The main workshop carries all of the cataloged parts and is operated by the enterprise wide computer package. The value of the stores is around £3 M (2000) involving some 12,500 grouping of items. The turnover was estimated at 60% of the value per annum. The main stores had recently introduced an open stores policy (serve yourself). The parts can be located via the computer system and withdrawn after a WO has been raised.

In terms of inventory policy the items are divided into six categories to include a 'slow moving parts' category. The initial ordering procedure for parts ('what to hold' and 'how many to hold' for new equipment) is taken by the Unit Engineers as part of their 'life plan analysis'. A stand-alone software package (SCAS) is used to establish the policy for the 'slow moving expensive category or parts'. The main stores are the responsibility of the site services manager via the stores superintendent (see Figure 11.11).

The sub-stores carry a mixture of consumables, non-stores controlled parts and tools and are the responsibility of the area facilitators.

The reconditioned items are supplied to the stores from the workshop and also direct from outside contractors (see Figure 11.9). The workshop is currently the responsibility of the site services manager but will come within the proposed contractor alliance.

Comments and recommendations
- The auditors were told that the SCAS system for establishing the level of slow moving parts was not being used. In addition the inventory policy for parts holding had not been reviewed for upwards of 20 years. During this time the plant had gone through numerous major shutdowns. In the auditors opinion (backed up by the comments of interviewees) there is serious overstocking of the expensive slow moving parts.

  It is recommended that a review is carried out of the stock held in stores. This should included a Pareto analysis of parts by cost and turnover. All expensive slow moving parts should be subjected to a SCAS review.

- The proportion of reconditioned items (17%) going out to contract is low for a company located in an industrial area. It is recommended that a small project team be set up to study this problem in more detail with the objective of outsourcing as much as possible of the reconditioned items. This should start with the outsourcing of the reconditioning of the electric motors.
- There were very few performance indices (PIs) in operation in the stores management system. PIs should be introduced as soon as possible to include:
  - a service factor index (the number of times per period a request for parts was unable to be provided);
  - a rework index (for reconditioned items).

11.8 Maintenance control (see Chapters 3 and 4)

11.8.1 The control of overall maintenance performance

A conventional budgeting and cost control system was in use via the computer WO system of the kind outlined in Figure 11.14. The plant is divided into its main units of equipment and each given a functional location number, e.g.:

SGC	6	C	02
	Ammonia plant	Compressor	Unique number

The units are divided into their main assemblies or systems, e.g. Reaction Turbine RT02. The costs are also divided via an alpha-numeric code into trade/department/work type, etc. This allows cost reports to be generated against numerous criteria to include:

- Total cost per period per functional location/equipment number.
- Top 10's/20's/30's functional location by cost and work type.

A different system was in use to record plant and equipment uptime/availability and more recently a series of key PIs have been established. These include the following indices/graphs for each main plant:

- Monthly maintenance cost per ton produced.
- Monthly availability.
- Total cost of maintenance.

11.8.2 The control of organizational efficiency

Until recently no data was collected for this purpose. However, the recently introduced system of key PIs include the following organizational indices for each plant:

- Percentage of planned work.
- Percentage of unplanned work.
- Percentage of preventive man-hours.

- Percentage of rework man-hours.
- Time WO raised before completion.
- Units with a spare parts list.
- Backlog of man-hours.
- Percentage overtime.
- Inventory value.
- Percentage turnover.
- Stockout costs.

11.8.3 The control of maintenance effectiveness (plant reliability control)

The auditors summarized their comments about plant reliability control (PRC) at Fertec as follows:

- The PRC structure should be formalized and the roles of the people involved clarified *viz.*:
  - The level 1 system should be set up to include the involvement of the process and maintenance teams in continuous improvement (non-existent at the moment). The teams should also be involved in the improvement of the life plans and given increased training with a view to improving the quality of history feedback.
  - The roles of the Plant Engineer and Engineering Officers in PRC should be clarified (second level). Such clarification should include their inter-relationships and their relationships with the reliability group. It should be pointed out that they should be spending at least 30% of the time on 'design out maintenance problems'.
  - The role of the Reliability Group and their linkage to the Plant Engineers and the original equipment manufacturer.

11.9 Documentation (see Chapters 9 and 10)

The main computerized information system at Fertec is a fully integrated EWSP of which the maintenance management system is one of a number of functions. This main system is supplemented by a number of other computer systems and by hard paper documentation files.

The following are a list of the main observations made about documentation at Fertec:

- *Unit life plans*: Not as yet formally documented with the exception of the pressure vessels.
- *Standard job catalog*: Some of the original preventive routines for the ancillary equipment are in the EWSP. These need updating. There are a number of reconditioning specifications for the large machines held in hard copy.
- *Equipment drawings*: The main point was that many of the drawings are out of date.
- *Manuals*: There is no master library. The manuals investigated were in poor condition and held in a number of locations.

- *Spare parts lists by unit*: The electrical lists are only 50% complete.
- *History*: Held in a number of locations as follows:
  - The 'ancillary equipment' history was held in the EWSP and was of poor quality due to poor feedback from the teams.
  - The 'pressure vessel' history was held in a stand-alone computerized database which included job specifications, life plans and operating procedures. This history was of excellent quality.
  - The 'large machine' history was hard copy and held in a number of different locations.
- *Condition monitoring*: Each monitoring system seemed to be stand alone, e.g. the external consultant for the hand held vibration monitoring held their own records.
- *Short-term work planning*: Carried out via the WO system of the EWSP. This system also holds the preventive schedule for the ancillary equipment but not the shutdown schedule.
- *Shutdown planning*: Primavera is used to build the shutdown schedule and the WO system of the EWSP is used to allocate the jobs and collect the costs. XCEL is used to produce S curves.

11.9.1 Comments and recommendations

(i) The Reliability Group expressed the view that the EWSP was not suitable for holding and operating the kind of equipment that is needed for the maintenance of the large machines and pressure vessels *viz*. life plans, job specifications, history to include NDT mapping, case studies of overhaul, etc. The Reliability Group indicated their intention to develop stand-alone databases for the pressure vessels (existing), large machines and E/I equipment.

   The auditors had some sympathy with this view based on their audit. The EWSP had evolved out of the manufacturing industry where the major shutdowns are different to the process industries. However, the building of new databases and the interfacing costs is going to be an expensive business. The auditors recommend that a small project team is set up to examine this problem further to establish (via the EWSP experts) if the EWSP can be modified to satisfy the needs of the Reliability Group. For example, the auditors cannot see the need for a separate E/I database.

   The point being made is that if the EWSP is limited to its present equipment coverage then Fertec have paid a very heavy price for a simple WO – costing system.

(ii) At the moment the EWSP is not operating as well as it should. This is partly because the system is not user-friendly and partly because the training has fallen away. The auditors recommend that the EWSP training is reviewed and restarted to include its monitoring.

(iii) It is recommended that an equipment manuals master library is set up as soon as possible.

Reference

1. Kelly, A., *Maintenance Management Auditing*, Industrial Press, New York, 2005.

Appendix: Weibull analysis*

A.1 Weibull analysis of item lifetime

The Weibull *probability density function* (pdf) can represent *any* of the three basic types of failure *viz.* 'wear-out', 'random' and 'running in'. It has two other sovereign virtues:

(i) It can be applied via simple graphical techniques.
(ii) It is expressed by a formula in which all the terms have engineering significance.

The ideas underlying this pdf may be grasped from Weibull's own derivation, which was neither mathematical nor statistical, but was based on a few practical considerations.

Weibull was involved in analyzing the results of load tests on many nominally identical test specimens of a particular type of steel. Their ultimate tensile strengths exhibited random variability, as they always do. If $F(x)$ was defined as the cumulative fraction which exhibited strengths *less* than a particular load x (i.e. $F(x)$ was the *cumulative distribution function* (cdf), the distribution of the probability that a specimen would fail under the load x, then a plot of $F(x)$ looked like the one shown in Figure A.1. None failed before some given load x_0 (*guaranteed* strength) and a very few hung on to quite large loads.

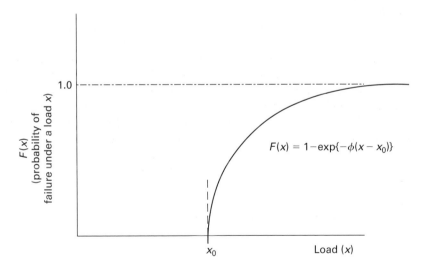

$$F(x) = 1 - \exp\{-\phi(x - x_0)\}$$

Figure A.1 Probability of failure of specimens as a function of load

* Extracted from '*Maintenance Strategy*', Kelly, A., Butterworth-Heinemann, 1997.

First, Weibull conjectured (see Figure A.1) that it might be possible to represent such a cdf fairly accurately by the expression:

$$F(x) = 1 - \exp\{-\phi(x - x_0)\}$$

where $\phi(x - x_0)$ would be some function of $(x - x_0)$, as yet undefined and which itself increased as x increased, e.g. $3(x - x_0)$, or $(x - x_0)^2$, or whatever. This would give a plot which started at x_0 and approached $F(x) = 1$ asymptotically, as required. However, $\phi(x - x_0)$ would have to be such that it gave the appropriate rate of rise of the value of $F(x)$, and would have to be dimensionless (because it is an exponent, a power).

Weibull found that the form:

$$\phi(x) = \left\{ \frac{x - x_0}{\eta} \right\}^{\beta}$$

where η was a characteristic load (determining, along with x_0, the scale of the loads involved), and β was a curve-shaping factor, gave him an expression for the cdf:

$$F(x) = 1 - \exp\left\{ -\left(\frac{x - x_0}{\eta} \right)^{\beta} \right\}$$

which enabled him to correlate his test data very well. In addition, the expression had some other very useful properties, as we shall see.

In the reliability problems that we are looking at here the stressing factor is not load but *running time t*, since new or last overhaul. The Weibull cdf for *times-for-failure* is, therefore, written as:

$$F(x) = 1 - \exp\left\{ -\left(\frac{t - t_0}{\eta} \right)^{\beta} \right\}$$

From this, some not very complicated mathematics (e.g. $R(t) = 1 - F(t)$) then leads to the appropriate expressions for the Weibull pdf $F(t)$, reliability $R(t)$ and hazard rate $Z(t)$:

$$f(t) = \frac{\beta(t - t_0)^{\beta-1}}{\eta^{\beta}} \exp\left\{ -\left(\frac{t - t_0}{\eta} \right)^{\beta} \right\}$$

$$R(t) = \exp\left\{ -\left(\frac{t - t_0}{\eta} \right)^{\beta} \right\}$$

$$Z(t) = \frac{\beta}{\eta^{\beta}} (t - t_0)^{\beta-1}$$

Each of the constants in these formulae has a practical meaning and significance.

The *threshold time-to-failure*, or *guaranteed life* t_0. In many cases of wear-out the first failure does not appear until some significant running time t_0 has elapsed. In the Weibull expressions the time factor is then the time interval $(t - t_0)$.

The *characteristic life*, η. When $t - t_0 = \eta$, $R(t) = \exp(-1) = 0.37$, i.e. η is the interval between t_0 and the time at which it can be expected that 37% of the items will have survived (and hence 63% will have failed).

The *shape factor*, β. Figure A.2 shows how the Weibull pdf of time-to-failure changes as β is changed (for clarity, on each plot $t_0 = 0$ and $\eta = 1$).

If β is significantly less than 1 the pdf approximates to the hyper-exponential, i.e. is characteristic of 'running in' failure.

If $\beta = 1$ the pdf becomes the simple negative exponential, characteristic of 'purely random' failure.

As β rises above a value of about 2 the pdf converges ever more closely to the normal pdf characteristic of 'wear-out' failure.

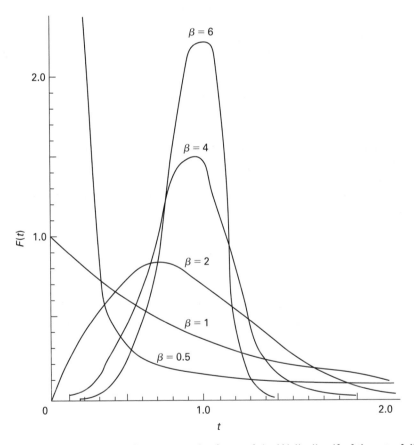

Figure A.2 Influence of shape factor β on the form of the Weibull pdf of time-to-failure

Note: For the first two cases t_0 must be zero, of course; for the wear-out case it may or may not be. Also note from Figure A.2 that β characterizes the consistency of failure occurrence. The larger its value the greater is the tendency for the failures to occur at about the same running time.

A.2 Weibull probability paper

How do we test whether several times-to-failure, collected from the history record of a particular type of component, look as if they could be plausibly represented by a Weibull cdf? In the language of statistics, whether they look as if they have been sampled from such a distribution? And if they do, how do we determine the values of t_0, η and β which will give the distribution which best fits the data?

One easy way is to use *Weibull probability graph paper*. There are several versions of this; we shall use the one, i.e. probably the most widely used in the UK, marketed by the Chartwell technical graph paper company (Ref. No. 6572 in their list. On this, the y-axis variable is the cumulative fraction failed, $F(t)$, expressed in percent, and the x-axis variable $(t - t_0)$, in whatever are the appropriate units of time for the particular component studied (as explained earlier in this section, 'time' in this context is a measure of usage and might appropriately be 'number of operational cycles'). The axial scales are so arranged that if a *theoretic* Weibull cdf were to be plotted on the paper, (i.e. using values of $F(t)$ calculated from the expression given earlier) they would lie on a perfectly straight line. The following example shows how the paper is used.

A.3 A Weibull analysis of a large and complete sample of times-to-failure

One hundred identical pumps have been run continuously and their times-to-failure recorded. To fit a Weibull expression to the data we proceed as follows:

1. The data are tabulated as in Columns 1 and 2 of Table A.1.
2. Successive addition of the figures in Column 2 leads to Column 3, the *cumulative* percentages of pumps failed by the *ends* of each of the class intervals of Column 1.
3. Three or four possible values, thought likely to span the actual value, are assigned to t_0 (*the guaranteed life*). The resulting values of $t - t_0$ are tabulated in Columns 4–6. *Note*: In each case t is the time of the *end* of the interval (e.g. in Column 4, Row 3):

$$t - t_0 = 1300 - 800 = 500 \text{ hours}$$

4. On the Weibull probability paper, the Column 3 figures are plotted first against those in Column 4, then against those in Columns 5 and 6, respectively.
   The result is shown in Figure A.3. The value of t_0 which results in the straight plot, in this case 900 hours, is the one which gives a Weibull cdf which best represents the data.
5. The characteristic life, η, is the value of $t - t_0$ at which the line fitted to the straightest plot reaches the 63% failed level, in this case 600 hours. (*Note*: $t - t_0 = 600$ hours corresponds to a total actual running time of $t = 1500$ hours, remembering that $t_0 = 900$ hours.)
6. As shown, a perpendicular is dropped from the fixed 'estimation point' (printed just above the too left-hand corner of the diagram) to the straightline fit. The point at which this perpendicular intersects the special β – scale at the top of the graph give the value of β for the best-fit cdf (in this case approximately 3.5, clearly pointing to a wear-out mode of failure).

Table A.1 Pump failure data

(1)	(2)	(3)	(4)	(5)	(6)
Time-to-failure (hour)	Number of pumps	Cumulative percentage failed	$t - t_0$ $t_0 = 800$ hours	$t - t_0$ $t_0 = 900$ hours	$t - t_0$ $t_0 = 1000$ hours
1000–1100	2	2	300	200	100
1100–1200	6	8	400	300	200
1200–1300	16	24	500	400	300
1300–1400	14	38	600	500	400
1400–1500	26	64	700	600	500
1500–1600	22	86	800	700	600
1600–1700	7	93	900	800	700
1700–1800	6	99	1000	900	800
1800–1900	1	100	1100	1000	900

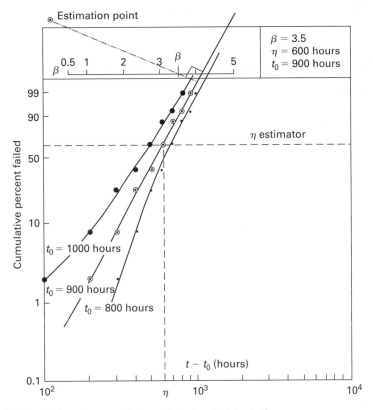

Figure A.3 Weibull plot of pump failure data (see Table A.1)

Index